From REBELLION to REDEMPTION

A Year of Reflections on the Heidelberg Catechism

From REBELLION to REDEMPTION

A Journey Through the Great
Themes of Christian Faith

Randal Working

Foreword by Richard J. Mouw

NAVPRESS

BRINGING TRUTH TO LIFE
P.O. Box 35001, Colorado Springs, Colorado 80935

OUR GUARANTEE TO YOU

We believe so strongly in the message of our books that we are making this quality guarantee to you. If for any reason you are disappointed with the content of this book, return the title page to us with your name and address and we will refund to you the list price of the book. To help us serve you better, please briefly describe why you were disappointed. Mail your refund request to: NavPress, P.O. Box 35002, Colorado Springs, CO 80935.

The Navigators is an international Christian organization. Our mission is to reach, disciple, and equip people to know Christ and to make Him known through successive generations. We envision multitudes of diverse people in the United States and every other nation who have a passionate love for Christ, live a lifestyle of sharing Christ's love, and multiply spiritual laborers among those without Christ.

NavPress is the publishing ministry of The Navigators. NavPress publications help believers learn biblical truth and apply what they learn to their lives and ministries. Our mission is to stimulate spiritual formation among our readers.

Library of Congress Catalog Card Number: 2001044212
ISBN 1-57683-285-6

Cover design by Jennifer Mahalik
Cover illustration by Photodisc
Creative Team: Don Simpson, Darla Hightower, Glynese Northam

Some of the anecdotal illustrations in this book are true to life and are included with the permission of the persons involved. All other illustrations are composites of real situations, and any resemblance to people living or dead is coincidental.

Unless otherwise identified, all Scripture quotations in this publication are taken from the *HOLY BIBLE: NEW INTERNATIONAL VERSION®* (NIV®). Copyright © 1973, 1978, 1984 by International Bible Society. Used by permission of Zondervan Publishing House. All rights reserved. Other versions include: the *New Revised Standard Version* (NRSV), copyright © 1989, by the Division of Christian Education of the National Council of the Churches of Christ in the USA, used by permission, all rights reserved; the *New King James Version* (NKJV), copyright © 1979, 1980, 1982, 1990, Thomas Nelson Inc., Publishers.

Working, Randal, 1958-
    From rebellion to redemption : a journey through the great themes of Christian faith : a year of reflections on the Heidelberg catechism / by Randal Working.
      p. cm.
    Includes bibliographical references.
    ISBN 1-57683-285-6
    1. Heidelberger Katechismus. 2. Devotional calendars. 3. Reformed Church--Doctrines. I. Title.

BX9428 .W67 2001
238'.42--dc21   2001044212

FOR A FREE CATALOG OF
NAVPRESS BOOKS & BIBLE STUDIES,
CALL 1-800-366-7788 (USA)
OR 1-416-499-4615 (CANADA)

Printed in the United States of America

1 2 3 4 5 6 7 8 9 10 / 05 04 03 02 01

To Evelyne,
full of joy and light, faithful wife and friend.

"Weiter, liebe Brüder: Was wahrhaftig ist, was ehrbar, was gerecht, was rein, was liebenswert, was einen guten Ruf hat, sei es eine Tugend, sei es ein Lob - darauf seid bedacht!" (die Philipper 4:8)

"Au reste, frères, que tout ce qui est vrai, tout ce qui est honorable, tout ce qui est juste, tout ce qui est pur, tout ce qui est aimable, tout ce qui mérite l'approbation, ce qui est vertueux et digne de louange, soit l'objet de vos pensées." (Philippiens 4:8)

Contents

Foreword   *11*

Introduction   *13*

Part One: Our Need

WEEK ONE: BELONGING TO GOD   22

WEEK TWO: HUMAN BROKENNESS   27

WEEK THREE: GOD'S ORIGINAL INTENT   32

WEEK FOUR: GOD'S COSTLY LOVE   37

Part Two: Our Lord's Provision

WEEK FIVE: A HOLY GOD WHO IS MERCIFUL   43

WEEK SIX: AMAZING LOVE   47

WEEK SEVEN: WHAT SHALL WE THEN DO?   51

WEEK EIGHT: GOD IN THREE PERSONS   56

WEEK NINE: GOD THE FATHER   61

WEEK TEN: GOD'S GUIDING HAND   66

WEEK ELEVEN: JESUS SAVES!   71

WEEK TWELVE: LORD, I WANT TO BE A CHRISTIAN IN MY HEART   75

WEEK THIRTEEN: WE ARE GOD'S CHILDREN   81

WEEK FOURTEEN: GOD IN THE FLESH   86

WEEK FIFTEEN: GOD'S GREATEST GIFT   91

WEEK SIXTEEN: DEATH, WHERE IS YOUR STING?   96

WEEK SEVENTEEN: GOD'S STAMP OF APPROVAL   101

WEEK EIGHTEEN: FULLY HUMAN, FULLY DIVINE   107

WEEK NINETEEN: COME, LORD JESUS!   111

WEEK TWENTY: THE COMFORTER   116

WEEK TWENTY-ONE: THE CHURCH   120

WEEK TWENTY-TWO: THE HOPE OF GLORY   127

WEEK TWENTY-THREE: BY GRACE ALONE THROUGH FAITH   133

WEEK TWENTY-FOUR: A RIGHT RELATIONSHIP WITH GOD   138

WEEK TWENTY-FIVE: A MINISTRY OF WORD AND SACRAMENT   144

WEEK TWENTY-SIX: WASHED CLEAN   151

WEEK TWENTY-SEVEN: CLEAN FROM THE INSIDE OUT   156

WEEK TWENTY-EIGHT: CHRIST'S BODY AND BLOOD FOR US   161

WEEK TWENTY-NINE: HIS SPIRITUAL PRESENCE   166

WEEK THIRTY: IF YOU LOVE JESUS AND HATE YOUR SIN   171

WEEK THIRTY-ONE: KEYS OF THE KINGDOM   176

Part Three: Our Living Sacrifice

WEEK THIRTY-TWO: BLESSED TO BE A BLESSING   184

WEEK THIRTY-THREE: INTO NEW LIFE   189

WEEK THIRTY-FOUR: A NEW WAY TO LIVE   195

WEEK THIRTY-FIVE: WORSHIP IN SPIRIT AND IN TRUTH   203

WEEK THIRTY-SIX: HONORING GOD'S GOOD NAME   209

WEEK THIRTY-SEVEN: ALLEGIANCE TO WHOM?   214

WEEK THIRTY-EIGHT: KEEPING GOD AT THE CENTER   219

WEEK THIRTY-NINE: HONORING OUR PARENTS   225

WEEK FORTY: LOVING MY NEIGHBOR   231

WEEK FORTY-ONE: SEEKING A PURE HEART   236

WEEK FORTY-TWO: CONTENT WITH WHAT I HAVE   242

WEEK FORTY-THREE: TELLING THE TRUTH   248

WEEK FORTY-FOUR: WANTING NOTHING BUT GOD   254

WEEK FORTY-FIVE: TALKING WITH THE FATHER   260

WEEK FORTY-SIX: TEACH US TO PRAY   266

WEEK FORTY-SEVEN: TO LIFT UP GOD'S NAME   271

WEEK FORTY-EIGHT: LONGING FOR GOD'S WHOLENESS   276

WEEK FORTY-NINE: NOT MY WILL BUT YOURS   282

WEEK FIFTY: EVERYTHING WE NEED   287

WEEK FIFTY-ONE: A CLEAN SLATE   292

WEEK FIFTY-TWO: NOT BY OUR OWN STRENGTH   298

Appendix   *305*

Bibliography   *311*

Notes   *317*

Author   *319*

Foreword

In the early 1960s, when I was a student at a Reformed seminary in Michigan, I heard some wonderful lectures by a visiting Dutch theologian, Dr. Hendrikus Berkhof of the University of Leiden. His subject was the Heidelberg Catechism, and even over the distance of four decades I can still remember how he compared that catechism, written in Germany, with its Scottish counterpart, the Westminster Shorter Catechism.

The Heidelberg and Westminster catechisms are two of the great doctrinal documents of the Reformation era. They both lay out in a systematic manner the basic teachings of the Christian faith as understood within the Reformed-Presbyterian tradition. But in spite of their theological similarities, Professor Berkhof pointed out, they have very different tones. This can be clearly seen in the way they begin. The first question and answer of the Westminster Shorter Catechism are stated, Berkhof noted, in quite abstract terms:

Question: "What is the chief end of man?"
Answer: "Man's chief end is to glorify God, and to enjoy him forever."

The Heidelberg, on the other hand, employs very personal language. It asks: "What is your only comfort in life and in death?" And the answer begins: "That I am not my own, but belong — body and soul, in life and death — to my faithful Savior Jesus Christ." While both questions are important ones, Berkhof insisted, there is something surprisingly contemporary about the tone of the Heidelberg Catechism. It asks us to speak, he said, existentially. It addresses us, not as "man" in general, but as flesh-and-blood individuals in the midst of the day-to-day realities of our lives. "What is your only comfort . . . ?" "That I am not my own."

And if Professor Berkhof thought that tone had a contemporary feel in the 1960s, this existential emphasis is perhaps even more fitting in these opening years of the twenty-first century. We live in a time when people think much about their own personal "journeys." We want to find ways in which our own individual stories can connect to the larger narratives about the human race. These concerns are certainly important for contemporary Christians. While the big-picture questions — about, for example, "the chief end" of human beings in general — are important to us, we also want to find our own personal place in this larger scheme of things: Where do I find my comfort as I seek to live out my calling as a Christian human being in the midst of the dilemmas and joys and sorrows of my life? Some cynics might want to dismiss this "I"-centered talk as too "individualistic," but those very personal questions are at the heart of biblical faith. There is a lot of first-person terminology in the Psalms!

A closely related feature that I also value greatly in the Heidelberg Catechism is its practical focus. It deals with important theological topics, but it regularly asks what those subjects mean to us as we seek to apply them in our actual lives as disciples of Christ. Take the doctrine of the Virgin Birth of Jesus. This has often been an important issue for those of us who want to defend theological orthodoxy against more liberal types, who like to cast doubt on the miraculous elements in Christian belief. Question 35 gives a good account of the why the Virgin Birth is good doctrine. But then it immediately asks, in Question 36: "How does the body conception and birth of Christ benefit you?" And this form of question appears repeatedly. One of my favorites is Question 52: "How does Christ's return to 'judge the living and the dead' comfort you?" The answer begins: "In all my distress and persecution I turn my eyes to the heavens and confidently await as judge the very One who has already stood trial in my place before God and so has removed the whole curse from me." The coming Judge is "the very One" who has already stood trial in my place! That kind of deep spiritual trust in the ministry of Jesus is a marvelous feature of this fine catechism.

I have long thought that outside the relatively small circles of conservative Reformed and Presbyterian groups, the Heidelberg Catechism has been — unfortunately — a well-kept secret. Now Randy Working has done the larger evangelical world the favor of making it accessible to what will surely be many new admirers. And he has given it just the kind of exposure that it deserves. He presents the questions and answers, and he gives us brief but very insightful expositions; then he adds some well-chosen reflections from a variety of spiritual writers representing a broad range of denominational and cultural traditions. And in all of this he honors — indeed he enhances — the wonderful spiritual riches of this marvelous catechism. This is a devotional resource that will have a long life. Many of us will want to start over again as soon as we have come to the last page. I am deeply grateful for this book. It is a gift from the past that will strengthen the faith of all Christian readers who want to think more deeply about their "only comfort in life and death."

RICHARD J. MOUW

Introduction:
Help for the Journey

Growing up, I became aware of the great creeds of the Christian church. I spent my early years in both Presbyterian and Methodist churches. When I was nine my family moved from the San Francisco Bay area to Southern California so my father could enter seminary, and we began to attend a large Methodist church, built in colonial style.

At ten years old I got tagged for the job of acolyte, a person who assists the clergy in the performance of liturgy. It meant I had to sit through the worship service rather than disappear into the bowels of the education building to go to Sunday school. It meant that I stayed in the sanctuary, where I heard the singing of hymns and the cadences of the corporate confession of sin and the sonorous recital of the Apostles Creed. I perceived that the creed was something important. I was impressed by the gravity it lent to the assembly. But I don't think it occurred to me to consider what it taught.

Later as a student at Whitworth College, a Presbyterian liberal-arts institution, I learned more about my faith. I took a freshman class that explored various life philosophies from the Western tradition. The case for each one seemed compelling. I thought, *I guess Plato explained life best,* and later, *How could I ever argue against this Machiavelli,* and *No, it's Kierkegaard who makes the most sense,* and then, *Existentialism really puts it all together.* The class was challenging to the point of inducing mental fatigue. After presenting the case for various ways of seeing the world, the professor took the class back around for a fresh look at the Christian perspective. By then I was able to see the uniqueness of the biblical faith.

In the class, I heard how the church articulated its faith in hymns, confessions, catechisms, and theological declarations. Those sources struck me as very important. Their perspectives came through for me in second-hand fashion in lectures and in the writings of modern commentators and historians. But I never had the time or inclination to delve into them myself.

In my junior year I had the opportunity to travel to Europe. I spent the spring semester studying the art, literature, and culture of France. In the fall I went to Geneva, Switzerland, for an internship with Youth for Christ in ministry to international students. In that environment far from friends and family, I began to more deeply examine my faith. I met Evelyne, a French-speaking Swiss citizen who worked in the Youth for Christ office, and the woman I would marry. I returned home at the end of the year to finish college and then pursue a graduate degree in drawing and painting. When Evelyne and I — now married — wanted to spend a year being trained in our faith, we returned to Geneva. We ended up spending three more years in campus ministry there.

Geneva, the city of John Calvin and the center of the Reformation, the place John Knox dubbed "the most perfect school of Christ since the days of the apostles," the city of refuge for persecuted Huguenots, the city of Rousseau and humanism — it was there I began to see more clearly the themes of the evangelical faith. I talked with students on frosty evenings on the Quais du Mont-Blanc when we warmed our hands with brown paper bags of roasted chestnuts. I drank strong coffee with youth workers in cafes while we planned club meetings. I led small-group discussions with students from Italy, Ireland, America, England, Japan, Iran, France, and Ghana, as we tried to come to terms with the significance of Christ. I studied Reformation theology and saw how the confessions of the church were attempts of my spiritual forerunners to articulate the gospel in response to crises in their own day. For the first time, I began to realize the importance of the church's historical witness to the faith. I came to see its relevance in the midst of our changing world.

The international community in Geneva is highly mobile. English-speaking professionals are there to work for the diplomatic corps, United Nations agencies like the High Commission on Refugees, the World Health Organization, or major corporations. There is about a one-third turnover every year. Many people who come through town have left much behind and are looking for purpose and security. I began to see how we live in what seems to be a "disposable world." From diapers to razors to relationships to the very environment in which we live, the tangible elements of our lives are used and then discarded. This impermanence and uncertainty makes us long for what is lasting and substantial. Many people in our time feel the insecurity of it all. They ask questions like "Where do we go to find meaning? Is there any hope for peace? How do we find direction in a perplexing world?"

Whether we live in the international community of Switzerland or in the suburbs of North America, many voices clamor for our attention. In the midst of the noise, the Lord of the universe is calling us still, as he did his very first followers by the Sea of Galilee long ago. As perhaps never before, it is easy to become distracted by the empty promises of the culture around us. But the invitation is still being spoken, "Come, follow me." Jesus seeks disciples who are willing to be transformed, who join him on the road and move into service.

This is the adventure to which we're invited: to live not as settlers, but as pilgrims on a journey toward heaven as disciples of Jesus the Nazarene. After all, everyone is a disciple of somebody or of something — of some commitment or ideology or program. A disciple is a follower, and every one of us is on a journey. The path we commit to — where we choose to invest our time and energy — reflects what's important to us. It exposes our most deeply held values, and it determines where we are going to end up. We are all disciples, because we are all pursuing something.

The question is not, then, whether we will be disciples. The question is rather whether we are disciples of one who is truly worthy of our lives. Some of us get so caught up in our daily routines and demands that we haven't considered what we're following. But we need to ask ourselves, "What will I commit to? What am I driving for? *Whose disciple will I be?*"

The Lord never promises the road will be easy. It is hard to live with courage in the face of life's dangers and temptations. But with God's companionship, the journey will be good. This book was prepared in the conviction that life can be a rich adventure because the Lord desires to give abundant life to all his children. It is offered in the hope that you will know, even in these turbulent times, the peace, power, and joy that are found when you travel with him.

Fulfillment doesn't come our way by accident. It is a byproduct of our journey with Christ, of an intimate connection with his life. That connection with him finds expression in and is nurtured by certain practices. These include study, prayer, meditation, and camaraderie with others who are also on the way. Their company encourages us to grow and to reflect on the progress we're making. God desires to reveal himself to those who belong to him. As we allow ourselves to be shaped by the Word of God, we will move toward God's goal for our lives. We will be able to draw from the resources of our heavenly Father.

But how do we begin? The way seems so arduous that one can become discouraged or confused before taking the first step of the journey. We need guidance to understand and make tangible our commitment to be a disciple of Jesus.

Thankfully, we are not alone on the pilgrimage of discipleship. For one thing, we join a community of brothers and sisters in Christ — his church — we have a family. We inherit the legacy of Christians throughout the centuries who have struggled to follow Christ faithfully. It is that legacy which C. S. Lewis referred to as "Christianity itself — the faith preached by the apostles, attested by the martyrs, embodied in the creeds, expounded by the fathers."[1] We find records of the convictions that gave them courage in the theological statements of the church known as creeds, confessions, or catechisms. As we look to these statements (the Apostles' Creed is the best known; other well-known examples include the Heidelberg Catechism, the Nicene Creed, the Canons of Dort, and the Westminster Confession of Faith, among many), we find that they are more than dusty, historical documents. Instead, they are vital expressions of the faith of our spiritual forebears. These theological statements help us discern the main themes of Scripture. They give us insight, encouragement, and accountability to historic, orthodox Christian faith. One of the ranges of meaning of the word "orthodox" is literally "right glory." Thus, orthodox faith is when one's beliefs and opinions give accurate credit to and understanding of God and his message to us. It is *the thinking* that glorifies God. The confessions as theological statements remind us that what we believe matters because those beliefs are the springboard for our values and our actions in life. There is an inseparable connection between what we believe and what we do, between our word and our work, between what we profess and what we practice.

Convictions make a difference. Our adventure is one of both heart and mind.

The Design of From Rebellion to Redemption

This study guide is designed around a catechism, which is a question-and-answer teaching tool. The catechism has been used from the earliest days in the Christian church and is still a helpful model for learning. This guide is structured upon the particular articulation of the Christian faith known as the Heidelberg Catechism. Like earlier editions, we have included the Scripture references to support the statements made in the answers. There is no need to look up all of the footnoted references, and you will find many of these in the assigned Daily Scripture Readings.

In the sixteenth century, the influence of Lutheranism flowed down the Neckar River from the north of Germany, and the influence of Calvinism flowed up the Rhine from Switzerland. The two streams met in the area of Heidelberg and spilled over their banks into bitter conflict.

Frederick III was a devout and thoughtful Protestant living at the time. He was one of the seven most powerful leaders of the Holy Roman Empire, which included four secular princes and three archbishops. As the governor of the German Palatinate province, he commissioned the catechism in 1562 for use in the churches under his jurisdiction. He hoped it would resolve the disputes between the Reformed and Lutheran camps of the Reformation. He called for a new catechism that would sum up the Christian faith from the Reformed perspective. Two gifted young men, still in their twenties, were assigned the task of writing the catechism. They were the preacher Kaspar Olevianus and the professor Zacharias Ursinus, both of whom had been influenced by Calvin and his Geneva Catechism. In short order, they produced "a catechism in our Christian religion" that simply but powerfully expressed the biblical faith, and it was published in 1563. It is personal, with the questions posed to "you" and the answers all in the first person. It has a universal appeal, a focus on the gospel, and a warm tenor to its language.

Popular response to the catechism was strong, and in its first year it went through three editions. It quickly became the most widely used of all Reformed confessions because of its highly personal and devotional tone, and because of its clear summary of the Protestant faith. Within a generation, the changing currents of political leadership would mean that the Reformed believers had to flee the city of Heidelberg. Still, the impact of the catechism would prove to be as wide as it was deep. The first Reformed confession to reach America, it appeared in the early seventeenth century, brought by Dutch settlers. It would eventually be translated into French, English, Greek, Polish, Spanish, Lithuanian, Italian, Bohemian, Malay, Javanese, Portuguese, Tamil, Chinese, Japanese, Arabic, and Hungarian, and used around the world to help Christians understand their faith.

The Heidelberg Catechism itself is structured around the movement of the apostle Paul's epistle to the Romans. In that pivotal New Testament letter Paul cries out, "Wretched man that I am! Who will rescue me from this body of death? Thanks be to God through Jesus Christ our Lord" (Romans 7:24-25, NRSV). The Heidelberg Catechism keys off each of these phrases, moving from humanity's "misery" (this term refers to the brokenness, or need, of the human race), through "redemption" (in other words, to what God has done to restore people to a right relationship to himself through the sacrificial death of his Son on a cross), to "thankfulness" (the way our lifestyle demonstrates the fact that God has brought us into new life, and we now live for him). The confession was divided into fifty-two sections so that a preacher could explain a different portion every Sunday of the year.

The structure of the catechism corresponds well to our purpose of discipleship. It covers the fundamentals that every Christian needs in order to progress into a mature understanding of the faith. *From Rebellion to Redemption* follows this outline: from guilt, to grace, to gratitude.

Part One: Our Need (Guilt) _____

How do we learn of our need of God? We learn it by seeing how far short we fall from God's good intention for humanity, which is summarized by Jesus in what is known as the "Great Commandment." All humanity has missed the mark and stands in need of renewal. The only way we are going to experience the life and help of God is if God himself makes a way.

Part Two: Our Lord's Provision (Grace) _____

How do we come into a saving relationship with God? How do we get in touch with his grace? Only through God's mediation for us in Christ. Our response is simply to believe, or as an old gospel song put it, "to trust and obey." What is the Christian to believe? The basic tenets of the Christian faith are outlined in the Apostles' Creed, with its statement on the nature of God in three persons: Father, Son, and Holy Spirit. The catechism also addresses the issue of how the Christian can enjoy the benefits of belonging to God. Baptism and the Lord's Supper are expounded as the manner in which God touches his people and nurtures their faith and life.

Part Three: Our Living Sacrifice (Gratitude)

How do we show that we've genuinely experienced God's love? We do it through a new kind of living. This section of *From Rebellion to Redemption* highlights the area traditionally known in Christian studies as "sanctification." This is the notion that those who belong to Jesus will come, with the help of the Holy Spirit, to look more and more like him. He has given us a way of knowing his will, a process of being stretched in our faith, and a practice to prove our appreciation for what he has done. God's intention for humanity is summed up in the Ten Commandments. They not only serve as a mirror by which we see our need for God's help in our lives — because we fall so far short of the ideal — but also as an expression of what is good for our lives.

In this section we will receive practical help for what it means to live as a Christian. For instance, how do we know how to pray? Jesus has given us an outline for communication with the Father in the "Lord's Prayer."

All followers of Christ need time for reflection and "Sabbath rest" in the midst of our distracted lives. Do we not long for meaningful quiet time, invigorating Bible study, dynamic personal worship, and authentic Christian community? We need hearts so inflamed and minds so captivated by Jesus that our lives bear witness to him in service and obedience. This endeavor is worth our best effort and thought, a way of worshiping him with our minds. This guide is an attempt to help believers move toward a more meaningful and transformational devotional life. I pray that the result for you might be a life more joyful, a life lived with abandon, a life more useful for God.

How to use From Rebellion to Redemption

This guide can be read straight through, or used periodically. It can also be studied in a weekly session of about an hour. Going at this pace, it will take a year to complete the material. In addition, you are encouraged to carve out a brief time every day for reflection, Scripture reading, and prayer, using this guide as a springboard. Consistency in devotions will bring the greatest benefit possible. Like learning to play the piano or make a three-point shot with a basketball, repetition will help make the skill second nature for us. Repetition can also build confidence with the practice of prayer and with learning Christian principles. Keep the goal of Christian growth in mind, yet don't be overly concerned about methodology. Discipleship is a process of development more than a destination. Building a relationship with the living Lord is the whole point.

The readings from the "Other Voices" section of each chapter are quotes from various Christian writers, many from the Reformed tradition. They are intended to amplify, illustrate, and help you reflect upon the topic at hand. There is no need to devour all of the selections at a time. The best approach may be to read one a day as a way to reflect further on the theme. The readings provide a way to scrutinize an idea from several different perspectives. They also give you a compendium of a theological library containing some of the best Christian thinkers. If a particular writer sparks special interest for you, I encourage you to go deeper. Get to know that person's writing until you have confidence that you understand how he or she thinks, and you will have made a friend and mentor for life.

This guide can be used by individuals. Others will prefer to have a partner through the process to help them keep on track. If that is the case for you, it is best to complete the study ahead of time to most meaningfully use the time together. *From Rebellion to Redemption* can also be used fruitfully in small groups or by mentoring partners.

The following elements make up the structure of the weekly selection:

Opening Prayer
Heidelberg Questions
Exposition
Other Voices
Daily Scripture Readings
Questions for Reflection and Discussion
Closing Prayer

Discipleship is the greatest endeavor we can imagine — responding to the claim of Christ on our lives. The quest ahead of us is an opportunity to take stock of ourselves. Maybe up to this point your road has been uneven and your progress haphazard. Through this study you will be able to take a spiritual inventory, as it were, and to use a systematic and personal approach that will enable you to consider the great themes of our faith. Through the course of time, you will find that your attitudes and actions will become more like Jesus'. Our goal is not simply to overload ourselves with information. It is to have our character transformed by Christ. We invite you to embark on this enterprise of faith. How you do it is not the critical issue; simply begin, and you will find the Lord ready to accompany you. Read his Word and pray daily, and you will find strength for your journey.

Part One
Our Need

Week One:
Belonging to God

Opening Prayer

Merciful and loving Father, I come to this place today hungering for communion with you. Here, away from the noise and confusion of the world, surround me with the sanctuary of your presence. In Jesus' name, amen.

Heidelberg Questions

QUESTION 1: What is your only comfort in life and in death?

That I am not my own,[1] but belong—body and soul, in life and death[2]—to my faithful Savior Jesus Christ.[3] He has fully paid for all my sins with his precious blood,[4] and has set me free from the tyranny of the devil.[5] He also watches over me in such a way[6] that not a hair can fall from my head without the will of my Father in heaven:[7] in fact, all things must work together for my salvation.[8]

Because I belong to him, Christ, by his Holy Spirit, assures me of eternal life[9] and makes me wholeheartedly willing and ready from now on to live for him.[10]

([1]*1 Corinthians 6:19-20;* [2]*Romans 14:7-9;* [3]*1 Corinthians 3:23; Titus 2:14;* [4]*1 Peter 1:18-19; 1 John 1:7-9; 2:2;* [5]*John 8:34-36; Hebrews 2:14-15; 1 John 3:1-11;* [6]*John 6:39-40; 10:27-30; 2 Thessalonians 3:3; 1 Peter 1:5;* [7]*Matthew 10:29-31; Luke 21:16-18;* [8]*Romans 8:28;* [9]*Romans 8:15-16; 2 Corinthians 1:21-22; 5:5; Ephesians 1:13-14;* [10]*Romans 8:1-17)*

QUESTION 2: What must you know to live and die in the joy of this comfort?

Three things: first, how great my sin and misery are;[1] second, how I am set free from all my sins and misery;[2] third, how I am to thank God for such deliverance.[3]

([1]*Romans 3:9-10; 1 John 1:10;* [2]*John 17:3; Acts 4:12; 10:43;* [3]*Matthew 5:16; Romans 6:13; Ephesians 5:8-10; 2 Timothy 2:15; 1 Peter 2:9-10)*

Exposition

These first two questions form a kind of preamble to the whole fifty-two week series. To the second question, the threefold response echoes the structure of the apostle Paul's epistle to the Romans: from "guilt" to "grace" to "gratitude." It also sums up the good news: we problematic human beings, who are overshadowed by death and its consequences, nevertheless belong to Jesus. We were made by him and for him, and because of that, we have a future that is secure if we trust in him even in all the vast uncertainties of life.

Why do we belong to Jesus Christ? On three accounts: first, because he made us. Second, because he died to buy us back from the dominion of sin — that is what the "payment with his precious blood" refers to. Third, because his Spirit has now been given to those who trust in him. When he was at the table with his disciples for their Last Supper, Jesus promised that it was better for them that he leave, because he would send a Comforter in his place. His words must have sounded incredible to the disciples — how could it possibly be *better* for them that he leave? It was better because as he resumed his place with the Father, his Spirit would be present for them and for all who believe, present with God's power and peace as never before. Our comfort is none other than the Spirit of Jesus himself.

The answer to question 2 comes as a surprise; to know God's comfort, we need to know of our own "misery"! That's a term not commonly used in our time, at least not in the sense used here. It doesn't refer to feeling unhappy, but rather to a condition of alienation from God, whether or not one feels that alienation. It is an objective reality, just as if one were to wake up and find oneself lost in a foreign country without wallet or passport. Synonyms would be "wretchedness" or "misfortune." In order to enjoy the benefits of God, we need to know our lostness or our deep need for God, because the benefits of God are not different from the person and character of God himself. We can't enjoy God in just the abstract. The goal of life is to "glorify" him by enjoying community with him and fulfilling his purpose for us. When we know how much we need him, we are receptive to the gift of himself he wants to give us. Jesus made clear this truth when he told his followers, "Blessed are the poor in spirit, for theirs is the kingdom of heaven" (Matthew 5:3). David said it another way: "Delight yourself in the LORD and he will give you the desires of your heart" (Psalm 37:4). When we long for God, he will fill the longing.

Other Voices

At issue here is the question: "To whom do I belong? To God or to the world?" Many of my daily preoccupations suggest that I belong more to the world than to God. A little criticism makes me angry, and a little rejection makes me depressed. A little praise raises my spirits, and a little success excites me. It takes very little to raise me up or thrust me down. Often I am like a small boat on the ocean, completely at the mercy of its waves. All the time and energy I spend in keeping some kind of balance and preventing myself from being tipped over and drowning shows that my life is mostly a struggle for survival: not a holy struggle, but an anxious struggle resulting from the mistaken idea that it is the world that defines me. . . . The world's love is and always will be conditional. As long as I keep looking for my true self in the world of conditional love, I will remain "hooked" to the world—trying, failing, and trying again. It is a world that fosters addictions because what it offers cannot satisfy the deepest craving of my heart.

— HENRI J. M. NOUWEN, *The Return of the Prodigal Son: A Story of Homecoming*

At the beginning of the film *The Neverending Story,* a young boy named Bastian finds himself in an old bookstore, inquiring of the bookstore owner about a special book that he has noticed.

"What's that book about?" asks Bastian.

"Oh, this is something *special*," says the bookstore owner.

"Well, what is it?"

"Look, your books are safe," the owner says. "By reading them you get to become Tarzan, or Robinson Crusoe."

"But that's what I like about them," replies Bastian.

"Ah, but afterwards you get to be a little boy again."

"What do you mean?" asks Bastian.

"Listen," says the man. "Have you ever been Captain Nemo, trapped inside your submarine while the giant squid is attacking you?"

"Yes," says Bastian.

"Weren't you afraid you couldn't escape?"

"But it's only a *story*!"

"That's what I'm talking about," says the man. "The ones *you* read are safe."

"And this one isn't?"

The biblical story that we have been exploring . . . is not safe. We cannot read this story without being caught up in its drama. We cannot claim to have genuinely understood the Bible without taking the risk of improvisation.

— J. RICHARD MIDDLETON AND BRIAN J. WALSH, *Truth Is Stranger Than It Used to Be: Biblical Faith in a Postmodern Age*

O God, immortal, eternal, invisible, I remember with gladness and thanksgiving all that Thou hast been to this world of men[2]:

Companion of the brave;

Upholder of the loyal;

Light of the wanderer;

Joy of the pilgrim;

Guide of the pioneer;

Helper of laboring men;

Refuge of the broken-hearted;

Deliverer of the oppressed;

Succor of the tempted;

Strength of the victorious;

Ruler of rulers;

Friend of the poor;

Rescuer of the perishing;

Hope of the dying.

Give me faith now to believe that Thou canst be all in all to me, according to my need, if only I renounce all proud self-dependence and put my trust in Thee.

— JOHN BAILLIE, *A Diary of
Private Prayer*

Speak to me low, my Saviour,
From out the hallelujahs, sweet and low,
Lest I should fear and fall, and miss thee so
Who art not missed by any that entreat.
Speak to me as to Mary at thy feet —
And if no precious gems my hands bestow,
Let my tears drop like amber, while I go
In reach of thy divinest voice complete
In humanest affection — thus, in sooth,
To lose the sense of losing! As a child,
Whose song-bird seeks the wood forevermore,
Is sung to in its stead by mother's mouth;
Till, sinking on her breast, love-reconciled,
He sleeps the faster that he wept before.

— ELIZABETH BARRETT BROWNING

Let him who cannot be alone beware of community. He will only do harm to himself and to the community. Alone you stood before God when he called you; alone you had to answer that call; alone you had to struggle and pray; and alone you will die and give an account to God. You cannot escape from yourself; for God has singled you out. If you refuse to be alone you are rejecting Christ's call to you, and you can have no part in the community to those who are called. 'The challenge of death comes to us all, and no one can die for another. Everyone must fight his own battle with death by himself, alone. . . . I will not be with you then, nor you with me' (Luther).

But the reverse is also true: *Let him who is not in community beware of being alone.* Into the community you were called, the call was not meant for you alone; in the community of the called you bear your cross, you struggle, you pray. You are not alone, even in death, and on the Last Day you will be only one member of the great congregation of Jesus Christ.

— DIETRICH BONHOEFFER, *Life Together*

After a few decades of cataloguing all the things Sunday school does not do, I now find myself impressed by all the vitally important things it does. All those interminable hospital reports . . . and the sending of get-well cards to the sick; the Sunday school attendance pins; the toe-tapping, maudlin music; the Hershey bars Miss Lewis gave us when we had memorized our Scripture verse for the day — all were part of my church's faltering attempts to make me a Christian. Whatever it was, it was the work of a church which still believed that Christians were made, not born; that someone had to get with you, for at least an hour on Sunday morning, or you would not make it.

Here was religion that took the formation of a community seriously. . . . Here was faith, not as a set of intellectual propositions or moral platitudes, but as a way of life together, a relationship, a familial, personal experience of God which could only be caught from someone else. Here was a view of the church not as an association of the ideologically pure or the aesthetically informed, but as one average Christian telling another average Christian where to find God.

> — WILLIAM H. WILLIMON, *On a Wild and Windy Mountain*

Daily Scripture Readings

KEY TEXT: 1 PETER 5:7
Sunday: Psalm 72
Monday: 1 Corinthians 6:19-20
Tuesday: Romans 14:7-9
Wednesday: John 10:27-30
Thursday: Matthew 10:29-30
Friday: Ephesians 1:13-14
Saturday: Romans 8:15-16

Questions for Reflection and Discussion

What are some of the ways people seek comfort for themselves? How have you seen God provide comfort for someone you know?

How does it make you feel to know that God is for you? What, if anything, makes it hard for you to believe that?

Closing Prayer

Lord, in all the uncertainties of this world, it's good to know I belong to you. Please help that reality to sink into the deepest levels of who I am, so that I can live my life with peace, confidence, and joy. In Jesus' name, amen.

Week Two:

Human Brokenness

Opening Prayer

Lord God, when I behold your majesty, I know I need you to make me clean if I am to be in fellowship with you. Renew me, I pray, and enable me to stand in your presence. In Jesus' name, amen.

Heidelberg Questions

QUESTION 3: How do you come to know your misery?
   The law of God tells me.[1]
(*[1]Romans 3:20; 7:7-25*)

QUESTION 4: What does God's law require of us?
   Christ teaches us this in summary in Matthew 22— Love the Lord your God with all your heart and with all your soul and with all your mind and with all your strength.[1] This is the first and greatest commandment.
   And the second is like it: Love your neighbor as yourself.[2]
   All the Law and the Prophets hang on these two commandments.
(*[1]Deuteronomy 6:5; [2]Leviticus 19:18*)

QUESTION 5: Can you live up to all this perfectly?
   No.[1] I have a natural tendency to hate God and my neighbor.[2]
(*[1]Romans 3:9-20; 1 John 1:8,10; [2]Genesis 6:5; Jeremiah 17:9; Romans 7:23-24; 8:7; Ephesians 2:1-3; Titus 3:3*)

Exposition

In order to enjoy the relationship with God for which we were created, we have to know of our need for him. If we are comfortable with our own resources and prospects without God, then we are smugly self-deceived, out of touch with the One who made us. It means we're wrapped up in the power of sin, that which keeps us going against the way of God.

Sin is more than weakness. It is squaring off against God's purposes in our lives, taking up arms against him. That is why sin is the root of all human miseries; it cuts us off from God and makes us hate our neighbor and ourselves. In this lifetime, it is a guarantee of despair and lack of fulfillment. In eternity, it is banishment from heavenly fellowship with God.

The first sin ruined the harmony our first human parents enjoyed with their Creator and made them refugees from Paradise. It then bled its influence into all the relationships of life, and epitomized itself in fratricide when Cain killed his brother Abel. The so-called "primeval prologue" of Genesis chapters 1 to 11 delineates the ways that sin permeates every aspect of the human experience. All the misery of our sad planet burst forth from the same Pandora's box of sin.

What is the meaning of the law of God? It is a standard beyond ourselves, something immutable and inviolable. It is not something established by humans; we get no vote in the matter, because it demands our obedience. The law is the will of God revealed. It leads us to what we could not discern on our own or achieve through reason or consensus. It goes beyond any kind of innate sense of what is good. Even though our conscience often confirms the standard of God, it can also deceive us. It is altogether too easy for us to rationalize an action or inaction until our conscience is anesthetized. The law of God stands beyond us as the touchstone of God's character.

What then is this law of God? It is the written Word of God in the Scriptures of the Old and New Testaments. The law of the Old Testament came in a three-fold form that included the ceremonial law, the civil law, and the moral law. The ceremonial law was made up of instructions for the worshiping life of Israel. The civil law was composed of instructions for the political and legal life of Israel. Both of these were intended for a particular cultural situation, the establishment of a nation singled out before God. But the moral law, summed up in the Ten Commandments delivered to Moses on Mount Sinai, stands forever. It offers a window into God's own heart, serving as shorthand for all of God's intentions for human behavior. That is why these ancient statutes have such contemporary meaning.

Sixteenth-century Reformer John Calvin came to see through Scripture that God has three purposes for the law to work in the world. For one thing, it reflects back to us our shortcomings. How would we know what wholesome living looks like without God's picture of it? When we see a dirty face in the mirror, we know we need a good scrubbing. So the law, representing the perfect righteousness of God, contrasts with our own condition and shows our need for moral cleansing. It leads us to see our sin. The ethical clarity of the commandments is a bracing tonic to our insensitivity. When we hear the Lord interpret the law, we begin to grasp its claim on us, and we stand rebuked. Who can measure up?

The law has a second purpose as well. This second function, which has been called the "civil use" of the law, is to restrain evil. The law of God does not have the capacity to change the heart. It cannot transform a person's inner motivation, but it can help to rein in the lawless tendencies of a society by inflicting penal sanctions. Because it threatens punishment to those who transgress and are convicted, it can secure civil order and protect people from violence and injustice.

The third function of the law of God is to guide regenerated men and women in the way of righteousness, the good works God has prepared for them to do (Ephesians 2:10). The law is how we know what pleases the Father; Jesus was reflecting this sense of the law when he told his disciples,

"Whoever has my commands and obeys them, he is the one who loves me," and "If you obey my commands, you will remain in my love, just as I have obeyed my Father's commands and remain in his love. I have told you this so that my joy may be in you and that your joy may be complete. My command is this: Love each other as I have loved you." (John 14:21; 15:10-12)

Sometimes Christians suppose the law to be a negative thing, now that we live by the grace of the gospel. But God's law is fulfilled and not canceled out in Christ. Because of that, as the catechism will later show us, it becomes the guide to a new way of life. That is to say, the Christian is free from the law as a way to try to get into God's good graces. But the Christian lives by the law as toward Christ. It is our rule for the Christian life.

But the catechism does not delineate the Ten Commandments here. The root problem in humanity is more profound than simply breaking commandments. The deeper issue is violating relationship with God. So it is that Jesus summed up the law with "Love the Lord your God with all your heart and with all your soul and with all your mind and with all your strength. . . . Love your neighbor as yourself" (Mark 12:30-31). The issue is not so much *sins* but a condition of *sin*. It is all too easy to trick ourselves into complacency by looking to particular commandments: "Well, at least I haven't committed *murder*!" But which of us is able to say we have loved God with every fiber of our being? Which of us is able to say we have always cared for our neighbor just as we care for ourselves? The answer is, none of us. Only Jesus has loved God perfectly and loved his neighbor as himself. The rest of us have spent our lives doing just the opposite. God is not concerned that we measure up well against a checklist. He is concerned with filling our souls with love.

Other Voices

Lord, You know what is most profitable to me; do this or that according to your will. Give me what you will, as much as you will, and when you will. Do with me as you know what is best to be done, as it shall please you, and as it shall be most to your honor. Put me where you will. I am your creature, and in your hands; lead me and turn me where you will. Lo, I am your servant, ready to do all things that you command, for I do not desire to live to myself, but to you. Would to God that I might live worthily and profitably, and to your honor.

— THOMAS À KEMPIS, *The Imitation of Christ*

Are we ignorant of what it means to be ignorant of God, not to understand, not to seek after God, not to fear God, to turn aside and become worthless? Are not the words entirely clear, and do not they teach us just this, that all men are devoid of the knowledge of God and full of contempt for him, and they all turn aside to evil and are worthless as regards the good? For it is not a question here of ignorance about where to find food or of contempt of money, but of ignorance and contempt for religion and godliness. And such ignorance and contempt are beyond doubt not in the flesh and the lower and grosser passions but in the highest and most excellent powers of men, in which there ought to reign righteousness, godliness, the knowledge of God and reverence for God. In other words, they are in the reason and the will, and

therefore in the power of free choice itself, or in the very seeds of virtue and the most excellent thing there is in man.

— MARTIN LUTHER, *The Bondage of the Will*

Can a person be so captured by God, so exclusively filled by and concerned with him? Do we know God as such a comprehensive and engaging reality? Hebrew poetry says, "Love is strong as death, jealousy is cruel as the grave. Its flashes are flashes of fire, a most vehement flame" (Song of Solomon 8:6). Is that our concept of love of God? Do we rejoice with God or suffer with him when his honor, the validity of his commandments, or the advance of his Gospel is at stake? Or do we remain cool with regard to the course of God's concerns in this world? Then we would not love God with all our soul. . . .

Whoever loves God, has it as his goal that God's will be done in all his creatures, in his whole creation. He strives to make of each of his works a ministration and "something beautiful for God."

— KLAUS BOCKMUEHL, *The Great Commandment*

God is none other than the Savior of our wretchedness. So we can only know God well by knowing our iniquities. . . . Those who have known God without knowing their wretchedness have not glorified him, but have glorified themselves.

— BLAISE PASCAL, *Pensées*

Daily Scripture Readings

KEY TEXT: ECCLESIASTES 2:11

Sunday: Psalm 51
Monday: Romans 3:9-20
Tuesday: Romans 7:7-25
Wednesday: Ephesians 2:1-3
Thursday: Titus 3:1-5
Friday: Mark 12:28-34
Saturday: Micah 6:6-8

Questions for Reflection and Discussion

Do you think many people today would have a hard time with the word "sin"? Why or why not?

Do you see it as valid to include time in a worship service for asking forgiveness, either in silent prayer or a printed prayer that is read by the congregation? How

does it apply to individuals if it's a prayer somebody else has written?

If you had to make a case to God for letting you into heaven, what would be your number one reason?

What does it mean to love the Lord with everything you've got?

Closing Prayer

O God, it isn't easy for me to admit, but I don't deserve you. I've done things, both petty and important, to tarnish your good name. I've neglected responsibilities that I should've embraced wholeheartedly to demonstrate my love for you. Lord, I'm sorry. Please don't let my sins ever drive me from you, but instead let them be one more occasion for you to show your goodness and power in my life. In Jesus' name, amen.

Week Three:
God's Original Intent

Opening Prayer

Gracious God, when I see the disorder of the world around me, and feel the disquiet within my own spirit, I remember that I am restless apart from the rest that is in you. In this quiet hour, would you meet me and restore my weary soul? Thank you for the life you have given me and keep giving me daily. Amen.

Heidelberg Questions

QUESTION 6: Did God create people so wicked and perverse?

No. God created them good[1] and in his own image,[2] that is, in true righteousness and holiness,[3] so that they might truly know God their creator,[4] love him with all their heart, and live with him in eternal happiness for his praise and glory.[5]

(*[1]Genesis 1:31; [2]Genesis 1:26-27; [3]Ephesians 4:24; [4]Colossians 3:10; [5]Psalm 8*)

QUESTION 7: Then where does this corrupt human nature come from?

From the fall and disobedience of our first parents, Adam and Eve, in Paradise.[1] This fall has so poisoned our nature[2] that we are born sinners — corrupt from conception on.[3]

(*[1]Genesis 3; [2]Romans 5:12,18-19; [3]Psalm 51:5*)

QUESTION 8: But are we so corrupt that we are totally unable to do any good and inclined toward all evil?

Yes,[1] unless we are born again, by the Spirit of God.[2]

(*[1]Genesis 6:5; 8:21; Job 14:4; Isaiah 53:6; [2]John 3:3-5*)

Exposition

The accounts from the book of Genesis, a name that means "beginning," make clear that God made humans to enjoy relationships. Bible scholar Dale Bruner has taught that the core relationships in life are with "God, a garden, and a good friend."[3] The Genesis story underscores that worship is primary, and that all the relationships of life are oriented and sustained in a right relationship with our Creator. It also suggests the need for vocation, and a relationship with creation itself. Lastly, it suggests that human beings are made to be in loving relationship with one another. In other words, Adam related to God and his world through "worship, work, and a woman," as Bruner says.

Questions 6 through 8 from the Heidelberg Catechism address the Christian doctrine of "the Fall." This idea suggests that, although humans were created to reflect the character of God and to enter into loving community with him, that community has been violated, broken because of human sin. The Bible teaches that historically, the progenitors of the human race, Adam and Eve, introduced sin into the world through their willful disobedience to God's instructions. Those instructions were not capriciously given, but reflected what is good and best for human well-being.

The Calvinist tradition has taught "original sin" and the "total depravity" of humankind. This is not to say that there is nothing good in human beings. Rather it is to say that all people have inherited Adam's sinful nature, and that there is not one part of the human personality that is not tainted by evil. In other words, no aspect of the human person is perfect; no element of any human endeavor is perfectly done. By implication, that brokenness affects our relationship with God, with creation, and with one another. Each human being since has repeated the evil that Adam and Eve, the first sinners, introduced into human behavior. Our natural propensity is neither toward God, nor toward the good of another person. We are selfishly oriented, and that is the human dilemma. There is no such thing as "enlightened self-interest." Without God, we're lost in our sin and self-focus.

This doctrine of good creation/fallen creation is important for a full-bodied Christian worldview. In this regard, we need to know three things as we look at the world around us.

First, we need to know that creation is good. God wove it together with symmetry and splendor. Because of its beauty, we are able to enjoy creation, to marvel at snow-capped mountains or a churning sea. Because people reflect the image of the Creator, we can be stirred by a great sculpture or moved by an opera's aria. We can be nurtured by friendships, find meaning in honest work. Because of that essential order, we can learn about our world through the insights of science.

But, second, we need to remember that our world is a broken place. Evidence for this is so overwhelming that we scarcely need to list examples. Simply to read the morning newspaper is to gain a sober view of human potential. The sadness of the human condition is seen on the macro and the micro scale, from the murderous sweep of history to the wasting of the earth's ecosystems; from the uglification of the urban landscape to the twisted examples of individual destructiveness. The Bible is very realistic about the human condition. Evil is not an illusion. It can — and does — rear its ugly head in each of us.

This means that we should not trust humanity unleashed. Given half a chance, people will pervert anything. This should not surprise us, because it is only an echoing of a root sickness in us. It is not simply that fundamentally nice persons occasionally lapse in their judgment. The Bible goes so far as to say we are absolutely incapable of good apart from the mercy of God. The only reason that the world now has any sanity to it at all is that God doesn't let it spin totally out of control.

And third, we Christians need to have a view large enough to encompass the hope and goodness offered in Christ. Part 2 of the catechism will take us into those liberating themes. But before we receive the good news of the salvation God offers, we need to understand the bad news of how much we need that salvation. We have to hear the next-to-the-last word before we can hear the last word.

Other Voices

So near is the relation between us and the Son of God that the Son of God Himself is the express image of the Father (Colossians 1:15). We are made after that image of Him. This nearness of relationship is further signified by use of the express phrase made "after His likeness" (Genesis 1:26) rather than the words "after His image." That which is made after the image of another must agree with the original mode. But it has only an empty name unless it has a real likeness to justify it.

Let us then be careful to express both the image and the likeness of God by desiring peace, contemplating truth, and loving charity. Let us keep God in our remembrance, having Him in our consciences and behaving ourselves with the deference and reverence that is becoming to those who believe God to be always present in them. For if our mind reflects His image, then it is capable of receiving and partaking of Him. It is *His* image because it is capable also of rising still higher to remember, consider, and love its Maker. In doing so, there consists true maturity and wisdom.

— BERNARD OF CLAIRVAUX, *The Love of God*

Against this background [of futile "modern answers to humanity's woes"] a few voices have continued to emphasize that the cause of the distressed human condition, individual and social — and its only possible cure — is a spiritual one. But what these voices are saying is not clear. They point out that social and political revolutions have shown no tendency to transform the heart of darkness that lies deep in the breast of every human being. That is evidently true. And amid a flood of techniques for self-fulfillment there is an epidemic of depression, suicide, personal emptiness, and escapism through drugs and alcohol, cultic obsession, consumerism, and sex and violence — all combined with an inability to sustain deep and enduring personal relationships.

So obviously the problem is a spiritual one. And so must be the cure.

— DALLAS WILLARD, *The Spirit of the Disciplines*

[T]here is something in human nature which will laugh in the face of every ideal you have. If you refuse to agree with the fact that there is vice and self-seeking, something downright spiteful and wrong in human beings, instead of reconciling yourself to it, when it strikes your life, you will compromise with it and say it is of no use to battle against it.

— OSWALD CHAMBERS, *My Utmost for His Highest*

The Fall of man in God's creation is both inconceivable and unalterably inexcusable, and therefore the word "disobedience" does not exhaust the facts of the case. It is revolt, it is the creature's departure from the attitude which is the only possible attitude for him, it is the creature's becoming Creator, it is the destruction of creatureliness. It is defection, it is the fall from being held in creatureliness. This defection is a continual falling, a plunging into bottom-

less depths, a being relinquished, a withdrawal ever farther and deeper. And in all this it is not simply a moral lapse but the destruction of creation by the creature. The Fall affects the whole of the created world which is henceforth plundered of its creatureliness as it crashes blindly into infinite space, like a meteor which has torn away from its nucleus.

— DIETRICH BONHOEFFER, *Creation and Fall/Temptation*

The butchers of the city of Melos were pagan in the hateful sense of the word, whereas their fathers had not been so. In a single sentence they completely and perfectly defined the pagan conception. "Concerning the gods we believe that by a necessity of nature each one always commands wherever he has the power to do so."

The Christian faith is nothing but the cry affirming the contrary. The same is true of the doctrines of China, India, Egypt, and Greece.

The act of creation is not an act of power. It is an abdication. Through this act a kingdom was established other than the kingdom of God. The reality of this world is constituted by the mechanism of matter and the autonomy of rational creatures. It is a kingdom from which God has withdrawn. God, having renounced being its king, can enter it only as a beggar.

As for the cause of this abdication, Plato expresses it thus: "He was good."

— SIMONE WEIL, *Are We Struggling for Justice?*

Daily Scripture Readings————

KEY TEXT: PROVERBS 13:15
>Sunday: Psalm 8
>Monday: Genesis 1:26-31
>Tuesday: Colossians 3:1-17
>Wednesday: Genesis 3
>Thursday: Genesis 6:5-6
>Friday: John 3:1-21
>Saturday: Psalm 139

Questions for Reflection and Discussion————

If you had to give two reasons for not believing in God, what would they be?

When reading the daily newspaper, do you see more evidence for a basic goodness or a basic evil in human nature? Why?

Given that the Bible affirms that humanity was created in the image of God, but does not define what that image is, what do you consider to be its signs in people?

Closing Prayer————

God, the world around me seems a dangerous place. Yet there are times when I see its poignant beauty, so much so that it catches me up short. In times like that I can't help but wonder at your creativity and majesty. I see echoes of you in your world, in spite of people's efforts to sully it. I see reflections of your love and purpose in people, even when there's much in the human character that has gone awry. Develop in me an instinct for what is good, and right, and honoring of you and of others. In Jesus' name, amen.

Week Four:
God's Costly Love

Opening Prayer

Father, I am amazed when I consider what it cost you to make me your own. I stand in awe before your deep, deep love in Jesus. He took on our humanity, suffered on the cross, and offers forgiveness to all who believe. Nothing else compares with what you have done. Help me to participate in the new life he brings. In Jesus' name, amen.

Heidelberg Questions

QUESTION 9: But doesn't God do us an injustice by requiring in his law what we are unable to do?

No, God created humans with the ability to keep the law.[1] They, however, tempted by the devil,[2] in reckless disobedience,[3] robbed themselves and all their descendants of these gifts.[4]

(*[1]Genesis 1:31; Ephesians 4:24; [2]Genesis 3:13; John 8:44; [3]Genesis 3:6; [4]Romans 5:12,18-19*)

QUESTION 10: Will God permit such disobedience and rebellion to go unpunished?

Certainly not. He is terribly angry about the sin we are born with as well as the sins we personally commit.

As a just judge he punishes them now and in eternity.[1]

He has declared: "Cursed is everyone who does not continue to do everything written in the Book of the Law."[2]

(*[1]Exodus 34:7; Psalm 5:4-6; Nahum 1:2; Romans 1:18; Ephesians 5:6; Hebrews 9:27; [2]Galatians 3:10; Deuteronomy 27:26*)

QUESTION 11: But isn't God also merciful?

God is certainly merciful,[1] but he is also just.[2] His justice demands that sin, committed against his supreme majesty, be punished with the supreme penalty — eternal punishment of body and soul.[3]

([1]*Exodus 34:6-7; Psalm 103:8-9;* [2]*Exodus 34:7; Deuteronomy 7:9-11; Psalm 5:4-6; Hebrews 10:30-31;* [3]*Matthew 25:35-46*)

Exposition

This is God's assessment of the human condition: broken, distorted, distant from his good design for humanity. And God's assessment is true; it isn't simply another opinion to add to the mix. Since his word is the final appraisal of humanity's moral situation, God also declares the *consequences* for human behavior. We can have no argument with God's judgment. When we refuse to do what's right, we give up our right to expect any different.

This is the second part of our misery. Not only are we stuck in sin, mired down in the weight of its destructive power, but also we stand under the judgment of God. The punishment of sin is upon us.

It is not as if God were violent or fickle. His anger is not the petty, self-indulgent anger of a peeved individual. God's anger is the expression of violated love. God's anger is a passionate hatred of everything opposed to righteousness. His anger is an expression of his good and holy character.

Thus it is that death is passed on to the whole human race. All the unhappiness of the world is passed on through the threefold consequence of death. First, physical: our bodies deteriorate until one day they give out. Second, spiritual: naturally at odds with our Creator, our hearts and our minds are clouded and we're incapable of knowing God. Third, eternal: sinful humans are unable to save themselves and are condemned to separation from God.

This seems a harsh word to our modern ears. Our culture is uncomfortable with any definition of right and wrong. Everything is relative, everything is negotiable, nothing is unequivocal, and the highest virtue is tolerance. Not even God, our culture claims, has the right to make absolutes. Further, we squirm at the idea of God unleashing upon us the consequences of our sinfulness.

But something in our being longs for moral clarity. We seem to know that a God who did not become angry about evil would not be a just God. We need to know that God cares passionately for wholeness, and will express that passion — that God's wholeness will one day be established, and that all that is false and destructive will one day be blotted out. We need to know that good will win out in the end. And we desperately need to be warned of the tendencies in us that would lead to our ruin.

Other Voices

Judge eternal, throned in splendor, Lord of Lords and King of Kings, With Thy living fire of judgment purge our land of bitter things: Solace all its wide dominion with the healing of Thy wings.

Still the weary folk are pining for the hour that brings release; And the city's crowded clangor cries aloud for sin to cease; And the homesteads and the woodlands plead in silence for their peace.

Crown, O God, thine own endeavor: Cleave our darkness with Thy sword; Feed the faint and hungry people with the richness of Thy word; Cleanse the body of this nation through the glory of the Lord.

— Henry Scott Holland, *Judge Eternal, Throned in Splendor*

Lord God, I have indeed transgressed your commandments. I have been impatient in reverses and trials. I am unsympathetic and unmerciful. I do not help my neighbor. I am unable to resist sin. I do not tire of doing wrong. Dear Lord, pour out your grace to me and give me your Holy Spirit so that I may be obedient and keep each of your commandments. Help me to be at odds with the world and to give my heart and soul to you. Amen.

— Martin Luther, *Luther's Prayers*

To Carthage I came, where all around me a cauldron of unholy loves rang in my ears. I did not love yet, yet I loved to love. Out of a deep-seated want, I hated myself for not wanting more. I sought what I might love, in love with loving, and I hated safety and a way without snares. Within me was a famine of that inward food — Yourself, my God — yet though that famine I was not hungry but was without all longing for imperishable sustenance, not because I was filled with it, but because the more empty I was, the more I loathed it. For this reason my soul was sick and full of sores; it miserable cast itself forth, desiring to be scraped by the touch of sensual things. . . .

Your faithful mercy hovered over me from afar. I found myself consumed with many grievous sins, pursuing a sacrilegious curiosity, that having forsaken you, it might bring me to the treacherous abyss and the beguiling service of devils to whom I sacrificed my evil actions. In all these things you scourged me!

— Augustine of Hippo, *Confessions*

In these days conscience seems to judge less severely. Who in our time ever thinks of Hell, or of being lost? Old wives' tales! We understand how to manipulate the register so that nothing causes us alarm. But such manipulation with the conscience really profits nothing. The register in eternity still shows the judgment — lost. Conscience still informs us secretly — you have not taken God's will in earnest. You cannot stand in His judgment. And secretly every one feels this. There is no one who does not fear God — even those who deny

God and laugh at faith in God. Beneath the surface, deep down in the soul, dwells the fear of God, the fear of being lost. . . . Such is the meaning of the word guilt.

What does God say to all this? He tells us that the voice within speaks truly. The conscience that accuses us does not lie. That meter, upon which our guilt mounts like the mileage of the automobile, is God's instrument. We said that conscience registers what God sees, what God says. In God's chancery the death sentence against us is made up.

— EMIL BRUNNER, *Our Faith*

Daily Scripture Readings

KEY TEXT: ISAIAH 13:11
  Sunday: Psalm 22
  Monday: Ephesians 4:17-24
  Tuesday: Psalm 5:4-6
  Wednesday: Galatians 3:10-11
  Thursday: Matthew 25:31-46
  Friday: Deuteronomy 27:26
  Saturday: Job 2:1-6

Questions for Reflection and Discussion

Why is it fair of God to require of people what we are unable to do?

How can God be merciful and yet demand that a penalty be paid for wrongdoing? Can you think of an example you've read where the consequences of an action still stand, even if the person could be forgiven for that action?

Can evil people get into heaven? Why or why not? What are God's criteria? Wouldn't the presence of any sin in heaven make it less than heavenly?

When did you long to see justice in some area of your life? Is there some area where God is calling you to show his justice now?

Closing Prayer

Father, thank you for all you have done for me. By your power, please let me feel again that I am really your child. Because — thanks to you — that is indeed my new reality. Empower me to be an agent of your costly love in the lives of those around me. Amen.

Part Two

Our Lord's Provision

WEEK FIVE:
A HOLY GOD WHO IS MERCIFUL

Opening Prayer

Lord, you are the Sovereign One. You alone hold the destiny of the world in your hands. You alone are pure and perfect. Let me not be threatened by your purity, but instead be drawn into your wholeness, and there find my fulfillment. Amen.

Heidelberg Questions

QUESTION 12: According to God's righteous judgment we deserve punishment both in this world and forever after: how then can we escape this punishment and return to God's favor?

God required that his justice be satisfied.[1] Therefore the claims of his justice must be paid in full, either by ourselves or another.[2]

([1]Exodus 23:7; Romans 2:1-11; [2]Isaiah 53:11; Romans 8:3-4)

QUESTION 13: Can we pay this debt ourselves?

Certainly not. Actually, we increase our guilt every day.[1]

([1]Matthew 6:12; Romans 2:4-5)

QUESTION 14: Can another creature — any at all — pay this debt for us?

No. To begin with, God will not punish another creature for what a human is guilty of.[1]

Besides, no mere creature can bear the weight of God's eternal anger against sin and release others from it.[2]

([1]Ezekiel 18:4,20; Hebrews 2:14-18; [2]Psalm 49:7-9; 130:3)

QUESTION 15: What kind of mediator and deliverer should we look for then?

One who is truly human[1] and truly righteous,[2] yet more powerful than all creatures, that is, one who is also true God.[3]

([1]Romans 1:3; 1 Corinthians 15:21; Hebrews 2:17; [2]Isaiah 53:9; 2 Corinthians 5:21; Hebrews 7:26; [3]Isaiah 7:14; 9:6; Jeremiah 23:6; John 1:1)

Exposition

The questions here begin to move into the solution to the human dilemma: God's radical intervention in the course of human history. God now restores the primal order of creation that people destroyed. The very evil that threatened to undo us is dealt with decisively. The abyss that gaped before humanity has been overcome, and now we can be free.

How has it taken place? All of it has happened through Jesus Christ. In him God brings together both holiness and mercy.

This is the opening of the second part of the catechism, the unfolding drama of "redemption." God, being holy and just, must himself make a way for us broken humans to be made whole again, if it is ever going to happen. Wholeness and healing come for us when we are restored to a relationship with God. This action of God to make us right with him is the core of the Christian faith, and it is the dominant theme of this catechism. (Of 129 questions in the catechism, two form the introduction, nine deal with our guilt, seventy-four deal with God's loving power at work to win us back, and forty-four deal with our thankful response. Far and away the prime theme is the deep, surprising, and efficacious love of God for his people.)

The Bible tells us that God's character is satisfied by the perfect fulfillment of his law — which humans never achieve; or by a perfect atonement — which we are powerless to provide. Perfect obedience or banishment from God. This is the great human dilemma: that we cannot save ourselves.

There is a striking scene in chapter 5 of the Revelation of John in the New Testament. John has a vision of a scroll and is asked by an angel, "Who is worthy to open the scroll and break its seal?" John relates that no one in heaven or on earth is able to open the scroll or to look into it. No one is able to make sense of the seeming randomness of history. No one is able to bring meaning to the chaos of our lives. No one is adequate to that task. And John breaks down and weeps bitterly.

That incident is a graphic reminder of the premise of the catechism that we need a savior. We cannot figure out the purpose of life from our own self-referential perspective. We need a savior from the outside, one of God's own choosing. In spite of all of the technological sophistication of our day, we are desperately in need. Only blindness and arrogance allow us to think otherwise. When we refuse to see the depth of our need, even the best among us, it only further distances us from God. The guilt of our predicament piles up higher every day.

Other Voices

Holiness together with love is the quintessential attribute of God. It includes his majesty, glory and power. James Leo Garrett expresses this well: "Eternity is the duration of God's holiness. Changelessness is the continuing stability or constancy of God's holiness. Wisdom is the truth of God's holiness. Power is the strength of God's holiness. Glory is the recognized manifestation of God's holiness as majesty." Righteousness, one might add, connotes the moral purity of God's holiness. It reminds us that obedience to the holy God involves moral excellence as well as separateness and apartness.

— DONALD G. BLOESCH, *God the Almighty*

As the Holy One, God wills that his holy will shall be realized in the whole of his human creation, by the fact that he is freely and willingly obeyed. Thus God wills that the creature should become full of his own nature — and that is the same as his will to impart himself, his love. God's holy will is fulfilled in the creature as perfect communion with him, the Holy One, and this is his love. The perfect rule of God is only realized where his love breaks down all resistance, and where his own love streams back to him from the hearts of his own people. Only in the fact that God gives himself wholly in his son do those who are his own wholly become his property. Thus holiness merges into love, and thus becomes complete.

— EMIL BRUNNER, *The Christian Doctrine of God*

Being a Christian, I first learned this word ["beloved"] from the story of the baptism of Jesus of Nazareth. "No sooner had Jesus come up out of the water than he saw the heavens torn apart and the Spirit, like a dove, descending on him. And a voice came from heaven: 'You are my Son, the Beloved; my favor rests on you.'" For many years I had read these words and even reflected upon them in sermons and lectures, but it is only since our talks in New York that they have taken on a meaning far beyond the boundaries of my own tradition. Our many conversations led me to the inner conviction that the words, "You are my Beloved" revealed the most intimate truth about all human beings. . . .

Yes, there is that voice, the voice that speaks from above and from within and that whispers softly or declares loudly: "You are my Beloved, on you my favor rests." It certainly is not easy to hear that voice in a world filled with voices that shout: "You are no good, you are ugly; you are worthless; you are despicable, you are nobody — unless you can demonstrate the opposite."

— HENRI J. M. NOUWEN, *Life of the Beloved*

Hear, Lord, my prayer; let not my soul faint under your discipline, nor let me faint in confessing your mercies, whereby you have drawn me out of all my most evil ways, that you might become a delight to me above all the allurements which I once pursued; that I may most entirely love you, and clasp your hand with all my affections, and you may yet rescue me from every temptation, even unto the end. For, O Lord, my King and my God, for your service be whatever useful thing my childhood learned; for your service, that I speak — write — read — reckon. For you granted me your discipline, while I was learning vanities; and my sin of delighting in those vanities you have forgiven. In them, indeed, I learned many a useful word, but these may as well be learned in things not vain; and that is the safe path for the steps of youth.

— AUGUSTINE OF HIPPO,
Confessions

Daily Scripture Readings

KEY TEXT: COLOSSIANS 2:9
    Sunday: Romans 8:3-4
    Monday: Hebrews 2:14-18
    Tuesday: Psalm 49:5-15
    Wednesday: Psalm 99
    Thursday: 1 Corinthians 15:20-28

    Friday: Exodus 15:1-18
    Saturday: Isaiah 53

Questions for Reflection and Discussion

Why does God demand a sacrifice to pay for our sins (see Hebrews 2:14-17)?

Why couldn't God have made some other sacrifice?

Is it easier for you to think of the justice or the grace of God? Why? How does God bring both aspects of his nature together in Jesus (see John 8:1-10)?

Closing Prayer

Gracious God, help me to see my need. Help me to be a person who searches for you, because in searching, there may be finding. In Jesus' name, amen.

Week Six:
Amazing Love

Opening Prayer

Gracious God, I need you even more than I can say. Teach me your way, and I will follow it, with your help. In Jesus' name, amen.

Heidelberg Questions

QUESTION 16: Why must he be truly human and truly righteous?

God's justice demands that human nature, which has sinned, must pay for its sin;[1] but a sinner could never pay for others.[2]

(*[1]Romans 5:12; 15:1; 1 Corinthians 15:21; Hebrews 2:14-16; [2]Hebrews 7:26-27; 1 Peter 3:18*)

QUESTION 17: Why must he also be true God?

So that, by the power of his divinity, he might bear the weight of God's anger in his humanity and earn for us and restore to us righteousness and life.[1]

(*[1]Isaiah 53; John 3:16; 2 Corinthians 5:21*)

QUESTION 18: And who is this mediator — true God and at the same time truly human and truly righteous?

Our Lord Jesus Christ,[1] who was given us to set us completely free and to make us right with God.[2]

(*[1]Matthew 1:21-23; Luke 2:11; 1 Timothy 2:5; [2]1 Corinthians 1:30*)

QUESTION 19: How do you come to know this?

The holy gospel tells me. God himself began to reveal the gospel already in Paradise;[1] later, he proclaimed it by the holy patriarchs[2] and prophets,[3] and portrayed it by the sacrifices and other ceremonies of the law;[4] finally, he fulfilled it through his own dear Son.[5]

(*[1]Genesis 3:15; [2]Genesis 22:18; 49:10; [3]Isaiah 53; Jeremiah 23:5-6; Micah 7:18-20; Acts 10:43; Hebrews 1:1-2; [4]Leviticus 1-7; John 5:46; Hebrews 10:1-10; [5]Romans 10:4; Galatians 4:4-5; Colossians 2:17*)

Exposition

The last section of the Heidelberg Catechism showed us that we need a Savior and that that Savior must be both fully human and fully divine in order to help us. If God's justice is to be satisfied on account of humanity, then the law of God must be fulfilled. After all, that law is not an arbitrary or capricious thing; it is a *righteous* law, that is, an expression of God's own pure and holy character. That is why sin, or rebellion against God, must be punished. Only a person who fully shares our human nature, who can suffer and die — and one who at the same time fully shares God's divine nature — is capable of standing in our place before God. Only such a one can suffer the punishment for the sins of others.

We cannot save ourselves. This idea rubs us the wrong way in our culture of rugged individualism because it means admitting our helplessness. In fact, we don't even like owning up to the fact that we are sinners. We would much rather make excuses: "My genetic code made me what I am . . . my family of origin is to blame for my shortcomings . . . if I had had more opportunities . . . if only I had had better information . . . anyway, other people have done far worse things."

But the beginning of health and hope in us is that point when we humbly admit our need. The Savior whom God has provided is Jesus of Nazareth, who mediates between frail humanity and Almighty God. Jesus is a true human being, body and soul. Jesus is the one righteous human being, without moral blemish of any kind. Jesus is the one who has the right to pronounce the last word on all things. Jesus is at the same time God and human, Immanuel, God with us. And Jesus is the one designated by God, the one whose holiness demands a resolution. Since all of God's prerogatives are found in Jesus, Jesus is able to reconcile us to God.

This message of the way of life is called "gospel," or good news. It's not something we could come up with on our own. It's not something we could figure out by being smart enough or spiritual enough or by working hard enough. It is a message from above from the God who desires to make himself known. In the Garden of Eden, God hinted that one day he would send a savior to cover human sin. Then, some four thousand years ago God reached down to Abraham and Sarah to speak his blessing. The kings of Israel reminded the people of God's sovereign reign, and the prophets called the people back to integrity before God. Throughout the history of Israel, through the cycles of grace, human rebellion, judgment, and more grace, God was expressing his holiness and love to his people, preparing the way for his

Son. The apostle Paul said, "Where sin increased, grace increased all the more"(Romans 5:20). The Bible is the account of the whole grand story, and all of the drama centers on Jesus, God's person for us.

Other Voices

Come, Thou long-expected Jesus, born to
    set Thy people free;
From our fears and sins release us, let us
    find our rest in Thee.
Israel's strength and consolation, hope of
    all the earth Thou art;
Dear desire of every nation, joy of every
    longing heart.
Born Thy people to deliver, born a child
    and yet a king.
Born to reign in us forever, now Thy gra-
    cious kingdom bring.
By Thine own eternal Spirit rule in all our
    hearts along;
By thine all-sufficient merit raise us to Thy
    glorious throne.
— CHARLES WESLEY, "Come, Thou
Long-expected Jesus"

Grant unto us, O God, the fullness of your
    promises.
where we have been weak, grant us your
    strength;
where we have been confused, grant us
    your guidance;
where we have been distraught, grant us
    your comfort;
where we have been dead, grant us your life.
Apart from you, O Lord, we are nothing,
in and with you we can do all things.
— CHRISTINA ROSSETTI

Looking down at night from the mountain top upon Zurich, the traveler sees a broad luminous strip in the midst of the confusing welter of the twinkling lights of the city. It is lovely and attractive although one does not understand the significance of this aggregation of lights. It is the park square in front of the railway station; each one of the hundreds of lights is in its place, but the wayfarer on the heights above knows nothing of this perfect order. Only the chief electrician knows why this arrangement has been made and not some other. He has the blue-print and can grasp the whole plan at a glance; it is his insight, his will that orders and guides the whole. . . .

God has done even more. He did not want to leave us in the dark, for it is not His will that we should go plodding through life fearful, troubled, and apathetic, but that we, mere men though we are, should know something of His great world plans. He has, therefore, revealed to us the counsels of His will in His Word. . . . Then He brought forth His plan out of the darkness of mystery and revealed it to all the world: Jesus Christ, the Word of God in person. . . . That is God's plan for the world.
— EMIL BRUNNER,
Our Faith

Daily Scripture Readings

KEY TEXT: 1 TIMOTHY 2:5
> Sunday: Psalm 99
> Monday: Psalm 110
> Tuesday: 1 Timothy 2:1-6
> Wednesday: 1 John 2:1-6
> Thursday: John 1:29-31
> Friday: Revelation 7:9-17
> Saturday: Hebrews 7:11-17

Questions for Reflection and Discussion

Question 16 tells us that "human nature, which has sinned, must pay for its sin." Why?

And why can't one sinner pay for another?

What does God's demand for righteousness say about God's character? What does his desire to forgive say about him?

Do you think that most people today would rather think of God as a holy God or a loving God? What evidence can you think of for your view? How can it help us to remember that God is both?

Closing Prayer

Thank you, Father, for sending us Jesus, fully human, fully divine. Show me how to share with others your justice and your love. Amen.

Week Seven:
What Shall We Then Do?

Opening Prayer

Lord, I need you. You know it full well, and I guess I know it too: my life just seems to be meaningless fragments without you. But I trust that you can put the pieces back together again, to integrate all the bits into a whole that makes sense. Show me how to live, how to be whole, how to be your child. In Jesus I pray. Amen.

Heidelberg Questions

QUESTION 20: Are all saved through Christ just as all were lost through Adam?

No. Only those are saved who by true faith are grafted into Christ and accept all his blessings.[1]

([1]*Matthew 7:14; John 3:16,18,36; Romans 11:16-21*)

QUESTION 21: What is true faith?

True faith is not only a knowledge and conviction that everything God reveals in his Word is true;[1] it is also a deep-rooted assurance,[2] created in me by the Holy Spirit[3] through the gospel,[4] that, out of sheer grace earned for us by Christ,[5] not only others, but I too,[6] have had my sins forgiven, have been made forever right with God, and have been granted salvation.[7]

([1]*John 17:3,17; Hebrews 11:1-3; James 2:19;* [2]*Romans 4:18-21; 5:1; 10:10; Hebrews 4:14-16;* [3]*Matthew 16:15-17; John 3:5; Acts 16:14;* [4]*Romans 1:16; 10:17; 1 Corinthians 1:21;* [5]*Romans 3:21-26; Galatians 2:16; Ephesians 2:8-10;* [6]*Galatians 2:20;* [7]*Romans 1:17; Hebrews 10:10*)

QUESTION 22: What then must a Christian believe?

Everything God promises us in the gospel.[1] That gospel is summarized for us in the articles of our Christian faith — a creed beyond doubt, and confessed throughout the world.

([1]*Matthew 28:18-20; John 20:30-31*)

QUESTION 23: What are these articles?

I believe in God, the Father almighty, creator of heaven and earth.

I believe in Jesus Christ, his only Son, our Lord, who was conceived by the Holy Spirit and born of the virgin Mary. He suffered under Pontius Pilate, was crucified, died, and was buried; he descended to hell. The third day he rose again from the dead. He ascended to heaven and is seated at the right hand of God the Father almighty. From there he will come to judge the living and the dead.

I believe in the Holy Spirit, the holy catholic church, the communion of saints, the forgiveness of sins, the resurrection of the body, and the life everlasting. Amen.

Exposition

Faith is the key for questions 20 through 23. It is the human response that allows us to tap into the saving power of God. God is the great actor in the drama of salvation. It is God who has worked in Christ to bring us to himself, and God who stirs in us so that we are even able to come to him.

Does this mean that we are merely acted *upon,* passive recipients of God's grace? If we cannot do anything to make ourselves right with God, then is it all a matter of resigning ourselves to our fate? No, the work of the Christian is this: to believe, or to trust God for what he has done.

Faith is more than just a warmth in my heart. It is more than just feeling good about God's love for me. There is content to the Christian faith. To be a Christian is to be sorry for the wrong I've done and to turn away from it; it is to trust in the work of Jesus dying in my place; and it is to commit myself to living for him.

Trusting in him: that's the key to it all. The most important thing about faith is not the amount of faith, but the object of one's faith. Have you ever heard somebody talking about a strong Christian, saying, "She has great faith"? Well, persons we perceive as having "great faith" are usually people who have discovered it's not about their faith at all. They are often people who are acutely aware of their own weakness and of their utter dependence on Christ.

This is the paradox of the Christian experience. People of great spiritual power are people who know they need God. The Lord pointed to this truth when he told the parable of the mustard seed. He used the example of the tiniest object known, a seed the size of the head of a pin, and told how it grows into a mighty tree. His point was that faith isn't an art form or a science. You don't need *great* faith. But you do need faith in the One who can do great things.

Every group of people is held together by what they believe. It's what you believe that shapes how you understand your world and your place in it. Perhaps we sometimes forget, in our anything-goes age of tolerance, that beliefs matter. And whether we're clear on our beliefs or not, all people have values and assumptions about how the world operates.

But where do we go to find spelled out the core of the Christian beliefs? The ultimate authority for us is the Word of God — Jesus, as Scripture bears witness to him. It's not ultimately a council of the church, as important as the voice of the church is for us. It's not tradition, as much as that adds to our understanding. It's not the inner witness of the Holy Spirit, as much as we want to be open to that voice. (That inner witness, too, has to conform to the clear witness of Scripture. Otherwise, how do you know that the feeling you have inside is really from God?) Our authority as Christians is the Word of God, received in the canon of Holy Scripture.

But the Bible is a very big book. How do you find the main themes, the really important ideas? How do you know you understand it rightly? One can spend a lifetime trying to absorb its truth and to grasp its complexity.

Since Christians are members of the body of Christ, the church, it is important to look to how the church has understood the Bible. Although the church is not infallible — it is a sinful institution like any other human institution — the church does provide tremendous help in discerning the essential stuff of the Bible. It does so through the creeds and confessions, the great, historic faith statements of the church.

So question 23 of the Heidelberg Catechism takes us to the core of Christianity. This "confession-within-a-confession" is the Apostles' Creed, one of the affirmations that the churches have embraced throughout the ages. This is what we are to believe.

In spite of the name, the apostles did not write the Apostles' Creed. But it is an ancient creed, dating in its present form back to the ninth century, and its content dates back to the second century and earlier. Its roots can be seen in the New Testament. The creed is built on a trinitarian outline, reflecting the nature of the one true God in the three persons of Father, Son, and Holy Spirit.

The word "creed" itself comes from the Latin, *credo,* "I believe." Here it is that we take our stand.

Other Voices

One man will love Rembrandt, genuinely, and that man will surely know there is a God, he will really believe it. Another will make a thorough study of the French Revolution — he will not be an unbeliever, he will see that there is a supreme authority that manifests itself in great affairs. Yet another has recently attended a free course of lectures at the great university of sorrow and has heeded the things he saw with his eyes and heard with his ears, and has reflected upon them. He too will come to believe in the end and will perhaps have learned more than he can tell.

Try to grasp the essence of what the great artists, the serious masters, say in their masterpieces, and you will again find God in them. One man has written or said it in a book, another in a painting. Just read the Bible and the Gospel, that will start you thinking, thinking about many things, thinking about everything, well then, think about many things, think about everything, that will lift your thoughts above the humdrum despite yourself. We know how to read, so let us read!

— VINCENT VAN GOGH, *The Letters of Vincent Van Gogh*

What every man looks for in life is his own salvation and the salvation of the men he lives with. By salvation I mean first of all the full discovery of who he himself really is. Then I mean something of the fulfill-ment of his own God-given powers, in the love of others and of God. I mean also the discovery that he cannot find himself in himself alone, but that he must find himself in and through others. Ultimately, these propositions are summed up in two lines of the Gospel: "If any man would save his life, he must lose it," and, "Love one another as I have loved you." It is also contained in another saying from St. Paul: "We are all members one of another."

— THOMAS MERTON, *No Man Is an Island*

["Repentance"] is always and everywhere the first word in the Christian life. . . . Repentance is not an emotion. It is not feeling sorry for your sins. It is a deci-sion. It is deciding that you have been wrong in supposing that you could man-age your own life and be your own god; it is deciding that you were wrong in think-ing that you had, or could get, the strength, education and training to make it on your own; it is deciding that you have been told a pack of lies about yourself and your neighbors and your world. And it is decid-ing that God in Jesus Christ is telling you the truth. Repentance is a realization that what God wants from you and what you want from God are not going to be achieved by doing the same old things, thinking the same old thoughts. Repentance is a decision to follow Jesus

Christ and become his pilgrim in the path of peace.

— EUGENE H. PETERSON, *A Long Obedience in the Same Direction*

One who dares not say an ill-natured word or do an unreasonable thing because he considers God as everywhere present performs a better devotion than he who dares not miss the church. To live in the world as a stranger and a pilgrim, using all its enjoyments as if we used them not, making all our actions as so many steps toward a better life, is offering a better sacrifice to God than any forms of holy and heavenly prayers.

To be humble in our actions, to avoid every appearance of pride and vanity, to be meek and lowly in our words, actions, dress, behavior, and designs — all in imitation of our blessed Savior — is worshipping God in a higher manner than do they who have only stated times to fall low on their knees in devotions. The man content with necessities that he may give the remainder to those who need it; who dares not spend any money foolishly, considering it as a talent from God which must be used according to his will, praises God with something that is more glorious than songs of praise.

— WILLIAM LAW, *A Serious Call to a Devout and Holy Life*

Daily Scripture Readings

KEY TEXT: ROMANS 10:9
  Sunday: Hebrews 11
  Monday: Romans 4:1-12
  Tuesday: Romans 4:13-25
  Wednesday: Galatians 3:1-14
  Thursday: Acts 11:1-18
  Friday: John 3:1-21; 11
  Saturday: Philippians 3:1-11

Questions for Reflection and Discussion

Do you know that if you died tonight, you would be welcomed into the presence of God? Here's how you can be sure:

> *Admit you are a sinner who needs God's forgiveness,*
>
> *Believe that Jesus died to pay for your sins,*
>
> *Commit your life to him as your Lord.*

What are some things that being a Christian means?

What are some things that being a Christian does not mean?

What are some of the reasons people don't believe in Christ?

*Closing Prayer*_____

Dear God, please break down any strong-hold of unbelief in me. Help me not to focus on my ability or inability, because in my self-absorption, I'm not at peace. Let me look instead upon your faithfulness to me and to your church. Because of the merit of Jesus, I can ask this. Amen.

Week Eight:
God in Three Persons

*Gracious God, thank you for your love
that follows me all the days of my life.
Thank you for every sign of your leading.
Don't let me ever refuse your work in me,
Father, Son, and Holy Spirit. Amen.*

Heidelberg Questions

QUESTION 24: How are these articles divided?
　　Into three parts:
　　God the Father and our creation;
God the Son and our deliverance;
God the Holy Spirit and our sanctification.

QUESTION 25: Since there is but one God,[1] why do you speak of three: Father, Son, and Holy Spirit?
　　Because that is how God has revealed himself in his Word:[2] these three distinct persons are one, true, eternal God.

([1]*Deuteronomy 6:4; 1 Corinthians 8:4,6;* [2]*Matthew 3:16-17; 28:18-19; Luke 4:18 (Isaiah 61:1); John 14:26; 15:26; 2 Corinthians 13:14; Galatians 4:6; Titus 3:5-6)*

Exposition

The Bible reveals God as Father, Son, and Holy Spirit. The Christian faith is unique in its understanding of God as Trinity, or three persons in one God. How are we to understand this? Would it be more comprehensible to talk of three distinct beings?

More comprehensible, perhaps, but not accurate. The revelation of God in Scripture has always been clear that there is an inscrutable mystery at the heart of God. We can only understand this experientially, not rationally, as we enter into relationship with the God who creates, redeems, and sustains us as his children. Looking from the outside, it doesn't seem to make sense; Muslims, for example, have accused Christians of polytheism — belief in many gods — because of the doctrine of the Trinity.

The term "Trinity" does not occur in Scripture. It is a theological formulation of the Christian community that helps us grasp how God has communicated himself to us. Yet the threefold character of God is deeply embedded in the scriptural testimony. Christians of all times and places have affirmed the truth that there is one God who exists in an eternal three-personed fellowship of love.

The Trinity is the primary doctrine of the Christian faith. In response to theological challenges in its first three centuries, the church rightly recognized the centrality of this belief. The trinitarian language made clear the conviction that the unity of God maintained the distinction of three persons — each one Lord, yet not three but one Lord.

This is an essential tenet of our faith, yet it remains a profound mystery. To attempt to conceive of analogies for the Trinity is to see the inability of human constructs. We cannot define a God who by nature is limitless. The immensity and grandeur of God simply outpace the power of human thought. We can only know God as God chooses to disclose himself to us. And he has chosen to do so in the persons of Father, Son, and Spirit.

God has given us his name. He appeared to Moses in the burning bush to commission Moses to lead the Hebrews out of oppression in Egypt. Moses was so bold as to ask the name of this God who speaks and sends. He implored, "If I come to the Israelites and say to them, 'The God of your ancestors has sent me to you,' and they ask me 'What is his name?', what shall I say to them?" God responded, "*Yahweh* — I am who I am. . . . This is my name forever, and this is my title for all generations" (Exodus 3:13-15, NRSV).

The response is enigmatic to contemporary ears, seeming to obscure as much as it reveals. Persons have speculated it could be understood ontologically, read "I am the one who exists." Perhaps it is better understood in the relational context of Hebrew theology. Moses was not requesting a philosophical formulation of divine being. He was instead pleading for reassurance. If he risked confrontation with the oppressive power of the pharaoh, could he count on God to back him up? If Moses stepped out in faith, would God be there for him? In light of his need, the Lord's answer is best understood relationally: "I am the one who causes to be," or "I am the one who will be there for you."

All the other scriptural designations for God, while highlighting different aspects of his character, are undergirded by this radical disclosure: the Eternal One is the One-*for*-us. The One who speaks is the One who is our Father; the One who has given us a Savior in his Son; the One who fills us with his Spirit.

God is order; God is truth; God is the only true God. God is all-powerful, all-knowing, all-present. He is spirit; he is light, perfect in all his ways. All of these attributes bring us both a challenge and a reassurance. The challenge is there because God sees everything, and doesn't tolerate darkness. We have to be aware of our responsibility before him. The reassurance is there because he is able to hold us up, to handle all the formidable issues of our lives. We can trust him to take care of us in all circumstances. His love is the characteristic that mediates all the other characteristics. God is not closed in upon himself, but pours himself out to communicate himself and his gifts, as Father, Son, and Spirit.

Other Voices

Belief in the Trinity has far-reaching implications for the spiritual life. It means that the God we worship is not a solitary, detached being but a living, personal God who can enter into meaningful relations with us. If God were simply an abysmal silence or infinite depth of being, we could not pray to this God, though we could meditate upon God. But if God is a heavenly Father who adopts us into his family as sons and daughters and who lovingly cares for his children, we can converse with him, knowing that he answers prayer. Arius hardly ever referred to the love of God, but a trinitarian God experiences self-giving love within his own life and can therefore bring this love to others. To depict God as love does not mean that God is absorbed in himself (as in Aristotle) but that he is capable of sharing and giving to others.

— DONALD G. BLOESCH, *God the Almighty*

Holy, Holy, Holy! Lord God almighty!
Early in the morning our song shall rise to
   Thee;
Holy, Holy, Holy! Merciful and mighty!
God in three Persons, blessed Trinity!
Holy, Holy, Holy! All the saints adore Thee,
Casting down their golden crowns around
   the glassy sea;
Cherubim and seraphim falling down
   before Thee,
Who wert, and art, and evermore shalt be.
Holy, Holy, Holy! Though the darkness
   hide Thee,
Though the eye of sinful man Thy glory
   may not see,
Only Thou are holy; there is none beside
   Thee
Perfect in power, in love, and purity.
Holy, Holy, Holy! Lord God Almighty!
All Thy works shall praise Thy name, in
   earth and sky and sea;

Holy, Holy, Holy! Merciful and mighty!
God in three Persons, blessed Trinity!
   Amen.
        — JOHN B. DYKES, "Holy, Holy, Holy!
                Lord God Almighty!"

We confess and acknowledge one God
alone, to whom alone we must cleave,
whom alone we must serve, whom only
we must worship, and in whom alone we
put our trust. Who is eternal, infinite,
immeasurable, incomprehensible, omnipotent, invisible; one in substance and yet distinct in three persons, the Father, the Son,
and the Holy Ghost. By whom we confess
and believe all things in heaven and earth,
visible and invisible, to have been created,
to be retained in their being, and to be
ruled and guided by his inscrutable providence for such end as his eternal wisdom,
goodness, and justice have appointed, and
to the manifestation of his own glory.
                — *The Scots Confession*

We must remind ourselves that Christian
theology does not believe God to be a person. It believes Him to be such that in Him
a trinity of persons is consistent with a
unity of Deity. In that sense it believes Him
to be something very different from a person, just as a cube, in which six squares are
consistent with unity of the body, is different from a square. (Flatlanders, attempting
to imagine a cube, would either imagine
the six squares coinciding, and thus
destroy their distinctness, or else imagine
them set out side by side, and thus destroy

the unity. Our difficulties about the Trinity
are of much the same kind.)
      — C. S. LEWIS, *The Poison of Subjectivism*

O holy and blessed Trinity, let me now so
dwell in the mystery of [your] heavenly love
that all hatred and malice may be rooted out
from my heart and life. Let me love Thee, as
Thou didst first love me; and in loving Thee
let me love also my neighbor; and in loving
Thee and my neighbor in Thee let me be
saved from all false love of myself; and to
Thee, Father, Son, and Holy Spirit, be all
glory and praise for ever. Amen.
      — JOHN BAILLIE, *A Diary of Private Prayer*

Daily Scripture Readings

KEY TEXT: JOHN 15:26
    Sunday: Deuteronomy 6:4-9
    Monday: Matthew 3:16-17
    Tuesday: 1 Corinthians 8:4-6
    Wednesday: 1 Corinthians 12:4-6
    Thursday: 2 Corinthians 13:14
    Friday: John 14
    Saturday: Matthew 28:16-20

Questions for Reflection and Discussion

Who are the three persons of God?

What are some analogies you've heard of the
Trinity? Are any of these satisfying? Do you
see any limitations to them?

What are some of the attributes of God that we learn in Scripture (such as holy, eternal, omniscience, or all-knowing)?

For you, what is the most meaningful name for God? (Master? Savior? Shepherd? Rock? Redeemer? Holy One? Father? Bright Morning Star?)

Closing Prayer

Lord, I don't want to follow anyone but you. That includes my own distorted ideas and misconceptions of you. Help me to know you as you are, and to enter into the fellowship that you created me to enjoy. In the name of Jesus, amen.

Week Nine:

God the Father

Opening Prayer

Father, incline your ear to me and hear my cry. Thank you for your promise to be there for me. Amen.

Heidelberg Questions

QUESTION 26: What do you believe when you say, "I believe in God, the Father almighty, creator of heaven and earth"?

That the eternal Father of our Lord Jesus Christ, who out of nothing created heaven and earth and everything in them,[1] who still upholds and rules them by his eternal counsel and providence,[2] is my God and Father because of Christ his Son.[3]

I trust him so much that I do not doubt he will provide whatever I need for body and soul,[4] and he will turn to my good whatever adversity he sends me in this sad world.[5]

He is able to do this because he is almighty God,[6] he desired to do this because he is a faithful Father.[7]

([1]*Genesis 1–2; Exodus 20:11; Psalm 33:6; Isaiah 44:24; Acts 4:24; 14:15;* [2]*Psalm 104; Matthew 6:30; 10:29; Ephesians 1:11;* [3]*John 1:12-13; Romans 8:15-16; Galatians 4:4-7; Ephesians 1:5;* [4]*Psalm 55:22; Matthew 6:25-26; Luke 12:22-31;* [5]*Romans 8:28;* [6]*Genesis 18:14; Romans 8:31-39;* [7]*Matthew 7:9-11*)

Exposition

There's a movement in some theological circles to do away with references to God as Father, for fear of conveying a patriarchal picture of God. That movement challenges the image of God as a distant, demanding, and domineering patriarch, one who crushes our spirits and establishes his will by force.

But that is not the God of the Bible. Scripture describes God in many different ways. These sometimes stand in dynamic tension with one another, because no description can encapsulate God. Most personal of these descriptions is the tenderhearted parent, like the father who reaches out to embrace his returning son (Luke 15:20), or like the mother who won't abandon the baby at her breast (Isaiah 49:15). If we jettison the biblical portrait of Father, we seriously misunderstand the reality of God. Because when we describe God as Father, we do not mean it as in contrast with a mother. Instead, we mean it as in contrast with some impersonal force of nature. Such fatalistic views of God had to be confronted by the biblical writers in their own setting. Such views of God need to be confronted in our day as well.

We have to be very careful not to project our own image onto the heavenly Father. When the disciple Philip asked to see the Father, Jesus responded, "Have I been with you all this time, Philip, and still you do not know me? Whoever has seen me has seen the Father. How can you say, 'Show us the Father?'" (John 14:9, NRSV). In effect, he was saying, "Do you want to see God? — then look at me — God is standing right in front of you."

What kind of father is God? Not an angry, punitive judge. He's just like Jesus — the One who brought a healing touch to so many, the One who delivered truth in a package of love, the One who showed a compassion and inclusiveness that gave a whole new understanding of the character of God, the One who longs to be called *Abba* — Daddy! — the One who sacrificially gave of himself so that his people can be whole. He is the Father who cares for us with the tenderness of a mother.

When we look at Jesus, we see the lofty summit of God's revelation. Look at him, and you see into the heart of God. The fatherhood of God answers the cry of our souls. It is much more profound than the idea of justification, for example, as great as that doctrine is. Justification means that God as the judge declares us right in his eyes by sheer grace. But the idea of fatherhood goes further. It tells us that God doesn't stay in the posture of judge. God says, "Not only do I find you not guilty, but I long to be in a relationship with you."

The Nicene Creed says it like this: "We believe in one God, the Father, the Almighty, maker of heaven and earth, of all that is seen and unseen." The great mystery at the heart of the cosmos is that almighty God is a suffering deity; the Savior of the world was nailed to a cross. The self-sacrificial, costly love of Jesus defines the character of the God. He is Father in that he saves and suffers for his people.

Jean Valjean is a figure of God's grace and tenderness in Victor Hugo's great novel, *Les Misérables*. Valjean has been caring for a destitute woman. He finds that the woman, in desperation, had boarded her little girl, Cosette, with the owners of a country inn. They turn out to be mean-spirited people who exploit her as a servant, but the poor mother had no other options. Now, on her deathbed, the mother makes Valjean promise to care for Cosette.

Valjean goes to get the child, and he doesn't let the manipulative innkeeper stop him from buying back the forlorn little girl. The innkeeper senses a strong resolve on the part of Jean Valjean that won't be deterred, just as a demon senses when it is in "the presence of a higher god."[4] The good man prevailed. Early the next morning, two dark figures could be seen making their way down the country road, away from the inn, a strong man holding the hand of the little girl who had so hated and who had *been* so hated in that place. In her other hand she clutched a new doll. And she looked up toward the face of the stranger who was her savior, feeling like she was walking with God.

Valjean is a symbol for the God who not only has bought our salvation, but who commits to caring for us. This is the God whom we call Father.

Other Voices

You sum up the whole of the New Testament teaching in a single phrase, if you speak of it as a revelation of the Fatherhood of the holy Creator . . . you sum up the whole of the New Testament religion if you describe it as the knowledge of God as one's Holy Father. If you want to judge how well a person understands Christianity, find out how much he makes of the thought of being God's child, and having God as his Father. If this is not the thought that prompts and controls his worship and prayers and his whole outlook on life it means that he does not understand Christianity very well at all. For everything that Christ taught, everything that makes the New Testament new, and better than the Old, everything that is distinctively Christian as opposed to merely Jewish, is summed up in the knowledge of the Fatherhood of God. "Father" is the Christian name for God.

— J. I. PACKER,
Knowing God

God is not a solitary being, detached and remote from the world of human discourse and activity, but a Trinitarian fellowship of love. Because he experiences love within himself he can relate in love to his creation. He is not simply the sustainer of the world but the suffering servant who redeems the world (Isaiah 53).

A too rigid adherence to the monarchy of the Father would cancel out the element of reciprocity in our relationship to God. The correct attitude would then simply be surrender and submission. But in biblical prayer we pour out our soul before God, we entreat him and beg him for his favor and mercy. We do not merely bring our requests before God, but we struggle with God, even wrestle with God. God is over us and above us to be sure, but he is also within us and beside us. He is not only Lord and Master but Friend and Brother. A purely monarchical view of God is challenged by Jesus: "No longer do I call you servants . . . but I have called you friends."

— DONALD G. BLOESCH,
God the Almighty

Jesus is my solace,
    so I won't need a thing.

⌒

He lets me stretch out in green meadows
    when I'm hot and tired,
        in a place where nobody's going to
        stumble upon me.
He takes me down to the water's edge
    where the currents run cool and deep and
where the trout are dark blurs on the
    granite pebbles of the stream bed.
The water's so clear you can drink it.
When I'm with him, I know who I am again.

⌒

I regard by the light of day the objects of
    my fear,
And the demons inside just evaporate in
    the warmth and light of his presence.
Jesus, you're here with everything I need.
You're here with what I never dreamed of
    asking, never dared to ask.

Goodness . . . mercy! Yes, they're here to
    stay
along with you.
— RANDY WORKING, "Jesus Is My Solace: A
                    Variation on Psalm 23"

Be Thou my vision, Lord of my heart;
Naught be all else to me, save that Thou art —
Thou my best thought, by day or by night,
Waking or sleeping, Thy presence my light.

⌒

Be Thou my Wisdom, and Thou my true
    Word,
I ever with Thee and Thou with me, Lord;
Thou my great Father, I Thy true son,
Thou in me dwelling, and I with Thee one.

⌒

Riches I heed not, nor vain, empty praise,
Thou mine inheritance, now and always;
Thou and Thou only, first in my heart,
high king of heaven, my Treasure Thou art.

⌒

High king of heaven, my victory won,
May I reach heaven's joys, O bright
    heaven's Sun,
Heart of my own heart, whatever befall,
Still be my Vision, O Ruler of all.
— ANCIENT IRISH POEM

Daily Scripture Readings

KEY TEXT: 1 PETER 1:17
    Sunday: Psalm 89:19-37
    Monday: Psalm 23
    Tuesday: Psalm 68:5-6
    Wednesday: Matthew 7:7-12

Thursday: Romans 8:12-17
Friday: John 1:10-13
Saturday: Galatians 3:26–4:7

Why do you suppose the Bible emphasizes that the Creator of the universe is a personal God?

Questions for Reflection and Discussion _____

What characteristics come to mind when you think of something as "mighty"? When you think of a father? What does putting the two together suggest?

Is there anything about "father" you think we have to overcome in order to more fully enjoy fellowship with God?

Closing Prayer _____

Abba Father, you created the cosmos, and you made me. You know me inside and out, and you love me. I'm so glad I get to know you intimately. Give me the grace to love those you lead into my life. Amen.

Week Ten:
God's Guiding Hand

Opening Prayer

Gracious God, you uphold all creation. You guide all things to their highest good. Thank you that I can count on you to provide everything I need. In Jesus' name, amen.

Heidelberg Questions

QUESTION 27: What do you understand by the providence of God?

Providence is the almighty and ever present power of God[1] by which he upholds, as with his hand, heaven and earth and all creatures,[2] and so rules them that leaf and blade, rain and drought, fruitful and lean years, food and drink, health and sickness, prosperity and poverty[3] — all things, in fact, come to us not by chance[4] but from his fatherly hand.[5]

([1]*Jeremiah 23:23-24; Acts 17:24-28;* [2]*Hebrews 1:3;* [3]*Jeremiah 5:24; Acts 14:15-17; John 9:3; Proverbs 22:2;* [4]*Proverbs 16:33;* [5]*Matthew 10:29*)

QUESTION 28: How does the knowledge of God's creation and providence help us?

We can be patient when things go against us,[1] thankful when things go well,[2] and for the future we can have good confidence in our faithful God and Father that nothing will separate us from his love.[3] All creatures are so completely in his hand that without his will they can neither move nor be moved.[4]

([1]*Job 1:21-22; James 1:3;* [2]*Deuteronomy 8:10; 1 Thessalonians 5:18;* [3]*Psalm 55:22; Romans 5:3-5; 8:38-39;* [4]*Job 1:12; 2:6; Proverbs 21:1; Acts 17:24-28*)

Exposition

To speak of "providence" is to speak of the care and protection of God. The providence of God entails at least a twofold work: first, God's holding together of the created order, and second, God's guidance of all things toward his ultimate purposes. This means that the living God, in goodness and power, directs and sustains the whole universe. He is intrinsically involved in caring for creation. God did not simply get things rolling and then step back to watch the action unfold.

God acts in freedom. He is not limited to the forces of nature, but acts to accomplish the fulfillment of all things. He is the one who made it all. He is the one who is moving all the events of history toward the good plan he had in mind when he created the world and when he revealed himself to a people in order to save them.

It means that there is a purpose to life, a grand design. Life is more than a random collection of events or an eternal cycle of birth and rebirth. Everything is in God's hands; God knows the ending-place to which he is guiding all things. The apostle Paul points to this when he writes in his letter to the Ephesians, "And he made known to us the mystery of his will according to his good pleasure, which he purposed in Christ, to be put into effect when the times will have reached their fulfillment — to bring all things in heaven and on earth together under one head, even Christ" (1:9).

Providence means that God takes care of us. Genesis 22 recounts the story of Abraham and Sarah's young son Isaac, the blessing of their old age and the hope for their progeny. Because of that son and his descendants, God had revealed the means by which he would bless all the peoples of the earth. Then, a shocking word from God came to Abraham in the command, "Take your son, your only son, Isaac, whom you love, and go to the region of Moriah. Sacrifice him there as a burnt offering on one of the mountains I will tell you about" (Genesis 22:2).

Imagine the profound sadness of the boy's parents! Is this, then, the way of the God who has called us out of a distant land to follow him in faith? Is he no different from the bloodthirsty idols of Canaan? With a broken heart, Abraham bundles up his supplies for the trek and makes his way toward the designated place.

But God knows what he's asking. He knows what Isaac means to his father and mother — "Your only son, Isaac, whom you love . . ." And Abraham, even in his devastation, still clings to faith. When Isaac sees that they have fire and wood for a burnt offering, but not a lamb, he asks, "[Father,] where is the lamb?" Abraham replies, "God . . . will provide, . . . my son" (22:7-8).

The place was probably the site of sacrifice to pagan idols from time out of memory. Abraham lays his son on the wood of the altar and lifts his hand to kill him. But the voice of the Lord's angel calls out, "Abraham! Abraham! . . . Do not lay a hand on the boy. . . . Now I know that you fear God" (verses 11-12).

Paintings throughout the ages have depicted that great scene, from medieval frescoes to the works of the Jewish Russian expressionist Chagall. Seventeenth-century Dutch painter Rembrandt has depicted the scene powerfully in a painting now hanging in the Alte Pinakotek in Munich. Other painters imagined the drama of the angel gripping the hand of the father just as he drove the dagger toward his son's heart. But Rembrandt, sensitive to the psychological underpinnings of the scene, did it differently. Brooding colors and chiaroscuro underscore the drama and electricity of the scene. Abraham has placed one hand over his young son's face so that the last image Isaac sees will not be his father laying a knife to his throat. The angel has appeared and seizes Abraham's wrist. His hand is open. The knife is falling to the ground. The father's eyes gaze heavenward, caught just at the moment of grace when stupefied grief turns to relief and joy.

In the shadows behind the figures, a ram struggles, caught in a thicket. Now Abraham can make a thank offering to the Lord. That's why the place is called, the writer of Genesis tells us, "The Lord will provide." The lesson: we cannot provide — but God can, and will. It is the Christian's comfort that God will take care of us, guide us, and through all the circumstances of life, work for our benefit.

Other Voices

[Jesus' word in Matthew 6:26] about the birds of the sky is only rightly understood if it is seen as counsel against anxiety, not as counsel for indolence. [Jerome writes,] "The birds are an example not of idleness but of freedom from anxiety." And yet Jesus is not asking here that we be as busy as sparrows, though the seeking of right-eousness that he commands in a moment includes seeking the righteousness of faith-ful work. If Jesus' reference to the birds is not pro-indolence, neither is it pro-industri-ousness; it is first of all and fundamentally pro-faith. We are asked not to limit our faith in the Father to spiritual things; we are asked to believe that the Father is active in economic matters, alive to physical need, and a provider of food no less than of mercy. We are asked, in a word, to believe that God is God. And as God he is not only Redeemer; he is Creator.

— FREDERICK DALE BRUNER, *The Christbook: A Historical/Theological Commentary*

If we could see what we will receive in the life to come (as a reward for what we have done here), we would cease to occupy our-selves with anything but the things of heaven. But God, who desires that we see by faith and who desires that we not do good because of selfish motives, gives us this vision little by little, sufficient to the level of faith of which we are capable. In this manner, God leads us into a greater vision of that which is to come until faith is no longer needed.

On the other hand, if we were somehow informed that we were about to die, and that the life that awaits us will be miserable because of our sins, and that we would have to suffer eternally, I feel sure that we — for fear of it — would rather let ourselves be killed than commit one single sin! But God — as unwilling as he is that we avoid sin out of the motive of fear and therefore never lets us see it — will show it in part to souls who are clothed and occupied with him.

— CATHERINE OF GENOA,
Life and Teachings

O the deep, deep love of Jesus, vast,
  unmeasured boundless, free!
Rolling as a mighty ocean in its fullness
  over me! Underneath me, all around me,
is the current of thy love — leading onward,
  leading homeward, to thy glorious rest
  above!

🙐

O the deep, deep love of Jesus — spread his
  praise from shore to shore!
How he loveth, ever loveth, changeth
  never, nevermore! How he watches o'er
  his loved ones,
Died to call them all his own;
How for them he intercedeth, watcheth
  o'er them from the throne!

🙐

O the deep, deep love of Jesus, Love of
  every love the best!
'Tis an ocean full of blessing, 'Tis a haven
  giving rest!

O the deep, deep love of Jesus — 'tis a
  heaven of heavens to me;
And it lifts me up to glory, for it lifts me up
  to Thee!

— SAMUEL FRANCIS,
"O the Deep, Deep Love of Jesus"

Therefore God, with his Word and Holy Spirit (which are three-in-One), one God omnipotent, creator and maker of every soul and every body; by whose gift all are happy who are happy through truth and not through vanity . . . that God can never be thought to have left the human kingdoms outside of the laws of his providence.

The sins of mortals and of angels do nothing to impede the great works of the Lord which accomplish his will. For he who by his providence and omnipotence distributes to every one his own portion, is able to make good use not only of the good, but also of the wicked.

— AUGUSTINE OF HIPPO, *The City of God*

Daily Scripture Readings

KEY TEXT: ISAIAH 46:4
  Sunday: Romans 8:28-39
  Monday: Genesis 28:10-17
  Tuesday: Exodus 23:20-33
  Wednesday: Matthew 6:25-34
  Thursday: Psalm 16
  Friday: Mark 10:27-31
  Saturday: Deuteronomy 28:1-14

Questions for Reflection and Discussion

Can you think of a time when you really needed direction at a crossroads in your life, and God "came through" for you? How did it happen?

Does God control everything? Even the details?

What are ways we can learn and practice the virtue of patience in adversity?

If someone is having problems in life, does that mean that God is punishing that person? How can knowing of God's providence comfort us in life?

Closing Prayer

Dear Father, you have given me so many blessings. I only ask for one more: please give me the gift of a grateful heart, now, and every day of my life. Amen.

WEEK ELEVEN:
JESUS SAVES!

Opening Prayer

Lord, pull me close to you, and fill me with praise for your salvation. Amen.

Heidelberg Questions

QUESTION 29: Why is the Son of God called "Jesus," meaning "savior"?

Because he saves us from our sins.[1] Salvation cannot be found in anyone else; it is futile to look for any salvation elsewhere.[2]

(*[1]Matthew 1:21; Hebrews 7:25; [2]Isaiah 43:11; John 15:5; Acts 4:11-12; 1 Timothy 2:5*)

QUESTION 30: Do those who look for their salvation and security in saints, in themselves or elsewhere really believe in the only savior, Jesus?

No. Although they boast of being his, by their deeds they deny the only savior and deliverer, Jesus.[1]

Either Jesus is not a perfect savior, or those who in true faith accept this savior have in him all they need for their salvation.[2]

(*[1]1 Corinthians 1:12-13; Galatians 5:4; [2]Colossians 1:19-20; 2:10; 1 John 1:7*)

Exposition

Question 23 introduced the Apostles' Creed as an outline of the Christian faith. Question 26 addressed the meaning of the title, "God, the Father almighty," the first person of the Trinity. Now, question 29 addresses the significance of God's Son, Jesus, the second person of the Trinity.

Here the church affirms its understanding of the *identity* of the Savior, "Jesus Christ, his only Son, our Lord, who was conceived by the Holy Spirit and born of the virgin Mary." Next, the creed will refer to the *work* of this Savior who "suffered under Pontius Pilate, was crucified, died, and was buried." In the following section, the questions will echo the movement of divine condescension: Jesus' descent from the glory he shared with the Father in heaven; the humility of his coming to earth as a servant; the shame of his death on a cross; and finally, his resurrection from the place of the dead and exaltation to God's right hand.

Each of these articles of the creed rests on the foundation of "I believe." They are articles of *faith*. The Christian embraces Jesus the unique Son of God just as he or she embraces the living God himself. Jesus shares the same nature as the Father. That is why the Christian sees Jesus as more than merely a prophet, more than simply a great moral teacher. He was more than a mystic or a miracle worker or some misguided messiah-figure. God himself attests to Jesus' unique stature and authority: "This is my Son, the Beloved, with whom I am well-pleased. Listen to him!" (Matthew 17:5, NRSV).

His name Jesus, in Hebrew "Joshua," or "Yeshua," means "God saves," or "Yahweh is salvation." His name reminds us that people need a savior. Humanity is unable to extract itself from the existential hole it's fallen into. And that from which we need saving is our sins. Ultimately, we don't need saving from ignorance, from intolerance, from primitive attitudes, from poverty. Humanity struggles with all of these ills, yet they are symptoms of the deeper disease of sin, or of attempting to live without reference to God. Various human responses to the brokenness of the world come and go, from stoicism to communism, but the only lasting solution is offered in the person of Jesus of Nazareth, the only begotten Son of the Father.

Has anyone ever asked you, "Are you saved?" The salvation of God is that which frees men and women from the guilt, the punishment, and the power of sin. It is to deliver needy humans, body and soul, and to bring them into communion with God. God accomplished it once for all in Christ; he continues it in his sanctifying work in those who believe; he will complete it at the consummation of history. This deliverance is a free gift of grace, one we are wholly unable to bring about by our own doing. How difficult it is to admit our need, to lay down all pretense of merit and affectation of pride, and to come to God with empty hands!

We need no other. Jesus our true Savior has everything we need.

Other Voices

What wondrous love is this, O my soul,
  O my soul,
What wondrous love is this, O my soul!
What wondrous love is this that caused the
  Lord of bliss
To bear the dreadful curse for my soul, for
  my soul,
To bear the dreadful curse for my soul!

To God and to the Lamb I will sing,
  I will sing,
To God and to the Lamb, I will sing;
To God and to the Lamb who is the
  great I Am,
While millions join the theme, I will sing,
  I will sing;
While millions join the theme, I will sing!

And when from death I'm free, I'll sing on,
  I'll sing on,
And when from death I'm free, I'll sing on;
And when from death I'm free, I'll sing
  and joyful be,
And through eternity I'll sing on,
  I'll sing on,
And through eternity I'll sing on!
— AMERICAN FOLK HYMN,
"What Wondrous Love Is This!"

Salvation must continue to come to human beings "from beyond": its source is God. That remains true, even though the human appropriation is such that the recipients are themselves being transformed in their inmost being in moral and spiritual assimi-lation to God. The motif of feeding allows an appropriate expression of the divine giving and the active human reception. The Psalmist confesses:

> The eyes of all look to thee,
>   and Thou givest them their food in
>   due season.
> Thou openest thy hand,
>   Thou satisfiest the desire of every
>   living thing (Psalm 145:15-16).

— GEOFFREY WAINWRIGHT, *Doxology: The Praise of God in Worship, Doctrine, and Life*

He so loves His world that He has given Himself to it, in the person of His Son, and thus He has again brought our race, and through our race, His whole Cosmos, into a renewed contact with eternal life. To be sure, many branches and leaves fell off the tree of the human race, yet the tree itself shall be saved; on its new root in Christ, it shall once more blossom gloriously. For regeneration does not save a few isolated individuals, finally to be joined together mechanically as an aggregate heap. Regeneration saves the organism, itself, of our race. And therefore all regenerate human life forms one organic body, of which Christ is the Head, and whose mem-bers are bound together by their mystical union with Him.

— ABRAHAM KUYPER, *Lectures on Calvinism*

Reader, had I the space to write at will,
  I should, if only briefly, sing a praise

of that sweet draught. Would I were
　drinking still!

❧

But I have filled all of the pages planned
　for this, my second canticle, and Art
　pulls at its iron bit with iron hand.

❧

I came back from those holiest waters new,
　remade, reborn, like a sun-wakened tree
　that spreads new foliage to the Spring
　dew

❧

in sweetest freshness, healed of Winter's
　scars;
perfect, pure, and ready for the Stars.
　　— DANTE ALIGHIERI, *The Divine Comedy*

Daily Scripture Readings

KEY TEXT: 1 TIMOTHY 1:15
　　Sunday: Matthew 1:18-25
　　Monday: Hebrews 7:18-28
　　Tuesday: Isaiah 43:1-13
　　Wednesday: Acts 4:1-12
　　Thursday: 1 Timothy 2:1-5
　　Friday: Galatians 5:1-6
　　Saturday: 1 John 1

Questions for Reflection and Discussion

What do you see as some of the great
questions of life that people have always
asked?

How do people try to overcome the moral
problems that plague humanity? What do
people do to "save" themselves?

Do you agree that Jesus is the only way to
God? What evidence from Scripture would
you cite in support of your view?

Closing Prayer

*Savior, embolden me to loosen my grip on
all the things I cling to, trying to justify
myself in your eyes. Then I will turn my
hands toward you to receive your happy
gift of salvation. I pray in the good name of
Jesus. Amen.*

Week Twelve: Lord, I Want to Be a Christian in My Heart

Opening Prayer

I love you, Lord, because you heard my cry and saved me from all my darkness. Give me the strength to live a life worthy of the name you have given me. In Jesus' name, amen.

Heidelberg Questions

QUESTION 31: Why is he called "Christ," meaning "anointed"?

Because he has been ordained by God the Father and has been anointed with the Holy Spirit[1] to be our chief prophet and teacher[2] who perfectly reveals to us the secret counsel and will of God for our deliverance;[3] our only high priest[4] who has set us free by the one sacrifice of his body,[5] and who continually pleads our cause with the Father;[6] and our eternal king[7] who governs us by his Word and Spirit, and who guards us and keeps us in the freedom he has won for us.[8]

[[1]*Luke 3:21-22; 4:14-19 (Isaiah 61:1); Hebrews 1:9 (Psalm 45:7);* [2]*Acts 3:22 (Deuteronomy 18:15);* [3]*John 1:18; 15:15;* [4]*Hebrews 7:17 (Psalm 110:4);* [5]*Hebrews 9:12; 10:11-14;* [6]*Romans 8:34; Hebrews 9:24;* [7]*Matthew 21:5 (Zechariah. 9:9);* [8]*Matthew 28:18-20; John 10:28; Revelation 12:10-11]*

QUESTION 32: But why are you called a Christian?

Because by faith I am a member of Christ[1] and so I share in his anointing.[2] I am anointed to confess his name,[3] to present myself to him as a living sacrifice of thanks,[4] to strive with a good conscience against sin and the devil in this life,[5] and afterward to reign with Christ over all creation for all eternity.[6]

([1]*1 Corinthians 12:12-27;* [2]*Acts 2:17 (Joel 2:28); 1 John 2:27;* [3]*Matthew 10:32; Romans 10:9-10; Hebrews 13:15;* [4]*Romans 12:1; 1 Peter 2:5,9;* [5]*Galatians 5:16-17; Ephesians 6:11; 1 Timothy 1:18-19;* [6]*Matthew 25:34; 2 Timothy 2:12)*

Exposition

The many scriptural titles for Jesus bring out the richness of his character and underscore the nature of his mission: Lord, God, Word, Son of David, Son of Man, Firstborn from the dead, Image of God, Alpha and Omega, Savior, Redeemer, Author and Perfecter of our faith, Light of the World, Lamb of God, High Priest, the Good Shepherd, the Way, the Truth, and the Life. These point to the role of mediator, one who stands between God and humanity to reveal the heart of God to his people and to make a way for sinful humans to come into his presence. He is the messenger, interpreter, and guarantor of the covenant. He confirms and fulfills the promises of God and makes peace between God and us. All of this is summed up in the terms of prophet, priest, and king.

These three titles represent the essential character of the Lord's redeeming work. The prophet teaches, the priest makes possible a way to God, and the king exercises sovereign authority and care for his people. Still, the prophets of the Old Testament who were true to God often had to speak out against priests and rulers who led the people astray. In the course of Israel's nation building it became clear that human society was incapable of fulfilling the plan of God in history. The hope of the people became focused upon a future messiah who would embody the three offices. These help us understand Christ's mission. Calvin said it this way:

> Therefore, in order that faith may find a firm basis for salvation in Christ, and thus
> rest in him, this principle must be laid down: the office enjoined upon Christ by the
> Father consists of three parts. For he was given to be prophet, king, and priest.[5]

The Old Testament writers longed for the coming of one who could fulfill the offices foreshadowed by Moses, Samuel, and David. Isaiah, though his prophetic mission to Israel would fail (Isaiah 49:4), told of the coming Servant of the Lord who would take upon himself God's penalty for sin and then reign as king (Isaiah 53). The Servant as prophet, priest, and king would reveal God.

In Jesus, the teacher of truth, the prophetic ministry comes to its pinnacle. The gospel accounts show the power and creativity of his teaching as he used questions, hyperbole, discourse, and parables filled with everyday images readily understood by his listeners. He taught with a kind of compelling authority unknown anywhere. The Sermon on the Mount recorded in Matthew chapters 5 through 7 pulls the curtains back on a whole new-world order for those who belong to his kingdom. He is the teacher still today as, through his Spirit, he interprets Scripture for his church to teach us about God, himself, his nature, his mission, his Spirit, and our place in the world.

In Jesus the High Priest, the sacrificial order of Israel accomplishes its goal. Israel practiced an extensive and elaborate sacrificial system. Priests conducted worship and made expiation for the sins of the people. Matthew says in the opening of his gospel that Jesus was to "save his people from their sins" (Matthew 1:21). He came to give his life "as a ransom for many" (Mark 10:45), as "the

Lamb of God, who takes away the sin of the world" (John 1:29). Redemption means forgiveness. In perhaps the high point of all the scriptural passages interpreting the Lord's sacrificial death, Hebrews 7 makes clear that he continues to intercede for us as High Priest in heaven. This role is twofold, because he is both the one who *offers* the sacrifice, and he is the sacrifice itself. It is because he entered the Holy of Holies, because he offered his own blood, that his sacrifice was effective.

In Jesus, the righteous one, the long-awaited king is revealed. Israel craved a king and cried out to God for one. This was seen by Samuel as a disobedient desire to be like the other nations. Nonetheless, it was through the Davidic line of kings that God prepared to send Jesus, the true king. When the monarchy failed time and time again to measure up morally, the prophets reminded the people that one day God would send a king who would rule over the nations with power and authority, a kingdom not like those of the world but one built on righteousness. The king was seen as the anointed of Yahweh, the one set apart for service.

The word "Christ" is Greek for "messiah," literally, "anointed one." In Old Testament times, those called by God to special office would be anointed with oil. People would submit to this rite as a consecration and a blessing for divine service. When the young David was designated for the kingship, the prophet Samuel anointed his head with oil. Later, the term "messiah" became a title of the one whom God would send on his behalf to the world. The Jews longed for a messiah who would be a military and political leader, one who would deliver his people from their enemies. Through Jesus, we have come to see that the messiah is the one who does more than that. The Redeemer of the world, he is the prophet who reveals God, the priest who mediates the grace of God, the king who rules in order to bring to the world the salvation of God. Jesus is the Christ, the one called by God to be our prophet, priest, and king.

Have you ever reflected on the fact that those who follow Christ as his disciples are called Christians? We, too, are now anointed, commissioned into his service as Christians — "little christs" called to make a difference in the world.

Other Voices

When I've thrown my books aside, being
  petulant and weary,
And have turned down the gas, and the
  firelight has sufficed,
When my brain's too stiff for prayer, and
  too indolent for theory,
Will You come and play with me, big
  Brother Christ?
　　　🙠

Will You slip behind the book-case? Will
  you stir the window-curtain,
Peeping from the shadow with Your eyes
  like flame?
Set me staring at the alcove where the
  flicker's so uncertain,
Then suddenly, at my elbow, leap up, catch
  me, call my name?
　　　🙠

Or take the great arm-chair, help me set the
    chestnuts roasting,
And tell me quiet stories, while the brown
    skins pop,
Of wayfarers and merchantmen and tramp
    of Roman hosting,
And how Joseph dwelt with Mary in the
    carpenter's shop?

                  ↜

When I drift away in dozing, will You
    softly light the candles
And touch the piano with Your kind,
    strong fingers,
Set stern fugues of Bach and stately themes
    of Handel's
Stalking through the corners where the last
    disquiet lingers?

                  ↜

And when we say good-night, and You kiss
    me on the landing,
Will You promise faithfully and make a
    solemn tryst:
You'll be just at hand if wanted, close by
    here where we are standing,
And be down in time for breakfast, big
    Brother Christ?
  —DOROTHY L. SAYERS, "Christ the Companion"
    from *Catholic Tales and Christian Songs*

All men are alike — true in that the difference
between those who received many talents
and those who received few is presently
erased without mercy. But untrue when it is a
question of how they employed them: then,
there still stands the frontier between life and
death, as it has been drawn for all eternity. In
the last analysis, however, true there also,
because we are, all of us, at all times, confronted with the possibility of taking the step
across that frontier — in either direction.
             — DAG HAMMARSKJOLD

In the *Epistle of Privy Counsel* there is a passage which expresses with singular com-
pleteness the author's theory of this
contemplative art — this silent yet ardent
encounter of the soul with God. Prayer, said
Mechthild of Magdeburg, brings together
two lovers, God and the soul, in a narrow
room where they speak much of love: and
here the rules which govern that meeting are
laid down by a master's hand. "When thou
comest by thyself," he says, "think not
before what thou shalt do after, but forsake
as well good thoughts as evil thoughts, and
pray not with thy mouth but list thee right
well. And then if thou aught shalt say, look
not how much nor how little that it be, nor
weigh not what it is nor what it bemeaneth
. . . and look that nothing live in thy working
mind but a naked intent stretching into God,
not clothed in any special thought of God in
Himself. . . . This naked intent freely fastened
and grounded in very belief shall be naught
else to thy thought and to thy feeling but a
naked thought and a blind feeling of thine
own being: as if thou saidest thus unto God,
within in thy meaning, 'That what I am,
Lord, I offer unto Thee, without any looking
to any quality of Thy Being, but only that
Thou art as Thou art, without any more.'"
    — EVELYN UNDERHILL, *Introduction to The*
      Cloud of Unknowing (Anonymous,
        fourteenth-century English)

"Christ-bearer; image of God; symbol of the sacred." Tom kept repeating these ideas to himself as he parked and made his way to the hospital elevator. He thought about all the tasks of ministry — preaching, teaching, counseling, baptizing, conducting funerals, offering the sacrament of the Lord's Supper — could he, in all these functions of ministry, be the bearer of Christ?

Perhaps more pressing, could he be the bearer of Christ to Juanita Jones in room 803, who had learned yesterday that she had an inoperable malignancy?

Tom MacGreggor has been confronted with an issue with which he must come to grips, a calling to re-present Jesus Christ in his life and ministry. This commission to be a Christ bearer has its source in the heart of the gospel — created in the image of God, re-created by Christ, called by God to be a servant in the church. These roots of pastoral spirituality must ripen into the fruits of Christian ministry.

— BEN CAMPBELL JOHNSON, *Pastoral Spirituality*

Chris: The essence of Christianity is a lived relationship with God, a love affair with God. It's more like marriage that anything else I can think of: a whole shared life. Those other three things we mentioned — shared ideas, shared values, and shared activities — they're only aspects of that shared life.

Sal: Let me get this straight. We talked about theology and doctrine last time, right? What you believe and why you believe it.

Chris: Right.

Sal: And now you're telling me that this isn't the heart of it all?

Chris: Right. Theology is knowing truth *about* God. That's important, all right, but not as important as *knowing* God; just as knowing things about your friend is not as important as knowing your friend.

Sal: I see. Christianity isn't just an idea; it's a relationship.

Chris: Exactly.

— PETER KREEFT, *Prayer, the Great Conversation*

Daily Scripture Readings

KEY TEXT: 1 CORINTHIANS 1:30
    Sunday: Psalm 116
    Monday: Luke 3:7-21
    Tuesday: Luke 4:14-20
    Wednesday: Acts 2:1-21
    Thursday: 1 Corinthians 1:4-17
    Friday: John 1:1-5, 9-13
    Saturday: Ephesians 1:3-14

Questions for Reflection and Discussion

What does it mean to you that you are called "Christian" if you belong to Jesus?

Do you think Christians basically do a good job of "giving Jesus a good name" in other people's minds? Why or why not? Do you have a responsibility to protect God's reputation? In what sense?

What roles do Christians play that are prophetic, priestly, or kingly?

Closing Prayer

Lord, thank you that you have given me the name Christian. You've called me your child. Let me have the integrity of life and witness to draw others to you. In Jesus' name, amen.

Week Thirteen:
We Are God's Children

Opening Prayer

Living God, I am bought with a price. Let that reality sink deep down in me. Now, help me to allow Jesus to be even more than my Savior, but my Lord as well — Lord over all of my life. Amen.

Heidelberg Questions

QUESTION 33: Why is he called God's "only Son" when we also are God's children?

Because Christ alone is the eternal, natural Son of God.[1] We, however, are adopted children of God — adopted by grace through Christ.[2]

([1]John 1:1-3,14,18; Hebrews 1; [2]John 1:12; Romans 8:14-17; Ephesians 1:5-6)

QUESTION 34: Why do you call him "our Lord"?

Because — not with gold or silver, but with his precious blood — [1] he has set us free from sin and from the tyranny of the devil,[2] and has bought us, body and soul, to be his very own.[3]

([1]1 Peter 1:18-19; [2]Colossians 1:13-14; Hebrews 2:14-15; [3]1 Corinthians 6:20; 1 Timothy 2:5-6)

Exposition

Language can be tricky. It is not reality in and of itself, but rather it describes and symbolizes reality. We know words are powerful. They help shape our values and perceptions as they bring understanding and insight. Still, words are limited in what they can do. That is why we sometimes need to look into a person's face or watch his "body language" in order to grasp his intended meaning.

Words symbolize realities like places, things, ideas, emotions, and people. Metaphors give us insight by saying such things as, "It *broke my heart* to see the man in that condition."

It's the same with trying to talk about God. Words fall short in describing his character and attributes. There's no way we can encapsulate him; we're never going to figure him out. So the Bible uses metaphors like "redeemer," "shepherd," "guardian" — even these tell only part of the story.

Nonetheless, these words are true in what they teach us about God. The language of the Bible is an example of God stooping to speak in baby talk, as it were, in terms we can understand on our own level. But they point to reality about God, about humanity, about our destiny. We can count on them and put our weight down on them.

Attempting to articulate the nature of Jesus is like trying to get our hands around an enigma wrapped in a mystery. The only way we can understand this God-in-human-flesh is by God's own self-disclosure. The term "only-begotten Son" gives us a pointer.

"Son" is sometimes used in Scripture of people who are anointed for special service, like the king. Sometimes it is used to indicate people who benefit from the special love and care of God, like the children of Israel. But the only-begotten Son is used for Jesus alone, who is in a unique relationship to God. It suggests that he is eternally coexistent with God — that is, there was never a time when he did not exist along with God the Father. What the Father is, so is the Son. What we can be through adoption — sons and daughters of God — Jesus is by nature. On account of who he is, we can be what we long to be.

If the first question for consideration this week deals with the sonship of Jesus, then the second deals with the *implication* of his being God's Son — he is Lord of all.

There was a cartoon some time ago that depicted a baby crawling on the floor. A little boy and a girl stood nearby watching. The boy asked the girl, "Why doesn't Baby get up and walk?" The girl answered, "Don't rush her. Once you stand and walk, you're committed for a lifetime!" Sometimes we're afraid of following Jesus. Perhaps we do not feel ready for such a serious commitment. We wonder what it will cost us to follow this One who claims to be the Son of God and our Lord. If I believe he is divine and commit my life to him, what does he intend?

Jesus intends to make disciples, those who acclaim him as Lord and then follow in his way. There's no need to be afraid of the word "Lord." We all have promised allegiance to some master. Master Jesus has laid down his life for us. If I'm afraid to allow him to be Lord of my life, then who is my lord? Jesus invites us to change from our allegiance to any other lord and to follow him. He is our rightful Lord because he has bought us for his own.

When we submit to him we are freed from the distorted view of reality that self-lordship breeds. People know there's more to existence than what one learns in school or reads in the daily newspaper. Christians are not bound by the narrowness of one-dimensional living. This is what Jesus was describing when he told Nathanael, considering the claims of discipleship, "You shall see heaven open, and the angels of God ascending and descending on the Son of Man" (John 1:51). It was as if Jesus was saying, "I am the bridge between heaven and earth, the connection between realities." He empowers us to see life as it really is.

The idea of lordship implies exclusivity. If you hold him as Lord, you cannot bow the knee to any other lord. Jesus himself said, "No one can serve two masters. Either he will hate the one and love the other, or he will be devoted to the one and despise the other" (Matthew 6:24). Jesus alone is the bridge between heaven and earth, between the human and the divine. He alone knows the heart of the Father. Nobody but the Son can personify the character of the Father and meet the needs of frail humanity. It means that I need to say "no" to any other influence as being ultimately authoritative for me, whether science, the state, my own feelings and experience, a lover, a career. These things might have their proper place in my life. But all of them must relinquish to Christ the throne of my life.

When we submit to him as Lord, we are drawn into a whole new life. The things that we are ashamed of, defeated by, utterly powerless to change, he will transform. It may not be immediate or dramatic, but inevitably, as we make the Son *our* Lord, we will experience new power and joy and effectiveness for his purposes.

Other Voices

How happy is each child of God
Who walks within God's ways!
You'll reap good fruit from honest work,
And joy in life always.

⤻

With fruitful spouse you'll parent now
Your children strong, adored;
Like olive shoots they shall surround
Your laden table board!

⤻

How happy is the family
Who honors God above!
The Lord shall send all help and grace
To bless your home with love.

⤻

May God's great peace, good health, and joy
Forever fill your home;
May you and your descendants know
Forever God's shalom!
— DWYN M. MOUNGER, "How Happy Is
Each Child of God"

[True grace] is costly because it costs a man his life, and it is grace because it gives a man the only true life. It is costly because it condemns sin, and grace because it justifies the sinner. Above all, it is *costly* because it cost God the life of his Son: "ye were bought at a price," and what has cost God much cannot be cheap for us. Above all, it is *grace* because God did not reckon his Son too dear a price to pay for our life, but delivered him up for us. Costly grace is the Incarnation of God.

Costly grace is the sanctuary of God; it has to be protected from the world, and not thrown to the dogs. It is therefore the living word, the Word of God, which he speaks as it pleases him. Costly grace confronts us as a gracious call to follow Jesus, it comes as a word of forgiveness to the broken spirit and the contrite heart. Grace is costly because it compels a man to submit to the yoke of Christ and follow him; it is grace because Jesus says: "My yoke is easy and my burden is light."

— DIETRICH BONHOEFFER,
The Cost of Discipleship

Though in our time motherhood has been greatly devalued, and the sick phrase "unwanted child" been given currency, it still remains true, as any nurse or gynecologist will confirm, that it is extremely rare for any child at the moment of birth to be other than wanted in its mother's eyes. Once when I was in Calcutta with Mother Teresa she picked up one of the so-called "unwanted" babies which had come into

the care of her Missionaries of Charity. It had been salvaged from a dustbin, and was so minute that one wondered it could exist at all. When I remarked on this, a look of exultation came into Mother Teresa's face. "See," she said, "there's life in it!" So there was; and suddenly it was as though I were present at the Bethlehem birth, and the baby Mother Teresa was holding was another Lamb of God sent into the world to lighten our darkness. How could we know? How dare we prognosticate upon what made life worth while for this or that child?

— MALCOLM MUGGERIDGE, "Mother Teresa
and the Baby Found in a Dustbin"

Passover marks not only exemption from divine wrath, but also the entire period of the exodus and its destruction of a way of life. . . . The fact that in the desert the bread was not able to rise became symbolic of all the disruption and tragedies, major and minor, that resulted from this abandonment of the life of the home. Now, centuries later, this unleavened bread is made a part of a family meal both to recognize the fact of the disruption and to value the power that, despite that disruption, allows the family to endure.

So also the Eucharist. It was over a meal — a Passover meal — that Jesus told his followers, his small family, that their time of sharing together would soon end. At that time he took bread, the one element that by its very commonness and importance to family life symbolized for them as it had for the followers of Moses an eternal presence, and broke it, saying, "This is my body." From that point on he would always be present with them. The most shattering incidence of Christian history became eternal by being drawn into the core of family activity.

— ERNEST BOYER, JR., *Finding God at Home: Family Life as Spiritual Discipline*

Daily Scripture Readings

KEY TEXT: JOHN 1:1-3,14
  Sunday: Ezekiel 18
  Monday: Hosea 11:1-11
  Tuesday: John 1:10-13
  Wednesday: Deuteronomy 14:1-2
  Thursday: 1 John 2:28–3:10
  Friday: Galatians 3:26–4:7
  Saturday: Romans 8:1-17

Questions for Reflection and Discussion

Should we consider all people "children of God"?

What does it mean to you to be God's child?

In Matthew 7:21 Jesus says, "Not everyone who says to me, 'Lord, Lord,' will enter the kingdom of heaven, but only he who does the will of my Father who is in heaven." How do you reconcile this with Paul saying in 1 Corinthians 12:3, "No one can say, 'Jesus is Lord,' except by the Holy Spirit"?

What would seem to be signs that someone takes seriously the lordship of Christ?

What is an area of your life where God might be calling you to another step of discipleship?

Closing Prayer

Lord Jesus Christ, you mean so much to me. In your presence, my fears and doubts have melted away. In your heart, I have found the truth and seen it in the shape of love. Change me so that when people look at me, they might see the one who rules me, you who gave up yourself for me. In your name I pray. Amen.

Week Fourteen:
God in the Flesh

Opening Prayer

Lord, long ago, your Holy Spirit inspired the writers of Holy Scripture to remember your saving activity and record it for our benefit. Please work in me by your same Spirit to make your Word come alive in me. I ask this in Jesus' name. Amen.

Heidelberg Questions

QUESTION 35: What does it mean that he "was conceived by the Holy Spirit and born of the Virgin Mary"?

That the eternal Son of God, who is and remains true and eternal God,[1] took to himself, through the working of the Holy Spirit,[2] from the flesh and blood of the virgin Mary,[3] a truly human nature so that he might become David's true descendant,[4] like his brothers in every way[5] except for sin.[6]

([1]John 1:1; 10:30-36; Acts 13:33 (Psalm 2:7); Colossians 1:15-17; 1 John 5:20; [2]Luke 1:35; [3]Matthew 1:18-23; John 1:14; Galatians 4:4; Hebrews 2:14; [4]2 Samuel 7:12-16; Psalm 132:11; Matthew 1:1; Romans 1:3; [5]Philippians 2:7; Hebrews 2:17; [6]Hebrews 4:15; 7:26-27)

QUESTION 36: How does the body conception and birth of Christ benefit you?

He is our mediator,[1] and with his innocence and perfect holiness he removes from God's sight my sin — mine since I was conceived.[2]

([1]1 Timothy 2:5-6; Hebrews 9:13-15; [2]Romans 8:3-4; 2 Corinthians 5:21; Galatians 4:4-5; 1 Peter 1:18-19)

Exposition

Last week's questions considered the theme of Jesus as God's Son, whom we know as Lord. This week's questions look back to his birth that was announced ahead of time through the Old Testament prophets. This promised birth is what we know as the Incarnation, the fleshing out of the eternal God into human form.

The gospel writers each have their own way of telling the story. Luke emphasizes the passivity of human response to God's action. When Mary hears the angel's announcement of her coming pregnancy, she replies, "Let it be with me according to your word" (Luke 1:38, NRSV). Matthew emphasizes the active component in the human response. Three times an angel instructs Joseph in a dream, and three times he has to do something, to obey, to act as a disciple. Together, the accounts make clear that God is the initiator in the drama of salvation. But even though God's grace is always first, we still need to actively respond to it. The call to action comes to a climax in the Sermon on the Mount, when Jesus says to his followers, "Not everyone who says to me, 'Lord, Lord,' will enter the kingdom of heaven, but only the one who does the will of my Father in heaven" (Matthew 7:21, NRSV).

In the setting of first-century Palestine, the engagement was often made when the couple were still children. Usually the parents would make the arrangements, but sometimes it would be done through a professional matchmaker. Often it was done without the couple ever having seen each other. Marriage was considered far too serious a thing to be done based on the emotions.

The betrothal was what we might think of as the ratifying of the engagement agreement already made. At this point the engagement entered into by the parents or matchmaker could be broken if the girl didn't want to continue. But once they entered into the agreement of the betrothal, then it was absolutely binding. This period lasted for about a year. During the course of the year, the couple were known as man and wife even though they hadn't yet come together sexually or lived together in the same household. The only way to get out of this was through death or divorce, and a girl whose fiancé died during the betrothal was known as "a virgin who is a widow." This was where Joseph and Mary were; if Joseph wanted to end the betrothal, he could only do it by divorce. Mary was already legally known as his wife.

The problem is that Joseph hears about the pregnancy before he hears about the cause. He knows he has to divorce her, not out of anger but out of deep conviction. No matter how much he still loves Mary, it's his religious obligation to annul the marriage contract, because she is apparently guilty of fornication. Deuteronomy lists it as a capital crime. According to Moses' law, Joseph doesn't have the right to forgive her and consummate the marriage, but he tempers judgment with mercy. Even though he has to demonstrate that his love for God is stronger than his love for Mary, he decides to do it quietly in order to avoid public scandal. His instinct is to show mercy.

The third stage was the marriage itself that took place at the end of the year of betrothal. The bride and her family wouldn't know exactly when the groom would come, so they would have to be ready for his sudden coming. The groom's reappearance would launch a weeklong celebration in the bride's village. This is the image the Lord uses in Matthew 25 with the parable of the bridesmaids waiting for the groom to come. In John 14 Jesus says that he is the groom who goes to prepare a place for the bride in his father's household, who will one day return with great joy to claim his bride — the church — and consummate their marriage.

It was during the betrothal stage that Joseph heard the staggering truth of what was to take place. The angel came and burst in on his plans, addressing him as "son of David." This tells us that Joseph's role in the story has to do with the fact that he's a descendant of David. It reminds us that this miraculous conception is God's way of bringing about the messiah awaited in the Davidic royal line.

The young woman Mary fulfills the prophesy of Isaiah that "the virgin will be with child and will give birth to a son" (Isaiah 7:14). The world cannot bring forth the savior it needs without God's intervention. But God has entered into the human story. This is the grand miracle of all history, that God would become flesh in order to save us. Jesus is the one through whom the people of God would be saved.

The virgin birth demonstrates that it is God's good pleasure to save sinners and to enter into communion with those he has created. It reminds us, too, that God's ways are not our ways. He came not in grandeur, nor in pomp and circumstance, but rather in the helplessness of a baby. Like the tiny mustard seed that grows into a mighty tree, the story of redemption begins inauspiciously. It tells us to see God in the small things, not to scorn the insignificant things, and to trust God in all things to work for our salvation.

Other Voices

"Very God and very man." If we consider this basic Christian truth first in the light of "conceived by the Holy Spirit", the truth is clear that the man Jesus Christ has His origin simply in God, that is, He owes His beginning in history to the fact that God in person became man. That means that Jesus Christ is indeed man, true man, but He is not just a man, not just an extraordinarily gifted or specially guided man, let alone a super-man; but, while being a man, He is God Himself. . . . God becomes man. In this way this story begins.

And now we have to turn the page and come to the second thing expressed thereby, when we say, "born of the Virgin Mary." Now the fact is underlined that we are on earth. There is a human child, the Virgin Mary; and as well as coming from

God, Jesus also comes from this human being. . . . Jesus Christ is not "only" true God; that would not be real incarnation — but neither is He an intermediate being; He is a man like us all, a man without reservation. He not only resembles us men; He is the same as us.

— KARL BARTH,
Dogmatics in Outline

Low, how a rose e'er blooming
From tender stem hath sprung,
Of Jesse's lineage coming,
As men of old have sung.
It came a floweret bright,
Amid the cold of winter
When half spent was the night.
Isaiah 'twas foretold it,
The rose I have in mind,
With Mary we behold it,
The virgin Mother kind.
To show God's love aright
She bore to men a Savior,
When half spent was the night.

— GERMAN, FIFTEENTH CENTURY,
"Lo, How a Rose E'er Blooming"

What, then, can be said about God and suffering? Can anything be said which is of comfort? In the history of the world, four answers have been given. First, suffering is real and will not go away, but death comes as the end, and in death there is an end of suffering and eventual peace. Second, suffering is an illusion. It simply is not there, but is imagined. Third, suffering is real, but we ought to be able to rise above it and rec-

ognize that it is of little importance. The Christian has the fourth answer: God suffered in Christ.

— ALISTER E. McGRATH,
Studies in Doctrine

We don't have to become like God before we can encounter him, because God became *like us* first. God meets us right where we are, without preconditions. A very famous saying of Athanasius is worth noting here: "God became man so that we might become God." By this, he simply meant that God became man in order that man might enter into a relationship and fellowship with him.

— ALISTER E. McGRATH,
Studies in Doctrine

From the Christian point of view there is no special problem about Christmas in a prison cell. For many people in this building it will probably be a more sincere and genuine occasion than in places where nothing but the name is kept. That misery, suffering, poverty, loneliness, helplessness, and guilt mean something quite different in the eyes of God from what they mean in the judgment of man, that God will approach where men turn away, that Christ was born in a stable because there was no room for him in the inn — these are things that a prisoner can understand better than other people; for him they really are glad tidings, and that faith gives him a part in the communion of saints, a Christian fellowship breaking the bounds of time and space and reducing the months of confinement here to insignificance.

> — DIETRICH BONHOEFFER, *Letters and Papers from Prison*

[It] was a cave used as a stable by the mountaineers of the uplands about Bethlehem; who still drive their cattle into such holes and caverns at night. It was here that a homeless couple had crept underground with the cattle when the doors of the crowded caravanserai had been shut in their faces; and it was here beneath the very feet of the passers-by, in a cellar under the very floor of the world, that Jesus Christ was born.

Omnipotence and impotence, or divinity and infancy, do definitely make a sort of epigram which a million repetitions cannot turn into a platitude. It is not unreasonable to call it unique. Bethlehem is emphatically a place where extremes meet.

> — G. K. CHESTERTON, *The Everlasting Man*

Daily Scripture Readings

KEY TEXT: 1 TIMOTHY 3:16
  Sunday: Isaiah 9:1-7
  Monday: Matthew 1:18-24
  Tuesday: Luke 1:26-38,46-55
  Wednesday: Luke 2:1-20
  Thursday: John 1:1-9,14-18
  Friday: Philippians 2:5-11
  Saturday: Romans 8:1-17

Questions for Reflection and Discussion

Do you consider the doctrine of the virgin birth of Jesus to be essential for salvation? Explain.

What are the implications for us that Jesus of Nazareth was fully human? That he was fully divine?

Does it matter that Jesus was born in a stable? How might that humble place for the birth of the King of the world change your perspective on Christmas? Are there practices in our culture that you think could be modified to better reflect the meaning of Christmas?

Can you think of a work that started small, but produced dramatic results in the long run?

Closing Prayer

O God, how incredible it is that you visited this earth in the person of Jesus of Nazareth. Thank you for the life he lived and the death he died so that I could know your love. Amen.

Week Fifteen:
God's Greatest Gift

Opening Prayer

Dear Father, your gifts to me are so many — when I consider them, I'm caught up short by your generosity. Please help me remember that your greatest gift is the gift of yourself, and to desire that gift the most. In Jesus' name, amen.

Heidelberg Questions

QUESTION 37: What do you understand by the word "suffered"?

That during his whole life on earth, but especially at the end, Christ sustained in body and soul the anger of God against the sin of the whole human race.[1]

This he did in order that, by his suffering as the only atoning sacrifice,[2] he might set us free, body and soul, from eternal condemnation,[3] and gain for us God's grace, righteousness, and eternal life.[4]

(*[1]Isaiah 53; 1 Peter 2:24; 3:18; [2]Romans 3:25; Hebrews 10:14; 1 John 2:2; 4:10; [3]Romans 8:1-4; Galatians 3:13; [4]John 3:16; Romans 3:24-26)*

QUESTION 38: Why did he suffer "under Pontius Pilate" as judge?

So that he, though innocent, might be condemned by a civil judge,[1] and so free us from the severe judgment of God that was to fall on us.[2]

(*[1]Luke 23:13-24; John 19:4,12-16; [2]Isaiah 53:4-5; 2 Corinthians 5:21; Galatians 3:13)*

QUESTION 39: Is it significant that he was "crucified" instead of dying some other way?

Yes. This death convinces me that he shouldered the curse which lay on me, since death by crucifixion was accursed by God.[1]

[*[1]Galatians 3:10-13 (Deuteronomy 21:23)]*

Exposition

The first thing to notice about the biblical accounts of Jesus' death is their striking earthiness. They don't "over-spiritualize" the event. They make it clear that he wasn't just taken up into heaven one day, but that he really died, just as he really lived, in history. We even know more or less when and where it took place: he was executed on a cross in the Roman province of Palestine, outside the city gates of Jerusalem, about A.D. 29.

You can visit the place today. When we visited, my wife, Evelyne, and I took a taxi from where we were staying on the Mount of Olives to the Old City, where we planned to worship at Christ Church just inside the Jaffa Gate. We were dropped off outside the Old City and walked through the breach in the wall that was opened by the Ottoman Turks in 1898 for the visit of Kaiser Wilhelm. It was the same place where General Allenby entered when he took Jerusalem for the British in 1917. Allenby rode up to the gate on his stallion, and then dismounted, saying he would not *ride* on the stones over which his Lord had had to carry his cross.

After worship at Christ Church, we headed north toward the Armenian and the Christian quarters: down stone alleyways into hidden courtyards; up flights of stairs, looking through ancient grating to see passersby in the alleys below. Streams of pilgrims headed into the Church of the Holy Sepulchre, the shrine begun in the fourth century over the place that is almost certainly where the Lord's death, burial, and resurrection took place. Crusader columns in front are inscribed with the crosses of illiterate Russian peasants who walked as many as three years to make their pilgrimage to the Holy Land. Countless Christians still make the pilgrimage today.

It takes a real act of will to visualize the first-century setting, with an "old rugged cross" on a faraway hill. Nothing of the original setting remains; all has been covered with the gilded encrustation of the ages: candles, ornate shrines, marble, paintings and icons, incense, and the ever-present throngs. One is perhaps shocked by the sense of decay. As H. V. Morton observed, it seems that "extreme devotion" and "extreme neglect" can produce the same result: nobody will easily alter any of the aspects of that expansive church.[6] Centuries-old paintings hang in shreds, and repair of generations-old earthquake damage goes undone.

To many Western Christians, the place is quite disappointing. We go looking for vestiges of Jesus' own day and feel distanced by all the shabby trappings of piousness. Even more, it is disillusioning to see the bitter rivalries between the branches of the church that occupy the site and continue the venerable rites. Armenian, Greek, Coptic, and Roman Catholic all have their allotted sections of the buildings, and fights have broken out between them over who controls what. The Crimean War in 1854 was incited by the competing claims of Russia and the Balkan countries on the Holy Sepulchre. Even in our day, high emotions and tensions have sometimes erupted into fisticuffs.

The vast, murky labyrinth of a church is not what one would call beautiful, but it is fascinating with its tortured passageways so laden with history. It is also strangely moving to see where God accomplished our atonement. To think that the events of Jesus' death, burial, and resurrection happened in a real place. They didn't only take place in the geography of the imagination.

I found it poignant to consider the multitudes of people, like sheep without a shepherd, longing for an encounter with God. If a space is sanctified by the prayers of believers, flawed and limited though we are, then this indeed would seem to be the holiest place on earth, the very navel of the world (as medieval Christians believed). The Lord's death took place in what is now one of the most hotly contested corners of the planet. It was no different in his day. This is the very world he entered into in order to save.

If the gospel accounts are straightforward about the fact of the Crucifixion, they are understated in regard to its physical details. It is almost as if modesty prevented the evangelists from describing the ghastly scene (in contrast to some of the T-shirt designs one sees in Christian bookstores today). They simply state the basic facts; Matthew writes only, "And when they had crucified him, they divided his clothes . . . by casting lots" (Matthew 27:35, NRSV).

But for all the simplicity of the accounts, the fact of the Crucifixion is of utmost importance. For the gospel writers, it conjured up the image of the Old Testament warning: "anyone hung on a tree is under God's curse" (Deuteronomy 21:23, NRSV). Matthew, Mark, Luke, and John all portray this real historical event in such a way as to show us that Jesus took upon himself the curse we deserved to bear. The brokenness of our own lives, and sometimes the brokenness of the church, remind us how much we need that saving work of Jesus. He bore in his body the punishment we rightly deserve, so that we could be forever free.

Other Voices

[Malcolm Muggeridge] became uneasy about "this whole concept of a Jesus of good causes". Then:

I would catch a glimpse of a cross — not necessarily a crucifix; maybe two pieces of wood accidentally nailed together, on a telegraph pole, for instance — and suddenly my heart would stand still. In an instinctive, intuitive way I understood that something more important, more tumultuous, more passionate, was at issue than our good causes, however admirable they might be.

It was, I know, an obsessive interest. . . . I might fasten bits of wood together myself, or doodle it. This symbol, which was considered to be derisory in my home, was yet also the focus of inconceivable hopes and desires.

— JOHN R. W. STOTT,
The Cross of Christ

Jesus was *brought to the place* where it was customary to execute criminals, that his death might be more ignominious. Now though this was done according to custom, still we ought to consider the loftier purpose of God. He determined that his Son should be cast out of the city as unworthy of human intercourse, that he might admit us into his heavenly kingdom with the angels. For this reason the apostle in Hebrews 13:12 compares it to the ancient figure of the law. For as God commanded his people to *burn outside the camp* the bodies of those animals, the blood of which was carried into the sanctuary to make atonement for sins (Exodus 29:14; Leviticus 16:27), so he says that Christ went out of the gate of the city, so that, by taking upon him the curse which pressed us down, he might be regarded as accursed. In this manner, he atones for our sins.

Now the greater the disgrace which he endured before the world, the more acceptable and noble a spectacle did he exhibit in his death to God and to the angels.

— JOHN CALVIN, *Commentary on Matthew*

O, Lord Jesus Christ, would that we also might be contemporary with you; to see you in your true form and in the actual environment in which you walked here on earth; not in the form in which an empty and meaningless tradition or a thoughtless and superstitious tradition or a gossipy historical tradition has deformed you. These cannot possibly be the form of glory in which no man has yet seen you. Would that we might see you as you are and were

and will be until your return in glory, to see you as the sign of offense and object of faith, the lowly man, and yet the Savior and Redeemer of the race, who out of love came to earth in order to seek the lost, to suffer and to die. And yet troubled as you were on every step you took on earth, every time you stretched out your hand to perform signs and wonders, and every time without moving a hand, you suffered without defense my opposition, again and again. You were constrained to repeat, "Blessed is the one who is not offended because of me." Would that we might see you this way, and then that in spite of all of this, we might not be offended because of you.

— SØREN KIERKEGAARD, *Training in Christianity*

As the self-offering of the Son for the reconciliation of the world and his being offered up by the Father are one and the same event and form a single process, so we are to see the work of the exalted Christ and that of the Spirit in us as different aspects of one and same divine action for the reconciliation of the world.

— WOLFHART PANNENBERG, *Systematic Theology*

Daily Scripture Readings

KEY TEXT: HEBREWS 13:12
  Sunday: Psalm 22
  Monday: Matthew 26:36-56

Tuesday: Mark 14:53-65; 15:1-15
Wednesday: Matthew 27:27-31
Thursday: Luke 23:26-43;
               Matthew 27:45-54
Friday: Galatians 6:11-16
Saturday: 1 Corinthians 1:17-25

Questions for Reflection and Discussion

Why do you think Jesus had to die? Couldn't God have come up with another way to save us from our sins?

The early church shied away from images of the cross. Why does the church today use the cross as its central symbol — why not the manger, or a boat, or a fish, or a fishing net, or carpenter's tools, or a towel and washbasin, or the rock that was rolled away from the empty tomb?

What might be a benefit to contemplating a crucifix or a painting of Jesus on the cross?

What does Jesus' death on the cross do for your perspective on life? On the world? On your responsibility as a Christian?

Closing Prayer

Lord Jesus, your cross was raised on a hill to pay for my sins. Let the shadow of your cross fall across my life, and so make right all my thoughts and ambitions. Let me carry in myself your death wherever I go, so that your life can also be in me. Amen.

Week Sixteen:
Death, Where Is Your Sting?

Opening Prayer

Gracious God, you sent Jesus into the world not to condemn the world, but that through him the world might be saved. Thank you that in his dying you destroyed the power of death. Save me from hardness of heart. Help me to confess my sin and receive your overflowing love. Amen.

Heidelberg Questions

QUESTION 40: Why did Christ have to go all the way to death?
Because God's justice and truth demand it:[1] only the death of God's Son could pay for our sin.[2]
(*[1]Genesis 2:17; [2]Romans 8:3-4; Philippians 2:8; Hebrews 2:9*)

QUESTION 41: Why was he "buried"?
His burial testifies that he really died.[1]
(*[1]Isaiah 53:9; John 19:38-42; Acts 13:29; 1 Corinthians 15:3-4*)

QUESTION 42: Since Christ has died for us, why do we still have to die?
Our death does not pay the debt of our sins.[1] Rather, it puts an end to our sinning and is our entrance into eternal life.[2]
(*[1]Psalm 49:7; [2]John 5:24; Philippians 1:21-23; 1 Thessalonians 5:9-10*)

QUESTION 43: What further advantage do we receive from Christ's sacrifice and death on the cross?
Through Christ's death our old selves are crucified, put to death, and buried

with him,[1] so that the evil desires of the flesh may no longer rule us,[2] but that instead we may dedicate ourselves as an offering of gratitude to him.[3]
(*[1]Romans 6:5-11; Colossians 2:11-12; [2]Romans 6:12-14; [3]Romans 12:1; Ephesians 5:1-2*)

QUESTION 44: Why does the creed add, "He descended to hell"?

To assure me in times of personal crisis and temptation that Christ my Lord, by suffering unspeakable anguish, pain, and terror of soul, especially on the cross but also earlier, has delivered me from the anguish and torment of hell.[1]
(*[1]Isaiah 53; Matthew 26:36-46; 27:45-46; Luke 22:44; Hebrews 5:7-10*)

Exposition

The payment for human sin — that event which is known as redemption — took place at the cross of Christ. The sequence of the redemptive drama went like this: God created the world good, and made human beings in his image to enjoy a relationship of love with him. Humans rebelled and set themselves up as their own gods. God spoke a word indicting sin and declaring that payment must be made. Then, surprisingly, God stepped into the human story in order to make that payment himself. The God who *made* us has acted to *save* us, because he *loves* us. Because of that, people can be restored to relationship with God if they accept in faith Jesus' death for them.

Why was this? Why was death the only way for us to be reconciled with God? It is because God is altogether holy. In order to meet the demands of his perfection, a sacrifice had to be made, and the sacrifice had to be a definitive one. Therefore, either the sacrifice had to be made again and again forever, or only the infinite God himself would be capable of offering it. Death was the natural consequence of human imperfection.

The story in the Garden of Eden illustrates this. The Lord warned Adam and Eve against eating of the fruit of the knowledge of good and evil, while permitting them to eat the fruit of all the other trees. God's reason for the prohibition was that "in the day that you eat of it you shall die." His warning was descriptive of the normal outcome of sin. The man and the woman did not physically die the moment they ate of the fruit. Instead, the death that came upon them was spiritual, a separation from the fellowship they had enjoyed with God. Suddenly, there was a rupture in the relationship that the humans were incapable of mending. Their eventual physical death was a gradual reflection of that spiritual sickness introduced into creation.

The garden story shows that sin must be dealt with. It also hints that God will send the One through the woman's seed who will crush, at great cost to himself, the stronghold of evil on creation.

It was necessary that God pay through Christ the penalty we are incapable of paying to make a perfect, once-for-all sacrifice. Yet there is irony in Governor Pilate's condemnation of the innocent Jesus.

On one hand, when Pilate washed his hands of Jesus, he was responsible for a stark and singular injustice.

But on the other hand, Jesus' death was not Pilate's doing at all. It was not a mere tragedy, something that went terribly wrong. The Roman and Jewish authorities were not the *cause* of what took place, only the instrument. In the midst of Pilate's decision, God was sovereignly at work. God's freedom was prevenient to Pilate's freedom, moving the events of the day to his intended conclusion. That conclusion was that his Son must die in order to accomplish our redemption.

Some people with a naturalistic worldview predetermine that Jesus could not have risen from the dead; therefore, some have conjectured he must not have really died that day on Golgotha. But historical accounts show that to be exceedingly unlikely. He was executed at the hands of professional soldiers ordered to carry out the death sentence. They verified his death by thrusting a spear into his side. The flow of blood and water from his side proved to their satisfaction that he had been dead for some time. His burial demonstrated that his death was real. All of this was in God's plan. To overcome death once and for all, Jesus really had to die. He had to pass through the gates of death itself for resurrection to be a real movement into life.

The account from Matthew's gospel illustrates this victory thrillingly. When Jesus cried out in a loud voice and breathed his last, "at that moment the curtain of the temple was torn in two from top to bottom" (Matthew 27:51). Whenever Israel had gathered in worship, that curtain demonstrated graphically that sinful humans were divided from the Holy One. They could not simply come crashing into the presence of the living God. Now, God declared that no barrier need stand between himself and the people he redeemed. Matthew reports that graves burst open and corpses were raised to life again. It's a picture that Jesus' sacrifice sets the prisoners free, even from the bonds of death itself. At the very moment he breathed his last, the power of death and evil was in fact overcome.

What does this mean for us? It means that we are his, once and for all. Nothing can undo what he did to make us his own — not our backsliding, not our poor discipleship, not our regret over the past, or our stress over the present, or our anxiety over the future. It means that if Jesus even went to hell and back for us, to the place of exclusion from fellowship with God, than we need never again be cut off from God. We do not have to be prisoners of our nothingness. Even in our worst trials, we can know that Jesus has saved us from hellish anxiety by the torment that he suffered. Nothing more needs to be done; it is finished!

Other Voices

The average person is just that — average. He or she has no great importance in the eyes of the world. Indeed that is one of life's frustrations. When an injustice is done to us we have no access to the great ones who might put things right. We are continually pushed around by low-grade bureaucrats and kept in our place by office receptionists. It is possible to spend hours awaiting the pleasure of some subordinate official.

This is part of life and if anything can be done about it I do not know what it is. But believers have access where it really counts. Christ's fulfillment of the Day of Atonement ceremonies has opened up the way into the very presence of God for the humblest of his people. Nothing on earth can take away what this means in terms of prayer and companionship.

— LEON MORRIS, *The Atonement: Its Meaning and Significance*

When God becomes man in Jesus of Nazareth, he not only enters into the finitude of man, but in his death on the cross he also enters into the situation of man's godforsakenness. In Jesus he does not die the natural death of a finite being, but the violent death of the criminal on the cross, the death of complete abandonment, rejection by God, his Father. God does not become a religion, so that man participates in him by corresponding religious thoughts and feelings. God does not become a law, so that man participates in him through obedience to a law. God does not become an ideal, so that man achieves community with him through constant striving. He humbles himself and takes upon himself the eternal death of the godless and the godforsaken, so that all the godless and the godforsaken can experience communion with him.

— JÜRGEN MOLTMANN, *The Crucified God*

So why did [his followers] go on regarding Jesus as special? With one voice they would reply: Because of what happened next. God raised him from the dead. We weren't expecting it, they would say; it wasn't part of our game-plan; but it happened. And gradually, bit by bit, we came to see that what happened here on that Friday afternoon was the drawing together of all those other Jerusalem-stories. This was how the kingdom was to come. This was how the prophecies would be fulfilled. This was what the temple was always pointing to. This was like Abraham sacrificing Isaac, only now it was the living God sacrificing his own beloved son. This was the place where the pain and the sin and the shame and the guilt of all the world, of all people, of all history before and since, was concentrated — and was dealt with once and for all. This was where the one true God acted to save and heal the whole world.

— N. T. WRIGHT, *The Original Jesus: The Life and Vision of a Revolutionary*

When I survey the wondrous cross on
  which the Prince of Glory died,
My richest gain I count but loss, and pour
  contempt on all my pride.

༄

Forbid it, Lord, that I should boast, save in
  the death of Christ my God,
All the vain things that charm me most, I
  sacrifice them to his blood.

༄

See, from his head, his hands, his feet,
    sorrow and love flow mingled down,
Did e'er such love and sorrow meet, or
    thorns compose so rich a crown?

                ✍

Were the whole realm of nature mine, that
    were a present far too small;
Love so amazing, so divine, demands my
    soul, my life, my all.
        — ISAAC WATTS, "When I Survey the
                      Wondrous Cross"

Daily Scripture Readings

KEY TEXT: 1 PETER 3:18
    Sunday: 1 Peter 2:21-25
    Monday: John 10:1-18
    Tuesday: John 19:38-42
    Wednesday: Isaiah 53:1-11
    Thursday: Psalm 49
    Friday: Romans 6:5-14
    Saturday: Matthew 26:36-46

Questions for Reflection and Discussion

How does the idea of spiritual burial remind us that we are separated from sin and the ways of the world?

Would you say that our society fears death? Or rather, that society is morbidly fascinated with death? Are the two mutually exclusive? What evidence might back up your answer?

How might your life look different if you really believed that the judgment of God against sin was finished at the cross? How might that strengthen your confidence in the heavenly Father?

Closing Prayer

Father, you have overcome death in order to give me life. Knowing that ought to give me a sense of humility, of gratitude, and of fearlessness for living the days you give me. May it be so! I ask it in Jesus' name.

Week Seventeen:
God's Stamp of Approval

Opening Prayer

Loving Father, restore life in me – in all your people – with the same power by which you raised Jesus from the dead. Bring me back from my doubt and discouragement to tell of your strength and love. I ask you this through Jesus. Amen.

Heidelberg Questions

QUESTION 45: How does Christ's resurrection benefit us?

First, by his resurrection he has overcome death, so that he might make us share in the righteousness he won for us by his death.[1]

Second, by his power we too are already now resurrected to a new life.[2]

Third, Christ's resurrection is a guarantee of our glorious resurrection.[3]

([1]*Romans 4:25; 1 Corinthians 15:16-20; 1 Peter 1:3-5;* [2]*Romans 6:5-11; Ephesians 2:4-6; Colossians 3:1-4;* [3]*Romans 8:11; 1 Corinthians 15:12-23; Philippians 3:20-21*)

QUESTION 46: What do you mean by saying, "He ascended to heaven"?

That Christ, while his disciples watched, was lifted up from the earth to heaven[1] and will be there for our good[2] until he comes again to judge the living and the dead.[3]

([1]*Luke 24:50-51; Acts 1:9-11;* [2]*Romans 8:34; Ephesians 4:8-10; Hebrews 7:23-25; 9:24;* [3]*Acts 1:11*)

QUESTION 47: But isn't Christ with us until the end of the world as he promised us?[1]

Christ is truly human and truly God. In his human nature Christ is not now on earth;[2] but in his divinity, majesty, grace, and Spirit he is not absent from us for a moment.[3]

([1]*Matthew 28:20;* [2]*Acts 1:9-11; 3:19-21;* [3]*Matthew 28:18-20; John 14:16-19*)

Exposition

Because of the death Christ died on the cross, the Christian shares in the life he lives in the Resurrection. Life in Jesus is more than life without him amplified. Though the Christian life means that the present time is now infused with new purpose, meaning, and help — and also trouble — life in Jesus has even more radical implications. His life bursts the shackles of earth-bound existence. It cannot be contained in the span of a person's years. This life is an eternal reality.

Jesus' resurrection bears witness that God will finish the work he began in creation, fulfilling his designs for a new creation that makes possible reconciliation between God and humanity. Death no longer speaks the final word for those who belong to Christ. Beyond the corridors of time, we will come into the fulfillment of the children of God.

The Resurrection, then, is a heavenly reality breaking into earthly existence. The promise of a new future comes to us in the midst of this life. The disciple Thomas's encounter with the risen Lord demonstrated this. John's gospel recounts how Thomas joined the disciples after the Resurrection. The others had seen Jesus alive again, but Thomas had not. He declared, "Unless I see the nail marks in his hands and put my finger where the nails were, and put my hand into his side, I will not believe it" (John 20:25).

Many have labeled Thomas "the doubter" because of his demand for empirical evidence. But nothing in the account suggests he should be looked down on for lack of faith. Indeed, any follower after the first generation of Jewish disciples owes a debt of gratitude to Thomas for his insistence that he needed to know in whom he was putting his trust. Thomas wouldn't bank his life on anything else than the same Rabbi he had accompanied for those past three years. The Christ of faith had to be for him the same as the Jesus of history. The Lord of whom the others spoke had to be the same body that was brutally executed and laid in the grave. No phantom would do. No mere apparition, or wishful sentiment that love might triumph over death, or longing that the ideal of Jesus would endure in the memory of his followers. Thomas needed to see Jesus; then he'd follow him anywhere. And because of his determination, we have the assurance that at least one person insisted on proof that the Resurrection was more than a vision.

The seeking heart was wonderfully filled as the Lord again appeared to the little band of followers, this time for the benefit of Thomas. He offered his hand and side to the disciple and invited him to come home to faith in the risen Savior. Seeing was believing for Thomas. He was convinced, stirred to the depth of his soul. His cry of response is the most profound faith affirmation of the gospels: "My Lord and my God!" (John 20:28).

It's worth noting that Jesus does not upbraid Thomas for his request. Rather, he observes that Thomas is *blessed,* and that those who hear and believe the apostolic witness to the Resurrection will also be blessed.

His resurrection is for all who believe. Jesus' death paid the penalty for our sin and freed us from its insidious power; his resurrection proved he had done his work. Death had no hold on him. Neither does it have any claim on us. His resurrection serves as the divine seal of *our* resurrection and forgiveness of sin. The cross and the empty tomb are the core proclamation of the Christian church because they are the epicenter of God's saving intervention in humanity.

Jesus showed himself to many others as testimony to his new life. Then, after forty days of communion with his disciples, he was taken up into heaven. Jesus ascended in the same body, now glorified, he had on earth. His physical absence is for our good. Because he ascended, he could pour out his Spirit upon us. Though in his human nature he is no longer on earth, he still is very much with us, closer to us than the very air we breathe. His Spirit is a down payment that says one day we will be taken into the heavenly home for which we were created.

Other Voices

They looked round. There, shining in the sunrise, larger than they had seen him before, shaking his mane (for it had apparently grown again) stood Aslan himself.

"Oh, Aslan!" cried both the children, staring up at him, almost as much frightened as they were glad.

"Aren't you dead then, dear Aslan?" said Lucy.

"Not now." said Aslan.

"You're not — not a — ?" asked Susan in a shaky voice. She couldn't bring herself to say the word *ghost*.

Aslan stooped his golden head and licked her forehead. The warmth of his breath and a rich sort of smell that seemed to hang about his hair came all over her.

"Do I look it?" he said.

"Oh, you're real, you're real! Oh, Aslan!" cried Lucy and both girls flung themselves upon him and covered him with kisses.

"But what does it all mean?" asked Susan when they were somewhat calmer.

"It means," said Aslan, "that though the Witch knew the Deep Magic, there is a magic deeper still which she did not know. Her knowledge goes back only to the dawn of Time. But if she could have looked a little further back, into the stillness and the darkness before Time dawned, she would have read there a different incantation. She would have known that when a willing victim who had committed no treachery was killed in a traitor's stead, the Table would crack and Death itself would start working backwards. And now — "

"Oh yes. Now?" said Lucy jumping up and clapping her hands.

"Oh, children," said the Lion, "I feel my strength coming back to me. Oh, children, catch me if you can!" He stood for a second, his eyes very bright, his limbs quivering, lashing himself with his tail. Then he made a leap high over their heads and landed on the other side of the Table. Laughing, though she didn't know why, Lucy scrambled over it to reach him. Aslan leaped again. A mad chase began. Round and round the hill-top he led them, now hopelessly out of their reach, now letting them almost catch his tail, now diving between them, now tossing them in the air with his huge and beautifully velveted paws and catching them again, and now stopping unexpectedly so that all three of them rolled over together in a happy laughing heap of fur and arms and legs. It was such a romp as no one has ever had except in Narnia; and whether it was more like playing with a thunderstorm or playing with a kitten Lucy could never make up her mind. And the funny thing was that when all three finally lay together panting in the sun the girls no longer felt in the least tired or hungry or thirsty.

— C. S. Lewis, *The Lion, the Witch and the Wardrobe*

Jesus Christ is risen today, Alleluia!
Our triumphant holy day, Alleluia!
Who did once, upon the cross, Alleluia!
Suffer to redeem our loss. Alleluia!
Hymns of praise then let us sing, Alleluia!
Unto Christ, our heavenly King, Alleluia!
Who endured the cross and grave, Alleluia!
Sinners to redeem and save. Alleluia!
But the pains which He endured, Alleluia!
Our salvation have procured; Alleluia!
Now above the sky He's King, Alleluia!
Where the angels ever sing. Alleluia!
Sing we to our God above, Alleluia!
Praise eternal as His love; Alleluia!

Praise Him, all ye heavenly host, Alleluia!
Father, Son, and Holy Ghost. Alleluia!

— Charles Wesley, "Jesus Christ Is Risen Today"

We are searching for the center of the wide circumference of Christian experience. What is the center? *Resurrection* as interpersonal meeting with the living Christ. Not resurrection as idea or past event but resurrection as a currently experienced interpersonal encounter. This is why interpersonal meeting has been the central feature of Christian theology from its inception.

Something so decisive happened anticipatively for human history in the resurrection of Jesus that it does not and cannot fit into our ordinary categories of understanding. We cannot rule out the resurrection of Jesus simply on the grounds (as Troeltsch's law of analogy would require) that nothing like this ever happened to us before. How could it! The event of which Christianity speaks is, like all truly significant interpersonal meeting, an event without analogy.

. . . Whatever it was, it was experienced as the resurrected or spiritual or glorified body of Jesus and understood as the final self-disclosure of God.

— Thomas C. Oden, *The Event Named Resurrection*

The resurrection . . . must be assessed as a historical fact. It is told as such in the narratives. Certainly, it is a mysterious event, but it is *not* presented as a dream, a theological inference, or an ineffable event in the hearts of those who loved him. It is told as another remarkable event within the narrative, as the bodily resurrection of the man Jesus, leaving the tomb empty, conversing with his disciples, showing them his hands and his feet, eating fish with them. This is the historical event that alone renders the development of the church historically explicable. This is the historical event in the light of which all our history must be interpreted anew.

. . . God did something beyond all power of human imagining by raising Jesus from the dead.

To make such a claim is to make an assertion that redefines reality. If such an event has happened in history, then history is not a closed system of immanent causes and effects. God is powerfully at work in the world in ways that defy common sense, redeeming the creation from its bondage to necessity and decay. That, of course, is precisely what the early Christians believed and proclaimed.

— RICHARD B. HAYS, *The Moral Vision of the New Testament: A Contemporary Introduction to New Testament Ethics*

The ultimate destination of Jesus' followers is the renewed earth, which will be joined together with the renewed heaven to make a world with extra dimensions — just as Jesus' new body seems to have had extra dimensions. When we speak of life after death, therefore, as of course we must both in comfort and in hope, let us school ourselves to speak of it Christianly, and not

slide back into the half-light of mere "immortality." . . . God's future for his people is a newly embodied life on a renewed earth, married to a renewed heaven. This is the hope that followers of Jesus must keep before their eyes.

— N. T. WRIGHT, *Following Jesus: Biblical Reflections on Discipleship*

Daily Scripture Readings

KEY TEXT: MATTHEW 27:62-64; 28:10
   Sunday: Luke 24:9-12
   Monday: Luke 24:13-35
   Tuesday: John 20:19-31
   Wednesday: John 21:1-14
   Thursday: Luke 24:36-53
   Friday: Matthew 28:18-20
   Saturday: 1 Corinthians 15:1-28

Questions for Reflection and Discussion

Why is Jesus' physical resurrection from the dead the touchstone of the Christian faith? What would have happened to this fledgling movement and the disciples' claims that they had met him again if authorities had been able to produce Jesus' body?

Does it make a difference to you to know Jesus has a "spiritual body" from now on? Why or why not? How might this reassure us that God has intrinsically tied himself into the human story? What hope does this suggest for our renewal as our bodies are subject to hurt, handicap, and aging?

How does Christ generally make himself present for his church? What are some ways he has reassured you with his presence when you've needed it?

Closing Prayer

Gracious God, it's amazing to me that you have given to me all that Jesus earned in his dying and that I am covered by his righteousness. Help me to live by that new reality, brave and ready to face the world with your help and presence. In Jesus' beautiful name I am bold to ask this. Amen.

Week Eighteen:
Fully Human, Fully Divine

Opening Prayer

Lord, it's unfathomable to me! How can you be all that you are? Your strength overcomes my weakness; your love overthrows my self-centeredness; your wisdom masters my foolishness; and your peace calms my fears. I thank you and praise you for your grandeur and for your care for this child. Please come and work in me through your Spirit, to bring me toward the wholeness that is found in you. Amen.

Heidelberg Questions

QUESTION 48: If his humanity is not present wherever his divinity is, then aren't the two natures of Christ separated from each other?

Certainly not. Since divinity is not limited and is present everywhere,[1] it is evident that Christ's divinity is surely beyond the bounds of the humanity he has taken on, but at the same time his divinity is in and remains personally united to his humanity.[2]

([1]*Jeremiah 23:23-24; Acts 7:48-49 (Isaiah 66:1);* [2]*John 1:14; 3:13; Colossians 2:9*)

QUESTION 49: How does Christ's ascension to heaven benefit us?

First, he pleads our cause in heaven in the presence of his Father.[1]

Second, we have our own flesh in heaven — a guarantee that Christ our head will take us, his members, to himself in heaven.[2]

Third, he sends his Spirit to us on earth as a further guarantee.[3] By the Spirit's power we make the goal of our lives, not earthly things, but the things above where Christ is, sitting at God's right hand.[4]

([1]*Romans 8:34; 1 John 2:1;* [2]*John 14:2; 17:24; Ephesians 2:4-6;* [3]*John 14:16; 2 Corinthians 1:21-22; 5:5;* [4]*Colossians 3:1-4*)

Exposition

Christian theology has affirmed from its inception that the divine and human come together in the person of Christ. The church has been most healthy when it has remembered both natures and held them in tension. To forget his God-nature, as revisionist scholars have done since the Enlightenment, is to reduce Jesus to the status of a mystic or a moralist with no saving relevance for our lives. To forget his human nature is the Docetic heresy that relegates his humanity and sufferings to the realm of illusion, where they can provide no help for our struggles. Both errors survive into our day, where one can discern their influence within the circles of the church and without. There is a kind of Gnostic impulse to be "in on" the secret knowledge of the initiated. From the radical demythologizing of the "Jesus Seminar" to the new age magazines at the newsstand, evidence says people keep trying to recreate Jesus according to their own needs, as merely human or as super-spiritual. But just as Jesus' two natures were united in his flesh on earth, so they are united in heaven. You cannot separate them. He was fully human, fully divine.

The same human tissue that formed in Mary's womb; the same body that they arrested, scourged, and nailed to a cross; the same flesh that Joseph of Arimathea wrapped in linen strips and laid in a borrowed tomb; the same muscles and bones that raised from the dead and appeared to his friends — this was the eternal self-expression of God in Jesus of Nazareth. We no longer have his earthly body with us, because he ascended to sit at God's right hand. Yet, he continues here with us, because his person is communicated to us in his divine nature, as he promised to be "with you always, to the end of the age" (Matthew 28:20, NRSV). He is present to us now by faith — as the praise chorus asks, "Have you seen Jesus my Lord? He's here in plain view."

How does his ascension help us? The catechism mentions three benefits.

First, Jesus is our intercessor in heaven. He represents us before the Father. Not that the Father is reluctant to grant us his blessing — after all, he is the one who expressed his tender care in coming to us in the person of his Son. The presence of Jesus of Nazareth at the right hand of the heavenly Father is the expression of humanity drawn into the heart of the divine fellowship. All believers are subsumed into his body so that we can enjoy the intimacy of this fellowship. Jesus intercedes for us, and the prayers we offer in his name are received into the Father's heart of love.

Second, since we are a part of Christ's body, we are in a sense already a part of heaven; we already have a foot in the door. This is our assurance that not only our souls but also our whole person, bodies included, participate in the salvation of God. The Bible affirms the goodness of creation — of *matter* — and never suggests that matter in and of its self is evil. The primeval litany at creation, "It is good," declares God's blessing on the material world. God's surprising visitation through the Incarnation crowns his plan. And God's resurrection in his Son climaxes the purpose of it all, promising that there is hope for all who groan for wholeness in their body.

The broken, the disabled, those who are bent under a load of pain — the Christian hope is that all who belong to Christ will be restored in body and in soul to God's original intention for humanity. The Christian shares in indissoluble communion with God; Jesus' flesh is our flesh, a sign that he will take us to himself as he has promised. We will be made whole.

Third, his Spirit is the pledge of salvation on our hearts. In his physical absence, Jesus is no longer bound by the limitations of time and space. He has sent his Spirit, whom he called the Advocate, who helps us realize we are children of God, who look forward to eternal life with him.

Other Voices

In Acts two languages are used to describe what has happened in Christ — one, the language of *resurrection* victory over death; the other, the language of *ascension*, sitting at the right hand of God and empowerment. These two motifs shall meet in Acts 2 at Pentecost when the life and power of Christ shall be given to disciples through the Spirit. When things go poorly for . . . the church, when the world falls apart, things come loose, and chaos threatens, it is good to know who is in charge, who rules. In the words of the ancient Ascension Day anthem, *Deus Ascendit*, "God Has Gone Up," not gone away from the church but gone up to be the empowerment for the church.

— WILLIAM H. WILLIMON, *Acts*

If Jesus had gone to heaven from the Mount of Transfiguration, He would have gone alone; He would have been nothing more to us than a glorious Figure. But He turned His back on the glory, and came down from the Mount to identify Himself with fallen humanity.

The Ascension is the consummation of the Transfiguration. Our Lord does now go back into His primal glory . . . [but now] He goes back to God as *Son of Man* as well as Son of God. There is now freedom of access for anyone straight to the very throne of God.

— OSWALD CHAMBERS, *My Utmost for His Highest*

I believe there is nothing lovelier, deeper, more sympathetic and more perfect than the Savior; I say to myself with jealous love that not only is there no one else like Him, but that there could be no one. I would say even more. If any one could prove to me that Christ is outside the truth, and if the truth really did exclude Christ, I should prefer to stay with Christ and not with truth. There is in the world only one figure of absolute beauty: Christ. That infinitely lovely figure is as a matter of course an infinite marvel.

— FYODOR DOSTOEVSKY, *The Brothers Karamazov*

We stand with unveiled face continuously gazing at the face of Christ as the center of our attention and love, and we are gradually and continuously changed into the likeness of Christ, thus proceeding from one degree of glory to another, the Spirit within us being the silent Artist who makes us into His image. It is a breath-taking conception and so simple! And yet how profound!

First of all, it is sound in that it gets you to look beyond yourself to another. It frees you from self-preoccupation and gets you to look at someone outside yourself. All the cults that get you to look within to discover Christ within you end in self-preoccupation with your own states of mind and emotion. As someone has said, "If Smith worships the divinity within Smith, he will probably end in worshipping Smith." In any case, he is tangled up with Smith. This verse gets our gaze fastened at the right place — the face of Christ. That fulfills the law of losing your life and finding it again. The attention is important, "for whatever gets your attention gets you." Christ gets attention, so He gets you. And what a getting!

— E. STANLEY JONES, *How to Be a Transformed Person*

Daily Scripture Readings

KEY TEXT: JOHN 10:22-42
    Sunday: Luke 24:50-51
    Monday: Romans 8:28-39
    Tuesday: 2 Corinthians 5:1-10
    Wednesday: Ephesians 2:1-10
    Thursday: Colossians 2:6-15
    Friday: Colossians 3:1-4
    Saturday: 1 Corinthians 1:18-22

Questions for Reflection and Discussion

As you consider the earthly career of Jesus Christ, what do you think of as indications of his divine nature? Of his human nature? Why is it important to remember both natures are perfectly held together in Jesus of Nazareth?

The modern perspective has changed from the time when people thought that God was "up there" in the sky. Why did God use the Ascension to demonstrate that he was bringing Jesus back into his heavenly presence?

What might it do for your perspective in life if you lived as if heaven were your real home, with Christ there to plead your cause before the Father? What do you need to be freed of in order to live that way?

Closing Prayer

God, I'm so glad you're on my side — that the story of your involvement with people didn't end at Calvary and that it didn't end at the empty tomb. Thank you that even in your heavenly glory, you think of me. In Jesus' name, amen.

Week Nineteen:
Come, Lord Jesus!

Opening Prayer

Lord, it's good to know that in these times when life often seems disorienting and disquieting, you are in control. Root me in the certainty that you are the reigning King. Amen.

Heidelberg Questions

QUESTION 50: Why the next words: "and is seated at the right hand of God"?

Christ ascended to heaven, there to show that he is head of his church,[1] and that the Father rules all things through him.[2]

([1]*Ephesians 1:20-23; Colossians 1:18;* [2]*Matthew 28:18; John 5:22-23*)

QUESTION 51: How does this glory of Christ our head benefit us?

First, through his Holy Spirit he pours out his gifts from heaven upon us his members.[1]

Second, by his power he defends us and keeps us safe from all enemies.[2]

([1]*Acts 2:33; Ephesians 4:7-12;* [2]*Psalm 110:1-2; John 10:27-30; Revelation 19:11-16*)

QUESTION 52: How does Christ's return "to judge the living and the dead" comfort you?

In all my distress and persecution I turn my eyes to the heavens and confidently await as judge the very One who has already stood trial in my place before God and so has removed the whole curse from me.[1] All his enemies and mine he will condemn to everlasting punishment: but me and all his chosen ones he will take along with him into the joy and the glory of heaven.[2]

([1]*Luke 21:28; Romans 8:22-25; Philippians 3:20-21; Titus 2:13-14;* [2]*Matthew 25:31-46; 2 Thessalonians 1:6-10*)

Exposition

From the Mount of Olives across the Kidron Valley you can see all Jerusalem spread out below: Mount Zion in the south, the Temple Mount to the north, the modern city toward the setting sun. The Old City with its labyrinthine alleys looks as if it was carved from a single layer of sandstone, following the contours of the land. The most imposing edifice is the massive, golden half-sphere of the Dome of the Rock, considered the third-holiest shrine in Islam. Spires and domes of ancient churches rise above the collage of roofs; out of sight is the Western Wall, the surviving wall of Herod's temple and the focus of Jewish piety. The thousands of graves spread across the slopes of the Mount of Olives look like endless stacks of marble slabs in a quarry. They attest to the belief of many that the resurrection will begin there when the Messiah returns. Somewhere near this place, Jesus gathered his disciples around him after his resurrection, blessed them, and was taken up into heaven before their eyes.

Jesus' ascension happened once in time. But it indicated to his disciples that while bodily apart from them, he now sits at the Father's right hand, an image for them of his continuing reign. One day, his disciples will ascend as he did into the presence of the heavenly Father. But only he is seated there.

The image of "seated at the right hand" reveals the highest honor accorded by a sovereign king. It is the right hand that holds the royal scepter, the symbol of supreme authority. Jesus has been given the highest honor because he shares God's nature. His work completed, he took up again the glory he set aside in order to express God's heart of servant-love to his creation. God's omnipotence expresses itself in Jesus, who rules with the power of God. God's majesty expresses itself in Jesus, who merits all worship and praise.

To be seated means to be at rest. Just as God the Creator rested after bringing the world into being — not because God was depleted, but because in his fullness he chose to enter into communion with his creation — so now God the Redeemer rests after bringing a broken world back to God. Everything that needed to be done has been done. Our destiny is secure.

Jesus has come into his throne as the sovereign ruler of the cosmos. He is the Head of the church, his body, through which he rules all things. In his place of highest dignity, a royal diadem has replaced the crown of thorns.

This says to us that he knows what's going on with our lives. When the world threatens to swirl out of control, he is still in charge. It is not the powers that be, not the political leaders of the day, not the genetic engineers, not the tyrants who brutalize their own people, not the forces of the world markets or the international corporations; Jesus governs all things.

It says to us that, though we cannot see him, we still share in intimate communion with him. We still enjoy his gifts of the Holy Spirit and the inner assurance of our future with him, along with faith, hope, love, and whatever else we need for salvation. Because he reigns in glory, we can count on God's protection from every enemy, whether the seductions of the world, or our own propensity to sin, or the distortions of the evil one, or death itself. We have the assurance that everything it costs us to keep true to Jesus he will repay us one hundredfold.

And it says to us that Jesus will come again. He will one day judge the world in righteousness and will eradicate evil. That which is fearful for those who ultimately reject God's reign is a source of dear comfort to Christians: We live in light of this final "putting-right" of all things. We live in the joyful expectation that he will deliver from all oppression, that he will glorify our bodies and redeem our brokenness, that he will wipe every tear from our eyes, and that he will restore us to the deepest longings of our souls. The implications are as cosmic as they are profound. The great consummation embraces not only humanity; Jesus' coming again will restore all of creation to the grand symphony of renewal, and we will join in the joy of eternity.

Other Voices

The matter of most crucial importance is this — a man is brought face to face with his own life — personal accountability is the keynote:

When the master calls me to him
I'll be somewhere sleeping in my grave.
In that great day when he calls us to him
I'll be somewhere sleeping in my grave.

The deep intimacy between the soul and God is constantly suggested. Even the true name of the individual is known only to God. There are references to the fact that the designation, Child of God, is the only name that is necessary. This gnosis of the individual is an amazing example of the mystical element present in the slave's religious experience. The slave's answer to the use of terms of personal designation that are degrading is to be found in his private knowledge that his name is known only to the God of the entire universe. In the

Judgment everybody will at last know who he is, a fact which he has known all along.

O' nobody knows who I am, who I am,
Till the Judgment morning.
> — HOWARD THURMAN,
> *For the Inward Journey*

The doctrine of the Second Coming teaches us that we do not and cannot know when the world drama will end. The curtain may be rung down at any moment: say, before you have finished reading this paragraph. This seems to some people intolerably frustrating. So many things would be interrupted. Perhaps you were going to get married next month, perhaps you were going to get a raise next week; you may be on the verge of a great scientific discovery; you may be maturing great social and political reforms. Surely no good and wise God would be so very unreasonable as to cut all this short? Not now, of all moments!

But we think thus because we keep on assuming that we know the play. We do not know the play. We do not even know whether we are in Act I or Act V. We do not know who are the major and who the minor characters. The Author knows. . . . That it has a meaning we may be sure, but we cannot see it. When it is over, we may be told . . . the playing it well is what matters infinitely.

> — C. S. LEWIS,
> *The World's Last Night*

God will not permit Satan to exercise his power in human history forever. Man will not destroy himself from the face of the earth, nor will this planet become a cold, life-less star. The day is surely coming when the knowledge of God shall cover the earth as the waters cover the sea, when peace and righteousness shall prevail instead of war and evil. The day is surely coming when God will take the reins of government into His hands and the kingdom of God will come on earth and His will be done even as it is in heaven. This glorious destiny for man will be achieved only by the personal, vis-ible, glorious return of Christ. He is destined to be Lord of lords and King of kings. The second coming of Jesus Christ is an absolutely indispensable doctrine in the Biblical teaching of redemption. Apart from His glorious return, God's work will forever be incomplete. At the center of redemption past is Christ on the cross; at the center of

redemption future is Christ returning in glory.

> — GEORGE ELDON LADD, *The Blessed Hope*

Jesus shall reign where'er the sun
Does his successive journeys run;
His Kingdom stretch from shore to shore,
Till moons shall wax and wane no more.

‿

For Him shall endless prayer be made,
And praises throng to crown His head;
His name, like sweet perfume, shall rise
With every morning sacrifice.

‿

People and realms of every tongue
Dwell on His love with sweetest song;
And infant voices shall proclaim
Their early blessings on His name.

‿

Blessings abound where'er He reigns;
The prisoner leaps to loose his chains,
The weary find eternal rest,
And all the sons of want are blest.

‿

Let every creature rise and bring
Peculiar honors to our King;
Angels descend with songs again,
And earth repeat the loud Amen! Amen.

> — ISAAC WATTS, "Jesus Shall Reign
> Where'er the Sun"

Daily Scripture Readings

KEY TEXT: PSALM 110:1
   Sunday: John 5:16-30
   Monday: Revelation 19:11-16

Tuesday: Luke 21:5-28
Wednesday: Mark 13:32-37
Thursday: Titus 2:11-15
Friday: 2 Thessalonians 1:3-12
Saturday: Matthew 19:23-30

Questions for Reflection and Discussion _____

What does it imply to you that Jesus now reigns in heaven? What does it mean when the world seems to spin out of control? What does it mean when your life lacks purpose or joy?

What would you say are the "enemies" all people struggle against? What are the particular enemies Christ is helping you overcome?

If you grew up in a Christian church, how did your tradition talk about "the end times"? Since no one knows when the Lord is coming back, what does it mean to live in expectation of his return? Do you anticipate that day with good feelings, with anxiety, with indifference? Why?

Closing Prayer _____

Jesus, I want to be with you. Please use every day of my life to make me more fit for heaven. I pray that you would come quickly to make this broken world right again. Remind us that our only hope is found in you. Amen.

Week Twenty:
The Comforter

Opening Prayer

Holy Spirit, I praise you for your work in creation and for your work in making a new creation as well. You are the source of ultimate peace and power that can bear me up when everything else fails. Help me to follow the example of Jesus. Breathe into me your sustaining breath, I pray. Amen.

Heidelberg Questions

QUESTION 53: What do you believe concerning "the Holy Spirit"?

First, he, as well as the Father and the Son, is eternal God.[1]

Second, he has been given to me personally,[2] so that, by true faith, he makes me share in Christ and his blessings,[3] comforts me,[4] and remains with me forever.[5]

([1]*Genesis 1:1-2; Matthew 28:19; Acts 5:3-4;* [2]*1 Corinthians 6:19; 2 Corinthians 1:21-22; Galatians 4:6;* [3]*Galatians 3:14;* [4]*John 15:26; Acts 9:31;* [5]*John 14:16-17; 1 Peter 4:14*)

Exposition

God sends the Holy Spirit into the hearts of those he has called. The Spirit is not only an energy or a force or an attribute of God. The Spirit is certainly more than divine awareness on the part of humans. The Holy Spirit is a person. The Spirit is the living God, just as much as the Father and the Son. He is distinct from the human spirit. He is holy, and he *makes* holy.

Gathered at the table with his disciples on their last night together before his death, Jesus promised that he would not leave them alone. He assured them that the Father would send his Spirit, which he called the "Paraclete." The disciples would have understood that term to mean a person who comes alongside. The word has been translated as Comforter, Advocate, Counselor, and Intercessor. Perhaps we best understand it as Helper, the friend who acts on our behalf. The Paraclete would come, Jesus said, to make his presence real even in his physical absence. The Spirit does not lead the church beyond Jesus as his successor, but continues the work already made clear in the Lord's earthly ministry. That work encompasses several areas: to teach his disciples the things of Christ; to witness to Christ; to enable the "greater works" of Christ; and to convict of sin, righteousness, and judgment.

So the Paraclete speaks *for* us, and he speaks *to* us. That is, he intercedes before God on our behalf in heaven, and he speaks in us to reassure us that we belong to him. He comes to testify, teach, make us more like Jesus, and more at peace in the assurance we belong to him. He comes to convict and to comfort: to convict of sin so that we will be moved to confess and find forgiveness, and to be wooed back into God's embrace to find the only comfort that is real comfort.

He awakens in us the longing to know God.

He illumines the heart to see our need for him.

He assures us we are his, as the bond by which Christ dwells in us and we in him, so that we might enjoy friendship with him.

The Spirit is also the one who gifts the body of Christ, the church, so that we can grow up into the full stature of the one who called us to himself. All believers have been baptized in the Holy Spirit and have a spiritual gift to share with the rest of the church. In the book of Acts, we see the Spirit coming in wind and fire, an image of cleansing, renewal, warmth, enlightenment, purification. These are the supernatural gifts connected with God himself, mediated through the third person of the Trinity.

Other Voices

So remember this; as long as you are willing to be Acceptance-with-Joy and Bearing-in-Love, you can never again become crippled, and you will be able to go wherever I lead you. You will be able to go down into the Valley of the world to work with Me there, for that is where the evil and sorrowful and ugly things are which need to be overcome.

— HANNAH HURNARD, *Hinds' Feet on High Places*

When [the apostle] Paul wants to find the distinctive mark of Spirit-given experience, he finds it not in the charismatic Spirit as such, nor in the eschatological Spirit as such, but in the Jesus Spirit, the Spirit whose characteristics are those of Christ; he experiences the Spirit as a power which owns the Lordship of Jesus, which reproduces for the believer Jesus' relationship of sonship with the Father, which creates the believer's character afresh after the pattern of Christ. The only charismata, the only charismatic Spirit Paul wants to know about is the Spirit of Christ, that is Christ the life-giving Spirit.

— JAMES D. G. DUNN, *Jesus and the Spirit*

It is the gift of the Spirit which enables human beings to love and therefore to worship.

Once given, the Spirit continues with believers as a "guarantee" or "earnest." The prospect is glory, and of this the Spirit is, in another image, the "firstfruits." This image is drawn from Old Testament worship: the firstfruits are the promise and anticipation of the whole. As Israel returned to God the firstfruits of his gifts to the people, so God's gift of the Spirit

enables the worshippers already to render God glory in anticipation of the final kingdom when God will be all in all.

— GEOFFREY WAINWRIGHT, *Doxology: The Praise of God in Worship, Doctrine, and Life*

Then a thought came to me. I said to myself, "I have been trying to keep this heart of mine clean and available for Christ, but it is hard work. I start on one room and no sooner have I cleaned it that I discover another room is dirty. I begin on the second room and the first one is already dusty again. I'm getting tired trying to maintain a clean heart and an obedient life. I just am not up to it!"

Suddenly I asked, "Lord, is there a possibility you would be willing to manage the whole house and operate it for me just as you did that closet? Could I give to you the responsibility of keeping my heart what it ought to be and myself doing what I ought to be doing?"

I could see his face light up as he replied, "I'd love to! This is exactly what I came to do. You can't live out the Christian life in your own strength. That is impossible. Let me do it for you and through you. That's the only way it will really work."

— ROBERT BOYD MUNGER, *My Heart — Christ's Home*

As the wind is your symbol, so forward
  our goings.
As the dove, so launch us heavenwards.
As water, so purify our spirits.
As a cloud, so abate our temptations.

As dew, so revive our languor.
As fire, so purge out our dross. Amen.
— Christina Rossetti,
Book of Common Worship

Daily Scripture Readings

Key Text: Joel 2:28-32
Sunday: Acts 2:1-13
Monday: John 14:16-31a
Tuesday: Ezekiel 36:22-28
Wednesday: 1 Corinthians 3:16-17
Thursday: Luke 11:5-13
Friday: 1 John 4:1-6
Saturday: Romans 8:1-11

Questions for Discussion and Reflection

Agree or disagree: "God does not only act upon human beings, but also in human beings who belong to him. Because of this, we can already live in the power of his resurrection." What are the reasons for your answer?

It seems many Christians are uncertain about the role of the Holy Spirit in their lives. Has there been a time when you have discerned the Spirit's presence to encourage you, to convict you, or to empower you for a special work? If so, describe this experience.

In the book of Galatians, the apostle Paul lists these characteristics as the fruit of the Spirit: love, joy, peace, patience, kindness, goodness, faithfulness, gentleness, and self-control. Name one or two that you have manifested lately. What where the effects of that in the lives of others? What is a characteristic that you would like to show in greater degree? What difference might that make in your life?

Closing Prayer

God, you are from eternity to eternity, and are not confined to one place and one time. The mountains and the seas, indeed the cosmos itself, cannot contain you. Yet you condescend to make your people into a holy temple. Thank you for the miracle of your indwelling Spirit that has come into my heart. Help me to give you free rein in my life. In Jesus' name, amen.

Week Twenty-one:
The Church

Opening Prayer

Lord, you have placed me in your family, the church. Thank you for those who have gone before me who have witnessed to Christ. I know that I have faith today because of those who passed it on to me. Meet me in the worship, the service, and the fellowship of your body. In Jesus' name, amen.

Heidelberg Questions

QUESTION 54: What do you believe concerning "the holy catholic church"?

I believe that the Son of God through his Spirit and Word,[1] out of the entire human race,[2] from the beginning of the world to its end,[3] gathers, protects, and preserves for himself a community chosen for eternal life[4] and united in true faith.[5] And of this community I am[6] and always will be[7] a living member.

([1]John 20:14-16; Acts 20:28; Romans 10:14-17; Colossians 1:18; [2]Genesis 26:3-4; Revelation 5:9; [3]Isaiah 59:21; 1 Corinthians 11:26; [4]Matthew 16:18; John 10:28-30; Ephesians 1:3-14; [5]Acts 2:42-47; Ephesians 4:1-6; [6]1 John 3:14,19-21; [7]John 10:27-28; 1 Corinthians 1:4-9; 1 Peter 1:3-5)

QUESTION 55: What do you understand by "the communion of saints"?

First, that believers one and all, as members of this community, share in Christ and in all his treasures and gifts.[1]

Second, that each member should consider it a duty to use these gifts readily and cheerfully for the service and enrichment of the other members.[2]

([1]Romans 8:32; 1 Corinthians 6:17; 12:4-7,12-13; 1 John 1:3; [2]Romans 12:4-8; 1 Corinthians 12:20-27; 13:1-7; Philippians 2:4-8)

QUESTION 56: What do you believe concerning "the forgiveness of sins"?

I believe that God, because of Christ's atonement, will never hold against me any of my sins[1] nor my sinful nature which I need to struggle against all my life.[2]

Rather, in his grace God grants me the righteousness of Christ to free me forever from judgment.[3]

(*[1]Psalm 103:3-4,10,12; Micah 7:18-19; 2 Corinthians 5:18-21; 1 John 1:7; 2:2; [2]Romans 7:21-25; [3]John 3:17-18; Romans 8:1-2)*

Exposition

Have you ever heard anybody say something like, "Jesus sounds good to me; it's just Christians I can't stand," or "I can follow God without having to be part of a church"? If you have been a Christian for long, you have heard statements like that. You have probably felt that way too. In fact, in the West a Christian perhaps endures more at the *hands* of the church than for the *sake* of the church.

To examine the history of the church is sometimes to grow disillusioned with its failure to live up to the model of Christ. Sometimes, it seems the history of the church is as filled with crimes as is the history of the world at large, from the Crusades to the corruption of the medieval papacy, from the Inquisition to the complacency of the state churches toward National Socialism in Nazi Germany or to systemic racism in our own society.

As a young man, I once had the chance to share Christ with a Muslim student from Syria. He listened politely until I had finished. Then he told me, "If Christianity is true, then how could the Crusades have taken place?" I wanted to protest, "What does that have to do with anything today? That happened nine hundred years ago!" At the time, I felt he was looking for some way to avoid the real issue — the character of Christ, not the integrity of those who claim to act in his name. And in a sense, it is true, we do need to look past the *members* of the church to the *Lord* of the church. When we pin our hopes on people, we can be disappointed. If we were only able to persevere with the Christian community as long as the church proved worthy of our allegiance, then none of us would be lifetime members of the body of Christ.

But could we not also agree with the complaint of the young Muslim student? We question whether real Christians, born again by the power of God, could even be capable of some of the things that have been done in the name of Christ. And are there not also times when our own Christian community disappoints? When people who should know and be better make the body of Christ a contentious place? Sometimes conflict erupts, and the resulting wounds hurt all the more precisely *because* they occur at the hands of those who are supposed to be our brothers and sisters. Why, then, persist with this problematic collection of people? Maybe it's like the adage that the church is an ark — you put up with the smell inside because of the terrible storm outside. The

Reformers of the sixteenth century believed, as did the Roman Catholic Church, that there truly was no salvation outside the church. That is, the church is God's chosen instrument for bringing the gospel to a needy world. Like any other human institution, it is distorted with sin. The church is broken because it is filled with broken people, who come into a new community of healing to begin to experience the salvation and the peace of God.

The apostle Paul saw the church as the people called by God through the proclamation of the gospel:

> How, then, can they call on the one they have not believed in? And how can they believe in the one of whom they have not heard? And how can they hear without someone preaching to them? And how can they preach unless they are sent? As it is written, "How beautiful are the feet of those who bring good news!". . . Consequently, faith comes from hearing the message, and the message is heard through the word of Christ. (Romans 10:14-15,17)

The church subsists as the people through whom the very Word of God was declared, the people in whom his presence is celebrated in the Lord's Supper. It consists of the people who respond to the good news of Jesus in confession, prayer, and service, traveling the road through the cross to the Resurrection.

In the catechism, the section on the church follows the section on the Holy Spirit, echoing the model of the Apostles' Creed. The order is important to notice; the Holy Spirit gives birth to the church by breathing it into being. God sovereignly and graciously created the church — the church didn't create or conjure up the Spirit. This reminds us, as Swiss theologian Karl Barth said, that there is no private Christianity. The salvation of individuals is not the end-all of God's activity in the universe. Yes, we *do* need to respond personally to Jesus Christ. We do bear responsibility as free agents before our Creator. We do need to come to the point where we *decide* to follow Christ. But God's goal is far more expansive than a private experience of "Jesus and me." To believe in God is also to believe in God's action on behalf of all creation. It is to long for the completion of God's work, which is through the church of Jesus Christ. This cosmic perspective contrasts starkly with the North American mentality of "rugged individualism" that many Christians have brought into their faith.

The initiative is Christ's — and wherever the church is, there he is active. But how do we recognize the church? What constitutes it? According to Calvin, there were two signs: the Word of God purely preached and the sacraments rightly administered. His twofold emphasis grew out of his conviction that God spoke the church into being, and continues to sustain it through his Word. We know that Word in the Bible, the faithful witness to Christ, and in the experience of worship. Proclamation and celebration, then, together form the primal experience of the church, and out of these flow mission and service to the poor in the name of the One who calls us into his presence. Further, the Reformers understood the church to be both visible and invisible. The visible church is composed of the structures, which anyone can see, and includes both the saved and the unsaved. The invisible church, on the other hand, is made up of the true believers of every age, known ultimately only to God. It is as if one drew a circle with a dotted line to delineate the circumference of the visible church. Anybody who professes Christ comes within that circle. A smaller circle would be situated within the larger to include only those who have experienced new life in Christ, the true children of God by adoption.

The Lord tells us of this reality in the parable of the wheat and the weeds in Matthew 13:

"The kingdom of heaven is like a man who sowed good seed in his field. But while everyone was sleeping, his enemy came and sowed weeds among the wheat, and went away. When the wheat sprouted and formed heads, then the weeds also appeared." (Matthew 13:24-26)

The man's employees wanted to pull up the weeds. But the man knew that would also uproot good wheat. Better to wait, he said, until the harvest, and separate the two at that time.

This tells us that the Lord is aware of the tension between where we are as a church and where we will be, between those who are truly in Christ and those who only appear to be. For the time being, our role is to confess our sin, to grow in obedience, and to carry our mission as we anticipate the church's consummation in Christ. We don't need to pretend that the wrongdoing of the church doesn't exist. Thank God that our salvation doesn't depend on our purity but on God's faithfulness. We are free to come to him, broken as we are, and move ahead in discipleship so that we might grow to more fully reflect the likeness of Christ.

So it is that we, along with all believers in Christ, compose the church — as the creed says, the "holy catholic church," that is, the church universal. The apostle Paul regularly addressed his letters to "the saints" of local congregations. He did not mean to single out the spiritual giants of his day, but to address the whole church made up of everyday Christians. Sinners though we are, the community of "saints" throughout the ages, regardless of denomination — that is the church, catholic and holy. May the church of Jesus Christ become a clearer sign of the kingdom of heaven in the midst of a dark world!

Other Voices

We are entering another Dark Age. The threat now comes not from savage tribes like the Vandals, Goths and Huns but from the brutalizing pressures of advertising and the mass media, the crudeness and violence of much popular music and entertainment and the inexorable rise of the consumer society with its rampant acquisitiveness and selfishness. If the churches are to make any kind of effective stand for the Christian values which are increasingly under attack it is surely by following the example of the Celtic monasteries and becoming little pools of gentleness and enlightenment, oases of compassion and charity in the ever extending desert of secular materialism. This will not be an easy calling. It will mean modern Christians becoming like the Celtic monks and pilgrims, never feeling quite at home or at rest in this world, ever seeking their place of resurrection and constantly invoking God's presence and protection against evil forces. But we will also have much to help us on our way: the inspiration of music, art and poetry, the refreshment of nature, and the companionship not just of fellow pilgrims among the living but also of the whole host of heaven, that great company who have already traveled the way before us.

— IAN BRADLEY, *The Celtic Way*

God created the Cosmos geocentrically, i.e., He placed the spiritual center of this Cosmos on our planet, and caused all the divisions of the kingdoms of nature, on this earth, to culminate in man, upon whom, as the bearer of His image He called to consecrate the Cosmos to His glory. . . .

For regeneration does not save a few isolated individuals, finally to be joined together mechanically as an aggregate heap. Regeneration saves the organism, itself, of our race. And therefore all regenerate human life forms one organic body, of which Christ is the Head, and whose members are bound together by their mystical union with Him.

But not before the Second Advent shall this new all-embracing organism manifest itself as the center of the cosmos. At present it is hidden. Here, on earth, it is only as it were its silhouette that can be dimly discerned. In the Future, *this New Jerusalem* shall descend from God, out of heaven, but at present it withdraws its beams from our sight in the mysteries of the invisible. And therefore the true sanctuary is now *above*.

— ABRAHAM KUYPER, *Lectures on Calvinism*

With these two themes of love and faith in Jesus Christ, other ideas, such as . . . the forgiveness of sin, the gift of the Spirit and of eternal life, are closely connected; nevertheless these two define the Christian life; no one can be a member of the Christian fellowship who does not acknowledge Jesus as the Christ and the Son of God and who does not love the brothers in obedience to the Lord. . . .

In faith in the faithfulness of God we count on being corrected, forgiven, complemented by the company of the faithful. . . .

To make our decisions in faith is to make them in view of the fact that no single man or group or historical time is the church; but that there is a church of faith in which we do our partial, relative work and on which we count. It is to make them in view of the fact that Christ is risen from the dead, and is not only the head of the church but the redeemer of the world. It is to make them in view of the fact that the world of culture — man's achievement — exists within the world of grace — God's Kingdom.

— H. Richard Niebuhr, *Christ and Culture*

We teach that the true Church is that in which the signs or marks of the true Church are to be found, especially the lawful and sincere preaching of the Word of God as it was delivered to us in the books of the prophets and the apostles, which all lead us unto Christ, who said in the Gospel: "My sheep hear my voice, and I know them, and they follow me; and I give unto them eternal life. A stranger they do not follow, but they flee from him for they do not know the voice of strangers." (John 10:5,27,28)

And those who are such in the Church have one faith and one spirit; and therefore they worship but one God, and him alone they worship in spirit and in truth, loving him alone with all their hearts and with all their strength, praying unto him alone through Jesus Christ, the only Mediator and Intercessor; and they do not seek righteousness and life outside Christ and faith in him. Because they acknowledge Christ the only head and foundation of the Church, and, resting on him, daily renew themselves by repentance, and patiently bear the cross laid upon them. Moreover, joined together with all the members of Christ by an unfeigned love, they show

that they are Christ's disciples by persevering in the bond of peace and holy unity. At the same time they participate in the Sacraments instituted by Christ, and delivered unto us by his apostles, using them in no other way than as they received them from the Lord.

— *The Second Helvetic Confession*

The task of the church in this society is not to turn from the world in order to affirm another. But neither is it called to baptize the world as it is or to run to do the world's bidding — to make a warm spot for troubled souls. Its task is to proclaim the total gospel message which affirms the world in order to transform it, which cooperates with but is not identical with secular programs and institutions because Christians seek "another city" — one which is only attained, however, through the effort to build the earthly *civitas*. When men deny the individual for the sake of society, then the Christian must proclaim the rights of each man. But, as has happened in industrial societies in the West, when individualism runs rampant over the common good, then the church must point out by deed and voice the message of human solidarity. It cannot expect other institutions to do this.

— W. Fred Graham, *The Constructive Revolutionary: John Calvin & His Socio-Economic Impact*

The church represents the presence of the reign of God in the life of the world, not in the triumphalist sense (as the "successful" cause) and not in the moralistic sense (as the "righteous" cause), but in the sense that it is the place where the mystery of the kingdom present in the dying and rising of Jesus is made present here and now so that all people, righteous and unrighteous, are enabled to taste and share the love of God before whom all are unrighteous and all are accepted as righteous. It is the place where the glory of God ("glory as of an only son") actually abides among us so that the love of God is available to sin-burdened men and women (John 17:22-23). It is the place where the power of God is manifested in a community of sinners. It is the place where the promise of Jesus is ful-filled: "I, when I am lifted up from the earth, will draw all men to myself" (John 12:32). It is the place where the reign of God is present as love shared among the unlovely.

> — LESLIE NEWBIGIN, *The Open Secret: An Introduction to the Theology of Mission*

Daily Scripture Readings

KEY TEXT: ACTS 2:42-47
    Sunday: Matthew 16:13-20
    Monday: Romans 12:1-8
    Tuesday: 1 Corinthians 12:1-30
    Wednesday: Ephesians 4:1-16
    Thursday: Matthew 18:15-35
    Friday: 1 Timothy 3:1-16
    Saturday: 2 Corinthians 6:14-18

Questions for Reflection and Discussion

Have you ever felt embarrassed by the church? Or felt you could do just as well following Christ on your own? When? In those times, what is it that pulls you back toward the church?

The writer Flannery O'Conner, talking with a friend who was a new Christian, said, "Remember that you will as often suffer because of the church as you will for the church." What do you think she meant by that statement? When, in your view, is the church closest to the character of Christ? When is it the most distant?

Jesus' parable of the wheat and the weeds in Matthew 13 suggests that in this life the good and bad are mixed together, but that God will sort out the true believers in the end. How does this encourage you to per-sist in these ambiguous days?

Closing Prayer

Lord of omnipotent love, you have gra-ciously elected to make me a member of your body. Glorify yourself in my life and in your church, I pray through Jesus. Amen.

Week Twenty-two:
The Hope of Glory

Opening Prayer

Shepherd of my soul, I need you to examine my heart and discern what is not of you. Test me, and see what needs cleansing; make me new, then lead me in your way. For Jesus' sake, amen.

Heidelberg Questions

QUESTION 57: How does "the resurrection of the body" comfort you?

Not only my soul will be taken immediately after this life to Christ its head,[1] but even my very flesh, raised by the power of Christ, will be reunited with my soul and made like Christ's glorious body.[2]

([1]*Luke 23:43; Philippians 1:21-23;* [2]*1 Corinthians 15:20,42-46,54; Philippians 3:21; 1 John 3:2*)

QUESTION 58: How does the article concerning "life everlasting" comfort you?

Even as I already now experience in my heart the beginning of eternal joy,[1] so after this life I will have perfect blessedness such as no eye has seen, no ear has heard, no human heart has ever imagined: a blessedness in which to praise God eternally.[2]

([1]*Romans 14:17;* [2]*John 17:3; 1 Corinthians 2:9*)

Exposition

My father's mother was one of God's dear people. She was a capable woman of intelligence and many gifts, having had a career as a schoolteacher. But the thing about Grandma that came through most clearly for me was always her gentleness and love for the family. She always seemed to express such pride in me — whether or not other family members felt it was justified — that I was likely to try to rise to her opinion of me. Sometimes when she was on the phone, talking with a relative or friend whose connection to me was obscure, I would squirm to hear her say, "My grandson Randy is here and would like to say hello."

After my grandfather passed away, I would come home from college for summer jobs and would get together with Grandma to go out to breakfast or to take a walk near the ocean where she lived in Southern California. I looked forward to those times; I'd often grill her for information about her growing-up years and about the joys and the hardships of raising a family and caring for grandchildren for over half a century. I had gotten to the point in my own faith journey that I wasn't embarrassed anymore by her sentimental stories or her childlike faith in Jesus. In fact, I found them an encouragement as I worked out my own worldview and system of values.

It was several years later, after I had gone through college and graduate school, served overseas in campus ministries, and returned to seminary in Southern California, that I got word that Grandma was gravely ill. She lingered for a couple days in the hospital, but her heart was worn out, and she longed "to go home to be with the Lord." I felt grateful for her life and for the friendship I had been gifted with since college days, but it was poignant to say goodbye. The simplicity and the tenor of thanksgiving at her memorial service was a tribute to the faithfulness of God, and was just what she had wanted.

Recently, she came to mind as I was daydreaming. I was formulating in my mind the words, "You know, I'll have to give Grandma a call one of these days," when I realized I couldn't do that any more. Funny how I almost said that. She had been gone for nearly ten years.

The Bible portrays death as an enemy. Not that there aren't times when the death of a loved one after an endless, agonizing illness seems like a relief. But the way in which death ends all of our plans, the way in which it clutches both the evil and the good, the way it separates a couple who have loved each other for most of a lifetime, the way it devours the innocent and the children, the way in which it takes people "before their time" like an unfinished portrait; all of this is overwhelming testimony that death is the great adversary of us all. We can pretend it doesn't exist or we can pay homage to it by morbid fascination, but the death rate of humanity is still universal. Death is the great destroyer of life.

But the Bible makes clear a new reality by the resurrection promise through Jesus. Death has lost its sting. It no longer has the last word on the human story and no longer has the last word in our lives. We find peace, assurance, and ultimately triumph in the declaration that

Christ has overcome death. The coming resurrection reminds us that death is not the end for the Christian.

What takes place then, when we die? The catechism echoes the two stages described in Scripture. The instant we breathe our last on earth, we draw our first breath in heaven. We leave our physical body and are immediately in the presence of the Lord. There is a separation of body and soul after death, as the body returns to the "dust" of the earth from which it was taken. There is no further intermediate state, no further purification from sin that needs to take place for the believer. That person's transgressions are completely forgiven, and the "slate is wiped clean." Then, in God's timing, we receive our resurrection bodies when Jesus returns in the Second Coming.

Nature provides analogies for this transformation: the butterfly that emerges from its inert cocoon; the lifeless seed of grain that is buried in the earth and comes up green. The analogies help us understand in part, but they fall short of the reality that goes beyond our modes of thinking. Resurrection is for the Christian the beginning of eternal bliss that can only be hinted at in earthly life. It is the onset of perfect salvation, of comfort. The Christian has the real hope that death is not the end, nor does it simply condemn us to go back and do it all over again as in reincarnation. Death is the indication that God will say to us an unqualified "yes," a welcome home into the arms of the One by whom and for whom we were made.

Do you look forward to heaven? The apostle Paul did, and he lived held together by the dual desires to serve Christ now and to go to be with him. He said, "For to me, living is Christ and dying is gain. If I am to live in the flesh, that means fruitful labor for me; and I do not know which I prefer. I am hard pressed between the two: my desire is to depart and be with Christ, for that is far better" (Philippians 1:21-23, NRSV).

That is the hope in whose light we live. The people we love who have died, along with all the great heroes and heroines of the faith who came before, have gone on ahead of us to heaven. Someday I'll continue that conversation with Grandma.

Other Voices

Throughout our culture we have been led to the idea that we accept death as the end of life on earth. Elisabeth Kübler-Ross, with her five stages of death, has indicated that the "acceptance" stage is the most healthful. The hope of heaven rarely enters into a therapy session. Philip Yancey said, "I have watched in hospital groups as dying patients worked desperately toward a calm stage of acceptance. Strangely, no one ever talked about heaven in those groups; it seemed embarrassing, somehow cowardly. What convulsion of values can have us holding up the prospect of annihilation as brave and that of blissful eternity as cowardly?" . . .

Every day of our lives we are just a breath away from eternity. The believer in Jesus Christ has the promises of heaven. If we believe them, the anticipation of heaven will never be boring. It will be more thrilling than any of the pleasures earth can offer.

— BILLY GRAHAM, *Facing Death and the Life After*

Heaven will be the fulfillment of that Sabbath rest foretold in the command: "Be still and see that I am God." . . .

Only when we are remade by God and perfected by a greater grace shall we have the eternal stillness of that rest in which we shall see that He is God. Then only shall we be filled with Him when He will be all in all. For, although our good works are, in reality, His, they will be put to our account as payment for this Sabbath peace, so long as we do not claim them as our own; but, if we do, they will be reckoned as servile and out of place on the Sabbath, as the text reminds us: "The seventh day . . . is the rest of the Lord. . . . You shall not do any work." In this connection, too, God has reminded us, through the Prophet Ezekiel: "I gave them my Sabbath, to be a sign between me and them, that they might know that I am the Lord that sanctifies them." It is this truth that we shall realize perfectly when we shall be perfectly at rest and shall perfectly see that it is He who is God.

— AUGUSTINE OF HIPPO, *The City of God*

And yet we can make no picture for ourselves of the Resurrection to eternal life. We only know that we shall not be submerged, melted and dissolved in a universal spirit. As God's confrontation of us is preserved intact, so is our confrontation of God. This confrontation is the presupposition of fellowship. . . .

There is one last truth contained in the paradoxical concept of the spiritual body. The body is the instrument of service and of communication, both of service of God, and of service among the many who are our equals. That which is given prominence as essential mark of the Ekklesia, the praise and worship of God and the brotherhood of mutual service, is also to be preserved in the Consummation. Thus the Pauline concept of the spiritual body becomes an expression of the decisively and specifically Biblical emphasis; fellowship instead of unity, answer and worship instead of monologue, love instead of the solitude of the self.

— EMIL BRUNNER, *The Christian Doctrine of the Church, Faith, and the Consummation*

But since the prophecy that death will be swallowed up in victory will only then be fulfilled, let us always have in mind the eternal happiness, the goal of resurrection. Human tongues can scarcely express the excellence of that happiness. We rightly hear that the Kingdom of God will be filled with splendor, joy, happiness, and glory. Still, when these things are spoken of, they remain utterly remote from our perception, and, as it were, wrapped in obscurities, until that day comes when he will reveal to us his glory, that we may behold it face to face. We know that "we are God's children," says John, but "it does not yet appear. . . But when we shall be like him . . . we shall see him as he is" (1 John 3:2).

Accordingly, the prophets, because they could not find words to express that spiritual blessedness in its own nature, merely sketched it in physical terms. Yet because any taste of that sweetness ought to kindle fervent desire in us, let us pause to reflect especially on this: If God contains the fullness of all good things in himself like an inexhaustible fountain, then those who strive after the highest good and happiness should search no further than God. Thus: "Abraham, . . . I am your very great reward" (Genesis 15:1). David's statement agrees with this: "The Lord is my portion . . . ; I shall be satisfied with your face." Indeed, Peter declares that believers are called in this to become partakers of the divine nature (2 Peter 1:4). How is this? Because "he will be . . . glorified in all his saints, and will be marveled at in all who have believed" (2 Thessalonians 1:10). The Lord will share his glory, power, and righteousness with the elect. In fact, he will give himself to be enjoyed by them and, will somehow make them to become one with himself! Therefore, let us remember that every sort of happiness is included under this benefit.

— JOHN CALVIN, *Institutes of the Christian Religion*

Daily Scripture Readings

KEY TEXT: PSALM 49
Sunday: John 5:16-30
Monday: John 11:1-44
Tuesday: Ecclesiastes 12:1-6
Wednesday: 1 Corinthians 15:12-58
Thursday: 1 Thessalonians 4:13-18
Friday: Isaiah 65:17-25
Saturday: Revelation 21:22-26

Questions for Reflection and Discussion

A friend says to you, "I can believe in the immortality of the soul, but it seems far-fetched to think a body that has been cremated can ever be reconstituted. Is it important to believe in a resurrection of the body?" What do you say?

How might it encourage you to anticipate our heavenly reunion with believers who have gone on before? Whom do you look forward to meeting in heaven?

Why do you suppose that Scripture does not dwell on physical descriptions of heaven? What are the ways that popular culture portrays heaven? How do you picture the place?

Given that it is communion with God that makes heaven heavenly, do you think the place itself matters? Why or why not? What does it mean to you that "creation itself will be liberated from its bondage to decay" (Romans 8:21)?

*Closing Prayer*_____

I'm so glad, Father, that this sad world is not all there is to our story: you have written eternity into our hearts and given us a great hope. Help me to live my life in the perspective of that hope, until you take me home to be with you. In Jesus, amen.

Week Twenty-three:
By Grace Alone Through Faith

Opening Prayer

Father, help me to grow in grace and in the knowledge of Jesus my Savior and Lord. Amen.

Heidelberg Questions

QUESTION 59: What good does it do you, however, to believe all this?

In Christ I am right with God and heir to life everlasting.[1]

(*[1]John 3:36; Romans 1:17 (Habakkuk 2:4); Romans 5:1-2*)

QUESTION 60: How are you right with God?

Only by true faith in Jesus Christ.[1]

Even though my conscience accuses me of having grievously sinned against all God's commandments and of never having kept any of them,[2] and even though I am still inclined toward all evil,[3] nevertheless, without my deserving it at all,[4] out of sheer grace,[5] God grants and credits to me the perfect satisfaction, righteousness, and holiness of Christ,[6] as if I had never sinned nor been a sinner, as if I had been as perfectly obedient as Christ was obedient for me.[7]

All I need to do is to accept this gift of God with a believing heart.[8]

(*[1]Romans 3:21-28; Galatians 2:16; Ephesians 2:8-9; Philippians 3:8-11; [2]Romans 3:9-10; [3]Romans 7:23; [4]Titus 3:4-5; [5]Romans 3:24; Ephesians 2:8; [6]Romans 4:3-5 (Genesis 15:6); 2 Corinthians 5:17-19; 1 John 2:1-2; [7]Romans 4:24-25; 2 Corinthians 5:21; [8]John 3:18; Acts 16:30-31*)

QUESTION 61: Why do you say that by faith alone you are right with God?

It is not because of any value my faith has that God is pleased with me. Only Christ's satisfaction, righteousness, and holiness make me right with God.[1] And I can receive this righteousness and make it mine in no other way than by faith alone.[2]

(*[1]1 Corinthians 1:30-31; [2]Romans 10:10; 1 John 5:10-12*)

Exposition

Faith places confidence in Jesus Christ. It trusts in the power of God to do what he intends to do in the world and in each of our lives. We hold onto this thankfully, because we know it is not due to any strength or merit on our part. That is also the basis for confidence. Confidence in ourselves is no sure confidence, but trust in the trustworthiness of God is as certain as his own unchanging character. Based on the perfection of God, and not on the whims of the human spirit, this faith is the basis for robust comfort in our lives.

This section of the catechism, as it comments on the Apostles' Creed, asserts our responsibility and freedom. The creed teaches us that God creates, that God redeems through the work of Jesus, and that God renews through the person of the Spirit; this is the God who calls us to respond to his powerful work with faith. We gain access to all that God has done with faith in Jesus Christ. By faith, we are made right with God and become the heir of all of God's blessings.

J. R. R. Tolkien's works, *The Hobbit* and the *The Lord of the Rings,* illustrate the idea of inheritance. Hobbits are a quiet, conservative, comfort-loving people about two-feet tall who live in underground houses shaped like tunnels. The story recounts how one hobbit named Bilbo Baggins was enticed into a wild adventure over mountains and into confrontations with hobbit-eating trolls, fierce goblins and werewolves, hunger, self-doubt, and a terrible dragon in order to restore the legacy of a group of dwarves.

The trip would mark the hobbit forever. He comes into possession of a mysterious ring that begins to exert its influence on him. The hobbit finds courage on the long sojourn and proves his value to the dwarves who began the trip dubious about his company. Ultimately, he makes a fortune for himself and lives to enjoy it for many years. On his "eleventy-first" birthday (that is, one hundred eleven) Bilbo throws a great party for himself and announces his young nephew Frodo as his heir. All that belongs to Bilbo would be his. Everything that Bilbo paid so dearly for in time, sacrifice, and hardship would now pass to the younger hobbit. The affection, the esteem, the name, the fortunes, and the privileges that the elder hobbit had bought at a great price became the prize of Frodo. In consequence, the young hobbit would discover he would have to make a choice whether to take these things along with the burden they implied.

The Christian participates in Christ, and through him his benefits. Jesus embodied these benefits: "perfect satisfaction, righteousness, and holiness." His work wins for us the justification we could never earn ourselves. He reinstates for us the eternal life we could never aspire to. The accuser, our tormented conscience, no longer carries the day with God the judge. The witnesses against us, the broken commandments, and our own thoughts and actions, are canceled out. Christ has paid the debt with the perfect payment, sufficient for the sins of the world. The Spirit of God announces the sentence — "not guilty!" — and makes it stick in the hearts of pardoned sinners.

How do we appropriate God's grace? Only by faith. The ABCs of faith are simple: we *admit* our sin by agreeing with God's assessment of us. We *believe* that Christ paid for our sins on the cross. We *confess* him before others as Savior and Lord. That faith in itself is not worthy or impressive to God. But it is pleasing to God nonetheless, just as a mother is pleased when a proud child brings home a clay project from school and offers it as a present. The project might be totally useless, yet it is beautiful to the mother because it expresses her child's love. In the same way, our faith pleases God not because it is a good work in itself, but because it reflects genuine love. Our faith is still anticipatory; for now, that faith looks forward to God's pronouncement at the last judgment. We trust that we are now rightly related to God, even though we have to keep on confessing our sins and continue to be restored to him. But when the end is certain, we know to whom we belong, and we have confidence for the living of our days. Christ has already spoken the last word.

Other Voices

A mighty Fortress is our God,
A Bulwark never failing;
Our Helper He amid the flood
Of mortal ills prevailing,
For still our ancient foe
Doth seek to work us woe;
His craft and power are great;
And, armed with cruel hate,
On earth is not his equal.

Did we in our own strength confide,
Our striving would be losing;
Were not the right man on our side,
The man of God's own choosing.
Dost ask who that may be?
Christ Jesus, it is He,
Lord Sabaoth His name,
From age to age the same,
And He must win the battle.

And though this world, with devils filled,
Should threaten to undo us,
We will not fear, for God hath willed
His truth to triumph through us.
The prince of darkness grim,
We tremble not for him;
His rage we can endure
For lo! his doom is sure;
One little word shall fell him.

That word above all earthly powers,
No thanks to them, abideth;
The Spirit and the gifts are ours
Through Him who with us sideth;
Let goods and kindred go,
This mortal life also;
The body they may kill:
God's truth abideth still;
His Kingdom is forever. Amen.

— MARTIN LUTHER, "A Mighty Fortress Is Our God"

Conversion is what happens between birth and death. By putting emphasis on conversion as a process, I do not mean to disclaim the many accounts of people being suddenly and mysteriously touched by God and changed tremendously. There are too many stories of radical change in people's lives to take them lightly. However, even people who have had a dramatic encounter with the Divine, still must go through that daily purifying process of continued conversion. A deep and lasting conversion is a process, an unfolding, a slow turning and turning again.

We are saved every day. We are saved from our self-righteousness, our narrow minds, our own wills, our obstinate clinging. We are saved from our blindness. Salvation stands before us at every moment. It meets us face to face. It asks us to make a choice. Do we have the courage to accept it? It is costly, yet it brings life. The cross is always costly. It costs us our lives. The dust of our Lenten ashes turns before our very eyes into Easter glory. Our frailty fades into splendor. Our life given becomes life received and renewed.

— Macrina Wiederkehr,
A Tree Full of Angels

Evangelical Christianity is a multifaceted subculture notoriously difficult to pin down. But two things especially characterize it, and they are the living legacies of Edwards the Puritan and Wesley the Methodist. First, evangelical theology and life are doctrinally conservative in the sense of seeking to preserve and maintain classical Christian doctrines of the church

fathers and Reformers. Both Edwards and Wesley resisted what they saw as impulses toward rationalism, heresy and accommodation to culture. They were committed to Christian orthodoxy.

The second legacy bequeathed by both Edwards and Wesley to contemporary evangelicalism is "orthodoxy on fire." That is, both of them averred that mere nominal Christian assent to doctrinal correctness does not automatically make one a real Christian. Transforming experience of God is what makes one a real Christian and is the best assurance of orthodoxy. They rejected sacramentalism, confessionalism and religious rationalism in favor of conversional piety, faith as trust and not merely assent, and belief in a supernatural God who works immediately in the world in often mysterious ways.

— Roger E. Olson, *The Story of Christian
Theology: Twenty Centuries of
Tradition and Reform*

When faith and love which parted from
thee never,
    Had ripened thy just soul to dwell with
      God,
    Meekly thou didst resign this earthy
      load
    Of death, called life; which us from life
      doth sever.

            ⌒

Thy works and alms and all thy good
endeavor
    Stayed not behind, nor in the grave were
      trod;

But, as faith pointed with her golden
rod,
Followed thee up to joy and bliss for
ever.

↬

Love led them on, and faith who knew
them best
Thy handmaids, clad them o'er with
purple beams
And azure wings, that up they flew so
dressed,

↬

And spake the truth of thee in glorious
themes
Before the Judge, who thenceforth bid
thee rest
And drink thy fill of pure immortal
streams.

— JOHN MILTON, *Paradise Lost*

Then Hopeful said, "My Brother, you've
quite forgotten the text where it is said of
the wicked, 'They have no struggle; their
bodies are healthy and strong. They are free
from the burdens common to man.' These
troubles and distresses that you go though
in these waters are no sign that God has forsaken you, but they're sent to try you, to see
whether you will call to mind that which
you've received before of His goodness and
depend upon Him in your distresses."

— JOHN BUNYAN, from *The Pilgrim's
Progress in Modern English*
by L. Edward Hazelbaker

Daily Scripture Readings

KEY TEXT: JOHN 3:36
Sunday: Ephesians 2:1-10
Monday: Romans 10:1-13
Tuesday: Galatians 5:1-6
Wednesday: 2 Chronicles 20:1-21
Thursday: Habakkuk 2:4; 3:1-19
Friday: Daniel 3:1-30
Saturday: Hebrews 11:1-30

Questions for Reflection and Discussion

How would you define faith? How can
you be sure if a person's faith is genuine?

What advice would you have for the
Christian who trusts in Christ but still
struggles with guilt?

Does it lead to bad self-image to teach that
we can do nothing pleasing to God apart
from faith? Why or why not?

Closing Prayer

*Dear God, my faith seems frail and puny
to me, but you are pleased when I simply
come to you in trust. I do believe; help me
in my unbelief. In Jesus' name and for his
sake, amen.*

Week Twenty-four:
A Right Relationship with God

Opening Prayer

Dear Father, help me to trust in your gracious mercy, to turn from the ways of sin, and to renounce evil in my life and in the world. With your help, I pledge this day to be your obedient disciple. In Christ, amen.

Heidelberg Questions

QUESTION 62: Why can't the good we do make us right with God, or at least help make us right with him?

Because the righteousness which can pass God's scrutiny must be entirely perfect and must in every way measure up to the divine law.[1] Even the very best we do in this life is imperfect and stained with sin.[2]

([1]*Romans 3:20; Galatians 3:10 [Deuteronomy 27:26];* [2]*Isaiah 64:6*)

QUESTION 63: How can you say that the good we do doesn't earn anything when God promises to reward it in this life and the next?[1]

This reward is not earned; it is a gift of grace.[2]

([1]*Matthew 5:12; Hebrews 11:6;* [2]*Luke 17:10; 2 Timothy 4:7-8*)

QUESTION 64: But doesn't this teaching make people indifferent and wicked?

No. It is impossible for those grafted into Christ by true faith not to produce fruits of gratitude.[1]

([1]*Luke 6:43-45; John 15:5*)

Exposition

If my experience can be trusted, then one of the most difficult lessons for Christians is also one of the most fundamental — that we live by grace, not by works. It is so easy to work ourselves into exhaustion by having to appear busy, busy, busy, as if anything less proves a lack of seriousness about life. Is being overwhelmed a sign of real discipleship, a mark that we're pulling our own weight? Might it not be that much of our "drivenness" results from inner emptiness, a vain craving for others' approval? Busyness is a demon of our preoccupied age. But the gospel invites us to come home to where we were meant to be, to a relationship of love with God. That implies simply *being* along with doing.

If our faith is not virtuous or worthy, as last week's answers proved, then how much less our works! The idea that works make us right with God betrays an insidious pride and a desire to control. Only perfect obedience to divine law counts as righteous before God. This is impossible, because even our best works are tainted by impure motives. Even if from this point onward we were to live flawlessly, we could never make up for the past sins. We cannot live up to God's standard of utter holiness.

Is God unfair to require what we are constitutionally unable to do? No, because God created the first man and woman unpolluted by sin and perfectly able to fulfill the demands of the law. It was after they fell from that pristine condition that sin was introduced into the human race. Like a drop of ink falling into a glass of spring water, its effects are ubiquitous. The only way for the demands of God's character to be fulfilled now is by God's own provision. That is precisely what he has done on the cross of Christ.

But good news hides in this dire assessment of the human condition. If our works in themselves avail nothing, we can be freed from our futile tactics of self-justification. Christians as well as anyone fall into this dismal habit; but to admit we cannot save ourselves is to embark on the path toward peace. If we set aside our compulsion to prove ourselves, we can relax, enjoy our service to the Lord, and be grateful for whatever comes. We don't have to insist on our own way, or to prove to others that we're competent persons, or squirm under constant, vague guilt about not measuring up.

Faith doesn't make us right with God because it makes us good. It doesn't make us right with God because it produces good works in us. It does that, but that is not why faith is acceptable to God. Faith doesn't make us right with God because of any quality in us. Faith makes us right with God because it is a response to the grace of God, an appropriation of Jesus' own work.

What now, in light of God's grace? Do good works count for nothing spiritually? Do Christians need not give of their resources, tithe to the church, get involved in mission, exercise their spiritual gifts, befriend the poor and homeless, study, work for social justice, and share the good news? Of course we do. In fact, the next major section of the Heidelberg

Catechism deals with the response to grace. Questions 86 through 129 occupy the section of "gratitude" in the catechism, or of the believer's response to what God has done. Sincere response means moving into a lifestyle of service, of making clear through our words and actions that we live now from a different center. Indeed, if a person lives sluggishly and without concern for others, then there's good reason to question whether he or she has made a commitment to Christ. Genuine faith always ensues in works, increasingly so as Christ gets a hold of every aspect of a person's life. Christians who see the depth and breadth of God's grace are empowered by a robust faith and an inclusive worldview, where nothing is outside the purview of the church's service in Jesus' name.

Other Voices

What we should do or say, Christ,
Is no longer clear.
Not so long ago
The lines were sharply drawn.
Now it seems as if
No line is clear,
Rules are an invitation
To do something else
And customs change as fast as the weather.
Grant me the grace to see things
As you see them, Christ,
And the strength and courage
To live in your light.

— AVERY BROOKE, *Plain Prayers in a
Complicated World*

None of us know much about where we are going really, not in the long run anyway, beyond the next mountain. We keep busy. We climb. We learn. We grow. Hopefully. But we are going, I believe, much, much further than at this point we can possibly see, and in everything we do or fail to do, much more is at stake, I believe, than we dream. In this life, and in whatever life awaits us, he is the way; that is our faith. And the way he is, is the way of taking time enough to love our little piece of time without forgetting that we live also beyond time. It is the way of hearing the lives that touch against our lives. It is the way of keeping silence from time to time before the holy mystery of life in this strange world and before the power and grace that surround us in this strange world. It is the way of love.

— FREDERICK BUECHNER,
The Hungering Dark

What is the chief distinguishing mark of a Christian? What is the hallmark which authenticates people as the children of God? Different answers are given by different people.

Some reply that what distinguishes the genuine Christian is *truth*, orthodoxy, correct belief, loyalty to the doctrines of Scripture, the Catholic Creeds and the Reformation Confessions. Right! Truth is sacred. Sound doctrine is vital to the health of the church. We are summoned to "fight the good fight of the faith", to "guard the deposit" of revealed religion, to "stand firm and hold to the teachings" of the apostles, and to "contend for the faith that was once for all entrusted to the saints". We must never forget these solemn exhortations. Nevertheless, "if I . . . can fathom all mysteries and all knowledge, . . . but have not love, I am nothing". Besides, "knowledge puffs up, but love builds up". So love is greater than knowledge.

Others insist that the hallmark of genuine disciples is *faith.* "For we maintain that a man is justified by faith apart from observing the law." As Luther wrote, justification by faith is "the principal article of all Christian doctrine" which "maketh true Christians indeed." And Cranmer added the negative counterpart: "This (*sc.* Doctrine) whosoever denieth is not to be counted for a true Christian man." Or to quote from a modern evangelical statement, justification by faith is "the heart and hub, the paradigm and essence, of the whole economy of God's saving grace." I agree. *Sola fide,* "by faith alone", which was the watchword of the Reformation, must be our watchword too. Nevertheless, "if I have a faith that can move mountains, but have not love, I am nothing". The great apostle of faith is clear that love is greater than faith.

A third group emphasizes *religious experience* as the hallmark of the Christian, often of a particular and vivid kind, which they believe must be reproduced in everybody. And this group also is to some extent cor-

rect. A first-hand personal relationship with God through Christ is essential. The internal witness of the Spirit is real. There is such a thing as "unutterable and exalted joy", and "compared to the surpassing greatness of knowing Christ Jesus my Lord" everything else is indeed a loss. Nevertheless, "if I speak in the tongues of men and of angels" and "if I have the gift of prophecy" (claiming a direct communication from God), "but have not love, I am nothing". So love is greater than experience.

A fourth and final category of people, being of a practical bent, emphasize *service* as the distinguishing mark of the people of God, especially the service of the poor. Right again. Without good works faith is dead. Since Jesus was himself a champion of the poor, his disciples must be also. If we see people in need, and have the wherewithal to meet it, but do not take pity on them, how can we claim to have God's love in us? Thank God for the renewed emphasis on his "preferential option" or priority or concern for the poor. Nevertheless, "if I give all I possess to the poor and surrender by body to the flames" (perhaps in a heroic gesture of sacrifice), "but have not love, I gain nothing". So love is greater than service.

To sum up, knowledge is vital, faith indispensable, religious experience necessary, and service essential, but Paul gives precedence to love. Love is the greatest thing in the world.

— JOHN R. W. STOTT,
The Contemporary Christian

For we teach that truly good works grow out of a living faith by the Holy Spirit and are done by the faithful according to the will or rule of God's Word. Now the apostle Peter says: "Make every effort to supplement your faith with virtue, and virtue with knowledge, and knowledge with self-control," etc. (2 Peter 1:5 ff.). But we have said above that the law of God, which is his will, prescribes for us the pattern of good works. . . .

Therefore, although we teach with the apostle that a man is justified by grace through faith in Christ and not through any good works, yet we do not think that good works are of little value and condemn them. We know that man was not created or regenerated through faith in order to be idle, but rather that without ceasing he should do those things which are good and useful. For in the Gospel the Lord says that a good tree brings forth good fruit (Matthew 12:33), and that he who abides in me bears much fruit (John 15:5).

— *The Second Helvetic Confession*

[Christ] himself and he alone, as Luther insisted again and again, is our righteousness and our life. No one else will ever be God incarnate, nor will anyone else ever die for the sins of the world. Only Jesus Christ is such a person, only he could do such a work, and he in fact has done it. He does not give us his righteousness and life except by giving us himself, as he does when we receive him through faith alone. We are not saved by reduplicating his spirituality, which Luther would have denounced as a new form of the law, but by the miraculous exchange whereby he has died in our place as sinners so that we might be clothed in his righteousness by grace and live though his body and blood in eternal fellowship with God. Our salvation is thus permanently anchored not in a repeatable, but in an unrepeatable, event, not in an event that takes place *in nobis,* but in one that has taken place *extra nos.*

— George Hunsinger, *Disruptive Grace: Studies in the Theology of Karl Barth*

Daily Scripture Readings

Key Text: Galatians 5:22
   Sunday: Titus 3:1-11
   Monday: Ephesians 2:11-22
   Tuesday: 1 John 3:1-24
   Wednesday: Luke 17:1-10
   Thursday: 2 Timothy 4:1-8
   Friday: James 2:14-26
   Saturday: 1 Peter 2:1-12

Questions for Reflection and Discussion

Have there been occasions in your life where you've really tried to "be good"? How successful were you? Have you ever had a relationship where you felt you needed to measure up to expectations or to prove yourself? What was that like?

The prophet Isaiah says that "all our righteous acts are like filthy rags" (Isaiah 64:6). How can that be? Is motivation just as important as results in the things we do? Explain.

The apostle Paul declares that we are "justified by faith apart from observing the law" (Romans 3:28), but James maintains "a person is justified by what he does and not by faith alone" (James 2:24). How do you reconcile the two statements? How might Paul's assertion that "the only thing that counts is faith expressing itself through love" (Galatians 5:6) help make sense of the apparent contradiction?

Closing Prayer

Great God, help me to love you more and more because of the great work you have done in me, and to express that love through all the works you have in mind for me to do. I pray this for your glory and my edification. Amen.

Week Twenty-five:
A Ministry of Word and Sacrament

Opening Prayer

Dear Father, you have revealed yourself in countless ways through the ages and have shown yourself most clearly in the person of your Son Jesus. I'm grateful that you bless us still with signs of your grace. Help me be attentive to you, and put your seal upon my heart. Amen.

Heidelberg Questions

QUESTION 65: It is by faith alone that we share in Christ and all his blessings: where then does that faith come from?

The Holy Spirit produces it in our hearts[1] by the preaching of the holy gospel,[2] and confirms it through our use of the holy sacraments.[3]

(*[1]John 3:5; 1 Corinthians 2:10-14; Ephesians 2:8; [2]Romans 10:17; 1 Peter 1:23-25; [3]Matthew 28:19-20; 1 Corinthians 10:16*)

QUESTION 66: What are sacraments?

Sacraments are holy signs and seals for us to see. They were instituted by God so that by our use of them he might make us understand more clearly the promise of the gospel, and might put his seal on that promise.[1]

And this is God's gospel promise: to forgive our sins and give us eternal life by grace alone because of Christ's one sacrifice finished on the cross.[2]

(*[1]Genesis 17:11; Deuteronomy 30:6; Romans 4:11; [2]Matthew 26:27-28; Acts 2:38; Hebrews 10:10*)

QUESTION 67: Are both the word and the sacraments then intended to focus our faith on the sacrifice of Jesus Christ on the cross as the only ground of our salvation?

Right! In the gospel the Holy Spirit teaches us and through the holy sacraments he assures us that our entire salvation rests on Christ's one sacrifice for us on the cross.[1]

(*[1]Romans 6:3; 1 Corinthians 11:26; Galatians 3:27*)

QUESTION 68: How many sacraments did Christ institute in the New Testament?

Two: Baptism and the Lord's Supper.[1]

(*[1]Matthew 28:19-20; 1 Corinthians 11:23-26*)

Exposition

Not long ago, I led a mission team of college students to Guatemala. Even on a short trip, we clearly saw the beauty of the country and its people, the sheer ugliness of the omnipresent poverty, and the life and hope of the Christian community there.

One afternoon, a social worker invited us to visit a juvenile detention center. We were to distribute some clothing and toothbrushes to the young men incarcerated there. The social worker asked if I would bring greetings from our group, and I responded that I would be glad for the chance to do so, as long as I could read a passage of Scripture to them. I was sure that the only thing I had relevant to their lives was God's Word; anything else I could have said would have been glib. The social worker agreed to let me read Scripture and pray for them along with bringing our greeting.

I wondered what to read from Scripture. Should I bring a word of encouragement, perhaps something about the love of God? Somehow, I felt drawn to Psalm 51.

Upon arrival, I felt the oppressive weight of those grim walls. The boys were under lock and key for everything from petty theft to murder. At night, the guards would simply lock them, unguarded, into two rooms. The despair of the place was palpable. We walked into the claustrophobic central court to face a hundred and fifty grim-faced boys, lined up military style, each one with a hand on the shoulder of the one in front of him. They looked ragged, and maybe half of them had bare feet. Their eyes had a haunted look of hardness and a sorrow for their age. The social worker had some words with the director of the detention center, then called me forward to talk through a translator. I opened my Bible and read, "Have mercy on me, O God . . . according to your great compassion . . . cleanse me from my sin . . . against you, you only have I sinned . . . so that you are . . . justified when you judge. . . . Create in me a pure heart, O God, and renew a steadfast spirit within me . . . a broken and contrite heart, O God, you will not despise."

I looked up from my Bible and said, "I want you to know today that no matter what you have done, no matter how you have sinned, no matter who you have hurt, no matter who has hurt you, no matter how your life has been torn apart, that Jesus loves you very much. He wants you to be his child, and he will never leave you, not even in this place." Then I said a prayer for them and walked back to our group while the director stepped up and told them to keep quiet while they distributed gifts. My cheeks reddened with embarrassment at the inadequacy of the used clothes and red and turquoise plastic toothbrushes. There were not enough shoes for all the boys who needed them.

Then I heard our translator call my name. "There's a boy who wants to accept Jesus," she said. "Really?" I thought, "Oh — I didn't even give an invitation!" By the time I could get over to where the boy was, there were six others. We brought them aside where we could talk: "Do you want to receive Jesus as your Savior? Do you trust that he died and rose again for you? Are you sorry for your sins, and ready from now on to live for him?" We asked each of their names, then had them kneel as we laid hands on them each in turn. They knelt in the dust, in plain sight of all the other boys, and received the light of Jesus in the midst of that dark place.

There's power in the plain Word of God. God has acted in Christ for our salvation. On the cross, Jesus accomplished everything we need in order to enjoy fellowship with God, to know that we are his children. We enter into this fellowship by faith in Jesus — through God's grace, not by any work of ours that makes us somehow deserving. How does faith happen? What conjures it up in us? And how do we "keep the faith"?

Bringing broken human beings to faith in Christ is the work of God's Spirit. He *creates* faith. But further, he also *confirms* it in us. God does this through two different mediums, which the church has known as "means of grace": the proclamation of the gospel in preaching and the enactment of the gospel in the sacraments.

The Protestant tradition has historically emphasized that preaching is the foundation of the church. The church didn't create the gospel message, but rather the gospel itself spoke the church into being. So it was that the Lord began his ministry by declaring, "The kingdom of heaven has come near" (Matthew 4:17, NRSV). Jesus, God's self-articulation, spoke words that brought light into darkness and new life out of deadness. This continues today as his word in Holy Scripture is exposited faithfully. Sixteenth-century Swiss theologian Heinrich Bullinger was convinced that the *preached* word actually is the Word of God.[7] That is a bold claim. How can mere humans, with all our foibles and frailty, speak the Word of God? Yet, this echoes the movement of the Incarnation: God descended to us on a level we could grasp in the person of Jesus. The Bible parallels the reality of the Incarnation, bringing the Word of God in human words, through the complexity of human culture. The apostle Paul saw how the proclamation of the church is the beginning of faith when he wrote, "Faith comes from what is heard, and what is heard comes through the word of Christ" (Romans 10:17, NRSV).

This suggests that the Word of God comes to the church in several manifestations, each one subordinate to the next level up. From the top, the priority would look like this:

The Eternal Word (Jesus Christ) and the Written Word (the Bible)

These two come hand in hand, because we *know* Jesus through the pages of Scripture. Anyone who offers a savior in contradiction to the Jesus of the New Testament is presenting a counterfeit. The One who longs to be known was pleased to reveal himself through the Bible.

The Historic Word (the creeds and confessions of the church)

How do we know we haven't steered off course in our interpretation of the Bible? By following the map, the historic witness to Christ through the creeds and confessions of the church. The map is not infallible. Still, developed over the course of hundreds of years by Christians seeking to hear God's voice, it serves as a faithful guide. The statements of the church are subordinate standards to Holy Scripture, but they are standards nonetheless.

The Contemporary Word (preaching)

Preaching that is true to the Bible and in conformity to the historic, orthodox faith of the church will lift up Christ and will transform lives.

The Inner Word (individual conscience)

Is there room for the whisperings of the Holy Spirit? Yes, but that word must be in conformity with the biblical witness. God's Spirit worked through the writers of the Bible to communicate his heart. By the same Holy Spirit, God illumines the meaning of Scripture through preaching and causes his Word to come alive in us. The Holy Spirit can speak to us in the impressions of our own hearts. Nonetheless, humans have an infinite capacity for self-deception. That is why the Christian must submit to the other clear expressions of God's will. God will never tell us to do something that is in conflict with the character of Jesus. He will never tell us to break the Ten Commandments. We never have warrant to go against God's revealed will.

Different manifestations, but the same God who comes to us supremely in the person of his Son. When we share God's Word that points to the Son, lives are changed.

You will not find the term "sacrament" in the Bible. It comes from the pledge that a soldier of Rome would have to make in allegiance to his emperor. In the Latin translation of the Bible, it was used to translate "mystery," or something that was consecrated, and it signified a sign of something secret. The church father Augustine called the sacrament "the visible Word." Calvin said that the purpose of the sacraments was to represent Christ to us and to make available for us the treasures of heaven. We should not see it so much as our promise to remain faithful as disciples, but as God's promise to keep us as his own. In the acts of baptism and the Lord's Supper, both practices instituted by Jesus during his earthly career, the Holy Spirit works to strengthen and establish the faith he has planted in our hearts. The believer who receives God's Word in preaching and sacraments is coming to reality at its deepest level, by encountering God who is for us.

We left those seven young men in the Guatemalan reformatory with a Bible, some all-too-brief instruction, and the promise of our prayers and a visit from our missionary. They seemed so frail in the face of their circumstances. But we left them in the trust that the God who called them to belong to him would sustain them as a witness. Even in that place.

Other Voices

It is true also in the sacrament that Jesus Christ is God's spoken Word. But against the attempt to limit Christ to doctrine, or to lose him in general truth, the Church stresses the sacramental form of Christ. He is not only doctrine, nor only idea, but nature and history. The inadequacies of nature and history are God's cloak. But not everything corporeal, not all nature and history, is meant to be sacramental. Nature as such does not symbolize Christ. His presence is confined to the forms of preaching and the two sacraments. . . .

The sacrament [of the Lord's Supper] is not a concealment of the incorporeal Word of God under the cover of a bodily form, so that one might think of the sacrament as a second incarnation. But the incarnate one, who has become flesh and blood, is in the sacrament as the stumbling block. The sacrament is not God becoming man, but the humiliation of the God-Man.

— DIETRICH BONHOEFFER, *Christ the Center*

"Are you not thirsty?" said the Lion.

"I'm *dying* of thirst," said Jill.

"Then drink," said the Lion.

"May I — could I — would you mind going away while I do?" said Jill.

The Lion answered this only by a look and a very low growl. And as Jill gazed at its motionless bulk, she realized that she might as well have asked the whole mountain to move aside for her convenience.

The delicious rippling noise of the stream was driving her nearly frantic.

"Will you promise not to — do anything to me, if I do come?" said Jill.

"I make no promise," said the Lion.

Jill was so thirsty now that, without noticing it, she had come a step nearer.

"Do you eat girls?" she said.

"I have swallowed up girls and boys, women and men, kings and emperors, cities and realms," said the Lion. . . .

"I daren't come and drink," said Jill.

"Then you will die of thirst," said the Lion.

"Oh dear!" said Jill, coming another step nearer.

"I suppose I must go and look for another stream then."

"There is no other stream," said the Lion.

— C. S. LEWIS, *The Silver Chair*

The Christian's redemption through Christ leads to a renewed relationship with the Creation. . . . Says Wolterstorff, "The image appropriate to subduing — to ordering nature for the benefit of man — is that of *gardening.* Man's vocation is to be the world's gardener." And the arts are a prime example of this "gardening" of Creation. . . .

Wolterstorff moves through many of the arts, showing how each is not so much a new creation as it is an elevation of unformed Creation into a higher possibility: a kind of gardening of Creation, till it blossoms into what that Creation can most fully be. So he concludes this description of the stewardly artist: "The artist, when he brings forth order for human benefit or divine honor, shares in man's vocation to master and subdue the earth."

The Reformed aesthetic, stemming from a strong sense of obedience to God and responsibility to act caringly in the world, rooted in the theological profundity of Calvinism, and in the godly activism of Abraham Kuyper, is a rich contribution to contemporary theological articulation of the nature of the arts.

— LOREN WILKINSON, "'Art as Creation' or 'Art as Work'?" from *With Heart, Mind & Strength*

We must expect some of Christian worship to seem strange, even unintelligible, to people who do not know Christ. Certainly all people are worshipers by nature; the impulse to worship is universal. But Christian worship is the worship of those who have died and risen again to a brand-new life and way of living. In this new community where Christ is head, things are different. Here people are less concerned with finding their life than with losing it for Christ. Here meekness, not muscle, is the mark of greatness. If the church is not radically different from the world, something is radically wrong. To be salt and light in the world implies a marked contrast between the way of life in the world and the way of life in the church. Peter says that Christians are aliens and strangers in the world (1 Peter 2:11). It follows, then, that Christian worship will have its peculiarities.

— *Authentic Worship in a Changing Culture*, Christian Reformed Church

In a society doing all it can to make people cozy, somehow we must convey the truth that God's Word, rightly read and heard, will shake us up. It will kill us, for God cannot bear our sin and wants to put to death our self-centeredness. The apostle Paul exclaims that he has been "crucified with Christ" and therefore that it is no longer he who lives, but Christ who lives in him (Gal. 2:19-20). Once worship kills us, we are born anew to worship God rightly.

Everything that we do in worship should kill us, but especially the parts of the service in which we hear the Word — the Scripture lessons and the sermon. One reason I especially treasure the Church's historic Mass is that so much of it is composed of direct quotations from the Scriptures, which kill me every time I sing them. I get more comfortable under liturgies composed of human words that make it easier to escape the death blow and remain satisfied with myself.

— MARVA DAWN, *Reaching Out Without Dumbing Down: A Theology of Worship for the Turn-of-the-Century Culture*

[T]heology (our belief about God) and doxology (our worship of God) should never be separated. On the one hand, there can be no doxology without theology. It is not possible to worship an unknown god. All true worship is a response to the self-revelation of God in Christ and Scripture, and arises from our reflection on who he is and what he has done. . . . Worship without theology is bound to degenerate into idolatry. Hence the indispensable place of Scripture in both public and private devotion. It is the Word of God which calls forth the worship of God.

On the other hand, there should be no theology without doxology. There is something fundamentally flawed about a purely academic interest in God. God is not an appropriate object for cool, critical, detached, scientific observation and evaluation. No, the true knowledge of God will always lead us to worship, as it did Paul. Our place is on our faces before him in adoration.

As I believe Bishop Handley Moule said at the end of the last century, we must "beware equally of an undevotional theology and of an untheological devotion."
— JOHN R. W. STOTT, *Romans: God's Good News for the World*

Daily Scripture Readings

KEY TEXT: DEUTERONOMY 30:6
  Sunday: Genesis 17:1-27
  Monday: Matthew 3:11-17
  Tuesday: Matthew 28:16-20
  Wednesday: Matthew 26:17-30
  Thursday: 1 Corinthians 11:17-34
  Friday: 1 Corinthians 10:14-24
  Saturday: 1 Corinthians 14:26-33,37-40

Questions for Reflection and Discussion

Think of a time when the Lord was especially present for you. What was that like?

Why do people need tangible signs to assure them of another person's love? What are some indications that love is real? What do you consider to be signs of God's presence and care for you?

How can baptism and the Lord's Supper — as well as other ordinances of the church like anointing with oil, laying on of hands, or marking a forehead with ashes to mark repentance — increase our faith? What does it mean to you to be sealed in Christ?

Closing Prayer

Lord, you have put upon me the seal of my union with Christ. Thank you for making that covenant of grace with me. I now consecrate myself to you and bind myself to your service. In Jesus' name, amen.

Week Twenty-six:
Washed Clean

I will praise you, O God, with all of my being; I lift up your name. May your transforming power be at work in me this day. Amen.

Heidelberg Questions

QUESTION 69: How does baptism remind you and assure you that Christ's one sacrifice on the cross is for you personally?

In this way: Christ instituted this outward washing[1] and with it gave the promise that, as surely as water washes away the dirt from the body, so certainly his blood and his Spirit wash away my soul's impurity, in other words, all my sins.[2]

(*[1]Acts 2:38; [2]Matthew 3:11; Romans 6:3-10; 1 Peter 3:21*)

QUESTION 70: What does it mean to be washed with Christ's blood and Spirit?

To be washed with Christ's blood means that God, by grace, has forgiven my sins because of Christ's blood poured out for me in his sacrifice on the cross.[1]

To be washed with Christ's Spirit means that the Holy Spirit has renewed me and set me apart to be a member of Christ so that more and more I become dead to sin and increasingly live a holy and blameless life.[2]

(*[1]Zechariah 13:1; Ephesians 1:7-8; Hebrews 12:24; 1 Peter 1:2; Revelation 1:5; [2]Ezekiel 36:25-27; John 3:5-8; Romans 6:4; 1 Corinthians 6:11; Colossians 2:11-12*)

QUESTION 71: Where does Christ promise that we are washed with his blood and Spirit as surely as we are washed with the water of baptism?

In the institution of baptism where he says: "Therefore go and make disciples of all nations, baptizing them in the name of the Father and of the Son and of the Holy Spirit."[1]

"Whoever believes and is baptized will be saved, but whoever does not believe will be condemned."[2]

This promise is repeated when Scripture calls baptism the washing of rebirth[3] and the washing away of sins.[4]

(*[1]Matthew 28:19; [2]Mark 16:16; [3]Titus 3:5; [4]Acts 22:16*)

Exposition

Have you ever wondered whether you are really a Christian? Baptism is a part of the answer; it asserts that you belong to Jesus if you have trusted in him. It is the outward sign that you are a member of his church and share in the benefits of God's family. But do you really believe? Do you have *enough* faith? The Holy Spirit alone gives assurance of salvation. It is not a result of our own confidence. The Spirit can assure us that we belong to Jesus. Until that happens, simply trust it is true. That is where faith comes in.

Ceremonial washings were established by Old Testament law. They symbolized purification and consecration to divine purposes. Water also recalls some of the great acts of God in history. In the beginning, God's Spirit moved over the waters. God sustains all life with the gift of water. In Noah's time, God destroyed the earth with water and saved his people in the ark, giving humanity a new beginning. In Moses' time, God led Israel out of Egypt and through the sea. God gave water from the rock to sustain his people in the desert and led them into the Promised Land. God led Jesus to be baptized in the waters of the Jordan.

Many people in the Christian community today are confused about the meaning of baptism. Various churches have different understandings of its meaning and purpose. The questions are deeper than simply the right ceremony or the mode of baptism. They have to do with who may be baptized and whether a person may be re-baptized. These questions have been around the church for a long time.

A baby's baptism is a happy occasion. People are touched and amused to see the baby's responses. But seldom is there a sense of the profound initiation that is taking place, of participating in the death and resurrection of Christ, of being welcomed into a new family that transcends all other natural ties. Not many would understand it to be a radically life-changing event.

John the Baptist offered a baptism of repentance, washing away sin and launching into a new direction of obedience to God. Jesus submitted to baptism at the beginning of his ministry not because he needed the cleansing of sins, but in order to open up for the new covenant people of God the promised kingdom. At his baptism, Jesus received God's confirmation that he was the beloved Son. That signals for us that one needs the Spirit to live the kingdom life.

Just as baptism stood at the beginning of all four Gospels, it stands at the beginning of the Christian life. It serves as a sign that we have turned away from the ways of the world and into the ways of the Spirit. We need to be converted in order to enter into the kingdom of God. Baptism points to life in the kingdom, life in the Spirit.

Jesus instituted baptism as a sign of our new covenant with God. Before his ascension, he commissioned his disciples to open his kingdom up to all peoples by baptizing disciples in the name of the Father, the Son, and the Holy Spirit. Our baptism represents a washing away of sin, marking our entering into fellowship with God and with Christ's body. It means that we share in the death and rising of Jesus. When he died, our old selves died with him. Now we can live as new persons. Our old self-referential lives pass away, and now we are included in his image. Baptism does not make this happen, but it bears witness to the fact that it has happened already. God has done it. His Spirit has given us a new birth.

Whether a person is submerged or sprinkled is of no importance. The word "baptism" signifies to immerse, and the ancient church practiced baptism in this manner. Still, according to Calvin, that can be left to the preference of the churches. The essential thing is that it is a sign that reminds us we belong to Jesus, washed by his blood and Spirit. His sacrifice is for *us*. Baptism is therefore more than just a sentimental rite of passage. It is for us who believe the water of rebirth into eternal life. His blood justifies, making us right with God. Then his Spirit sanctifies, making us more like him. Like varnish on a painting that keeps colors from fading, these benefits are sealed to us in our baptism.

Other Voices

Don't bother at all about the question of a person being "made a Christian" by baptism. It is only the usual trouble about words being used in more than one sense. Thus we might say a man "became a soldier" the moment that he joined the army. But his instructors might say six months later "I think we have made a soldier of him." Both usages are quite definable, only one wants to know which is being used in a given sentence.

— C. S. Lewis, *Letters of C. S. Lewis*

[Sin] is like a secret police force haunting us, tracking us, preparing to knock on our door in the middle of the night to claim us. It is like a man pressing a lawsuit against us. It is like a straitjacket that binds us. Being dead to sin, we are given asylum and citizenship in a totally new country, with new laws and new rulers; the old world has no claim on us and no power to extradite us for judgment.

Dying with Christ, then, is not a daily process of self-denial and cross-bearing. It is an event that happens *to* us. We perhaps do not live as men who died to sin; but this only demonstrates that we betray our origins. A political exile from Red China may still speak with a Chinese accent and feel at home with Chinese culture; similarly, we may still sound like sinners, enjoy acts of sin, and dream of judgment. But the Chinese person is dead to Chinese law and Chinese authority. So, while Christians may still enjoy the culture of sin, they are not under its power.

— LEWIS B. SMEDES, *Union with Christ*

Dear God, I know that though I have done my best, I am still to blame. Yet I am comforted, for you have died for me and covered me with blood from your holy wounds. I am surely baptized in you and have heard the word through which you have called me, have commanded me to believe, and have assured me grace and life. With these blessings I will gladly go ahead, not anxious and hesitating and asking in doubt and fear. Who knows what judgment God in heaven will hold against me? I now live in the assurance of the gracious decree which God in heaven has given against the curse of the law: Everyone who believes in the Son of Man has eternal life. Amen.

— MARTIN LUTHER, *Luther's Prayers*

In former times slaves were branded on the back with their master's name. In your baptism God laid hold upon you, called you by your name and stamped you as ever after — His own. Through the word and act of man in your baptism, the brand, "property of God" was stamped upon you. . . . God has laid claim upon you through the act of the Church.

. . . God does not make us His property in Jesus Christ to show that He can do with us what He wills, as the slaveholder stamps his name upon his slaves. He can to be sure, do with us what He wills; He is the Creator and we are His creatures. He does not want us to have to be afraid of Him as slaves before their master, but rather to love Him as the one who first loved us. "God so loved the world that He gave his only begotten Son that whosoever believes in Him should not perish but have everlasting life." *That* is the Gospel, in *this* way God claims us, in *this* way He means to proclaim to us by the Church the words, "Thou art mine."

— EMIL BRUNNER,
Our Faith

Christ orders that those who have subscribed to the Gospel, and professed themselves disciples are to be baptized, partly that Baptism may be for them a token of their eternal life in God's sight, partly an outward sign of faith before men. We know that God testifies to the grace of His adoption by this sign, for He engrafts us in the body of His Son, to reckon us among His flock. Thus our spiritual washing, in which He reconciles us to Himself, and our new righteousness are there represented. But as God affirms His grace to us with this sealing, so those who offer themselves for baptism in turn ratify their faith, as if by appending their signature.

— JOHN CALVIN, *Calvin's New Testament Commentaries*

Daily Scripture Readings

KEY TEXT: ACTS 2:38
>   Sunday: Zechariah 12:10–13:1
>   Monday: Romans 6:1-7
>   Tuesday: 1 Peter 3:18-21
>   Wednesday: Ezekiel 36:22-29
>   Thursday: John 3:1-8
>   Friday: Ephesians 1:3-14
>   Saturday: Colossians 2:6-12

Questions for Reflection and Discussion

What have you noticed about any baptisms you have witnessed?

Does baptism make a person a Christian? Why or why not? Is it imperative for a Christian to be baptized? Why or why not?

If you were baptized as a child, what have your parents told you about it? If you were baptized at a later age, what do you remember about it?

Since baptism reminds us of God's promise to wash away our sins, does the Christian need to feel guilty? What advice would you have for the Christian who still struggles with guilt?

Closing Prayer

Lord, defend me by your grace. May I continue to be yours forever, until I come into your kingdom. In Jesus' name, amen.

Week Twenty-seven:
Clean from the Inside Out

Opening Prayer

Gracious God, I'm well aware I need to come clean before you. In the confidence that you who have called me will make me transparent before you, I ask you to fill me today. Amen.

Heidelberg Questions

QUESTION 72: Does this outward washing with water itself wash away sins?

No, only Jesus Christ's blood and the Holy Spirit cleanse us from all sins.[1]

(*[1]Matthew 3:11; 1 Peter 3:21; John 1:7*)

QUESTION 73: Why then does the Holy Spirit call baptism the washing of rebirth and the washing away of sins?

God has good reason for these words. He wants to teach us that the blood and Spirit of Christ wash away our sins just as water washes away dirt from our bodies.[1]

But more important, he wants to assure us, by this divine pledge and sign, that the washing away of our sins spiritually is as real as physical washing with water.[2]

(*[1]1 Corinthians 6:11; Revelation 1:5; 7:14; [2]Acts 2:38; Romans 6:3-4; Galatians 3:27*)

QUESTION 74: Should infants, too, be baptized?

Yes. Infants as well as adults are in God's covenant and are his people.[1] They, no less than adults, are promised the forgiveness of sin through Christ's blood and the Holy Spirit who produces faith.[2]

Therefore, by baptism, the mark of the covenant, infants should be received into the Christian church and should be distinguished from the children of unbelievers.[3] This was done in the Old Testament by circumcision,[4] which was replaced in the New Testament by baptism.[5]

([1]*Genesis 17:7; Matthew 19:14;* [2]*Isaiah 44:1-3; Acts 2:38-39; 16:31;* [3]*Acts 10:47; 1 Corinthians 7:14;* [4]*Genesis 17:9-14;* [5]*Colossians 2:11-13*)

Exposition

The act of baptism in itself has no power. Scriptures nowhere maintain that the water is magical. If this were the case then faith would be of no avail. Every time a person is baptized in the New Testament, that person expressed saving faith in Jesus Christ (or, when a household was baptized, a parent expressed faith on a child's behalf). You can see this from the Ethiopian eunuch to the centurion Cornelius, from Lydia to the Philippian jailer. It is God's Spirit who transforms water from an everyday element into a supernatural one. Karl Barth said it this way: "Baptism cannot become a subject; it does not 'do' anything. But the Holy Spirit does something through baptism!"

Scripture claims that baptism washes away sins so that the outward symbol can make clear what is taking place on the inside, a "pledge and sign" that the invisible process of purification will be done in us. It is not unlike the ways people represent various commitments. A wedding band does not make a marriage; the committed love between a man and a woman does that. A presidential seal does not make an executive order; the authority of the president makes the order valid. A diploma on a woman's wall does not make her qualified to make a psychological assessment; her years of training and testing do.

What about baptizing children who are too young to make a profession of faith, too young to understand the inner reality to which the outer sign bears witness? Some would object that nowhere does Scripture direct us to baptize infants. It could be said, conversely, that nowhere does Scripture command that only adults be baptized. The Lord commanded his disciples to baptize all nations, and the book of Acts gives examples of whole families being baptized, because all ages were to be consecrated to the Lord. Furthermore, at what point is a person assured that he or she is *ever* ready for baptism — that they understand enough or are faithful enough? If it is God who brings us to himself before we have any inkling, then our conversion itself is an echo of the touch of God on the helplessness of a baby. If baptism parallels the Old Testament practice of circumcision, then it should rightly include Christians' babies. They, too, are included in the covenant family of God. Our children are holy. Not that they are without the capacity for sin, but they belong to the body of Christ. They are different from the children of unbelievers.

This has been a major point of contention between Christians of Anabaptist traditions on one hand and those of the Reformed tradition on the other. The former emphasize the importance of personal response to Christ seen in conversion and profession of faith. Baptizing infants can have no place in this view.

By contrast, the Reformed view has emphasized the sovereign work of God. It is God who takes the initiative, who acts graciously through baptism until we can respond with a life of discipleship. But our profession of faith is always a response to God, who helps us even before we know it. He acts to bring unqualified people into his kingdom. And whether we are two or ninety-two, we are all little children when it comes to faith, completely dependent on the grace of God and welcomed into the one holy, catholic church through baptism. Whatever our theological perspective on the issue, let us not allow baptism to become a subject of dissension among the churches. Jesus gave it in order to express our unity with him and among his body.

Other Voices

We gather for worship to remember who and whose we are. We come to recount the stories that shape our faith, stories that turn us from a collection of individuals into a community with a common source and vision. The church as a worshiping community carries our biblical faith and spiritual tradition down through the ages to each individual. We are joined to that community in Baptism, tutored in faith through the interpretation of scripture in preaching, and nourished at the Lord's Table *as a family of believers.* Life in the church teaches us that we are made for communion not only with God but with one another in Christ.

— Marjorie J. Thompson, *Soul Feast: An Invitation to the Christian Spiritual Life*

In many parts of the world baptism has degenerated into christening, a name-giving ceremony. . . . Baptism is regarded as a socially required rite of passage, celebrating a child's entrance into the world. The spiritual significance of the event is often buried under social custom. Often the baptized infant doesn't reappear at the church door until his or her wedding day. Thus in Scotland people often refer to Christianity as a "four-wheeled religion," with the wheels of the baby pram on the way to baptism, the limousine departing from a wedding, the hearse on the way to the grave.

If we really grasped the wonder (and even the horror) of what baptism represents, we wouldn't regard it with as much social sweetness. Once I was baptizing a most reluctant infant, who burst into tears as the water dribbled onto her forehead. The parents cringed in embarrassment, and the congregation shifted awkwardly in their seats. But it suddenly occurred to me: maybe this baby was one of the few people present who really understood what was happening! I commented to the congregation, "Dying to oneself is never easy. We seldom let go of ourselves without tears."

— Tim Dearborn, *Taste & See*

More and more the Reformers came to understand baptism in terms not only of the covenant signs found in Scripture but also in terms of the prophetic signs of Scripture. They identified a whole series of prophetic signs which they found in both the Old and New Testament. When Jacob laid hands on the two sons of Joseph it was clearly a prophetic act. Jeremiah took the potter's vessel and broke it as a prophetic act signaling the destruction of Jerusalem. Jesus' act of cleansing the Temple was a prophetic sign. Perhaps the prophetic sign most clearly analogous to the baptism of children is the story of Samuel anointing David to be king while David was still a shepherd boy. It would be many years before that prophetic act would be fulfilled. Surely David understood very little of what Samuel did to him. It was only as the years went by that the meaning of that act unfolded. Yet that act was there, it was there quite indelibly nurturing the faith of David. David believed God would be faithful to the promise and indeed God was. The sign was given to awaken faith and nurture faith.

— HUGHES OLIPHANT OLD, *Worship: Guides to the Reformed Tradition*

We must realize that at whatever time we are baptized, we are once for all washed and purged for our whole life. Therefore, as often as we fall away, we ought to recall the memory of our baptism and fortify our mind with it, that we may always be sure and confident of the forgiveness of sins. For, though baptism, administered only once, seemed to have passed, it was still not destroyed by subsequent sins. For Christ's purity has been offered us in it; his purity ever flourishes; it is defiled by no spots, but buries and cleanses away all our defilements.

— JOHN CALVIN, *Institutes of the Christian Religion, vol. 2*

Daily Scripture Readings

KEY TEXT: TITUS 3:1-8
    Sunday: Romans 6:8-14
    Monday: Ephesians 4:1-6
    Tuesday: Galatians 3:26–4:7
    Wednesday: 1 Peter 2:4-12
    Thursday: Romans 7:1-6
    Friday: Hosea 2:14-23
    Saturday: Acts 22:2-21

Questions for Reflection and Discussion

Have you experienced any rites of initiation in the secular realm? If so, how were these alike and unlike baptism as a welcome into God's family?

Do you have to remember your baptism for it to have an effect in your life? Why or why not? What makes it a sacrament — our faith, or the power of the Holy Spirit?

How is God at work in a person even before he or she comes to faith? For those that hold to "believer baptism," why might it be hard to qualify when some-body is ready for baptism?

Why is baptism such a gift for the church? Scripture tells us that there is "one Lord, one faith, one baptism"(Ephesians 4:5). Does that mean we should only be baptized once? Explain.

Closing Prayer

Dear God, strengthen me for your service by all your good gifts of grace. Give me wisdom and understanding, and reverence for you in all I do. Keep me safe in you until you bring me to my eternal home, I pray in Jesus' name, amen.

Week Twenty-eight:
Christ's Body and Blood for Us

Heidelberg Questions

QUESTION 75: How does the Lord's Supper remind you and assure you that you share in Christ's one sacrifice on the cross and in all his gifts?

In this way: Christ has commanded me and all believers to eat this broken bread and to drink this cup. With this command he gave this promise:[1]

First, as surely as I see with my eyes the bread of the Lord broken for me and the cup given to me, so surely his body was offered and broken for me and his blood poured out for me on the cross.

Second, as surely as I receive from the hand of the one who serves, and taste with my mouth the bread and cup of the Lord, given me as sure signs of Christ's body and blood, so surely he nourishes and refreshes my soul for eternal life with his crucified body and poured-out blood.

(*[1]Matthew 26:26-28; Mark 14:22-24; Luke 22:19-20; 1 Corinthians 11:23-25*)

QUESTION 76: What does it mean to eat the crucified body of Christ and to drink his poured-out blood?

It means to accept with a believing heart the entire suffering and death of Christ and by believing to receive forgiveness of sins and eternal life.[1]

But it means more. Through the Holy Spirit, who lives both in Christ and in us, we are united more and more to Christ's blessed body.[2] And so, although he is in heaven[3] and we are on earth, we are flesh of his flesh and bone of his bone.[4] And we forever live on and are governed by one Spirit, as members of our body are by one soul.[5]

(*[1]John 6:35,40,50-54; [2]John 6:55-56; 1 Corinthians 12–13; [3]Acts 1:9-11; 1 Corinthians 11:26; Colossians 3:1; [4]1 Corinthians 6:15-17; Ephesians 5:29-30; 1 John 4:13; [5]John 6:56-58; 15:1-6; Ephesians 4:15-16; 1 John 3:24*)

QUESTION 77: Where does Christ promise to nourish and refresh believers with his body and blood as surely as they eat this broken bread and drink this cup?

In the institution of the Lord's Supper:

"The Lord Jesus, on the night he was betrayed, took bread, and when he had given thanks, he broke it and said, 'This is my body, which is for you; do this in remembrance of me.' In the same way, after supper he took the cup, saying, 'This cup is the new covenant in my blood; do this, whenever you drink it, in remembrance of me.' For whenever you eat this bread and drink this cup, you proclaim the Lord's death until he comes."[1]

Paul repeats this promise in these words:

"Is not the cup of thanksgiving for which we give thanks a participation in the blood of Christ? And is not the bread that we break a participation in the body of Christ? Because there is one loaf, we, who are many, are the body, for we all partake of the one loaf."[2]

(*[1]1 Corinthians 11:23-26; [2]1 Corinthians 10:16-17*)

Exposition

The Lord's Supper bears witness to Christians that we will be sustained in fellowship with Jesus. Its name reminds us that he is the initiator. The sacrament is not a clever idea conceived by the church, but is a gift of the Lord of the church. It recalls the traditional Jewish Passover meal that Jesus celebrated with his disciples on the night he was betrayed and arrested by the authorities. Just as a healthy diet sustains our bodies, so the sacrament sustains our souls and nurtures our relationship with God.

The Passover meal distinguished one of the three great festivals of Israel and a highpoint of the Jewish year. It recalled the drama in Egypt, where God brought fierce punishment on the Egyptian oppressors, but spared his own people. The Hebrews were to prepare a meal, eaten in haste. They marked the lintel of their doors with the blood of a lamb; the angel took the life of every firstborn of Egypt, but not of the Hebrews. From that day forward, the people must remember with this somber feast — also called the Feast of Unleavened Bread — their deliverance from captivity.

The principal element of the Passover meal was a lamb, roasted over a fire. God commanded the people to eat all of it on the night of the feast; nothing could be saved. It reenacted the celebration of the first Passover, when the blood of the lamb protected them. Unleavened bread reminded them that they had to eat quickly in order to make their escape. Bitter herbs reminded them of the bitterness of their labor in Egypt. A paste of fruit reminded them of the clay for making bricks in captivity. A bowl of saltwater reminded them of tears and of God's leading the people through the waters of the Red Sea. Four cups of wine mixed with water reminded them of God's promises, recorded in Exodus 6:6-7. The fourth cup was the cup of blessing.

During the course of the meal together, the youngest son would ask the question, "Why is this night different from all other nights?" Then the host would retell the story for those gathered at the table. On the night of the Lord's last supper with his disciples, perhaps the beloved disciple John asked the question; then Jesus would have recounted the story. But as he did, he brought a startling difference. He took the bread and said, "This is *my* body, which is broken for you." Then he took the cup and said, "This is the cup of the *new covenant in my blood,* poured out for the remission of sins." The Passover's deepest meaning was clarified and fulfilled, and it could never be the same for the community of Jesus. The apostle Paul would later say, "As often as you eat this bread and drink the cup, you proclaim the Lord's death until he comes" (1 Corinthians 11:26, NRSV). Now we celebrate the meal as his supper, in remembrance of him.

Other names for the sacrament tell us of the richness of this act. We call it "the Lord's Table" because it is done at his invitation and in his name. Jesus is the one who invites us and who feeds us spiritually with his body and blood. Luke calls it "the breaking of the bread" in the second chapter of Acts because it points to the broken body of Jesus, put to death to provide the sacrifice for humanity. We call it the Eucharist, or "thanksgiving," because the cup of thanksgiving points to the shed blood of Jesus. We give thanks and praise for his great gifts, the life and salvation he purchased for us. We call it "communion" because through it we tangibly enter into fellowship with him and enjoy togetherness with him.

The Protestant Reformers objected to designating the Lord's Table as an "altar." The altar of ancient Israel was a place where the priests went to offer daily sacrifices. The whole sacrificial system underlined that no sacrifice would be enough to pay for sin and make us right with God. But God's perfect offering of his own Son was a once-for-all event. We cannot add to it, and indeed are freed from the futility of trying to add to it. God has made the way for us to him, and he invites us to share in fellowship with him at the table.

Other Voices

Even the Lord's Supper is not a cultic act, some sort of "high point of the worship service" or communion of the "nucleus of the congregation" (what is that anyway?). It should still be today what it was originally, namely, a strengthening for our departure, when we must go out again to the battle and the work and the testing, when we shall be sent as sheep among the wolves. That is no cultic celebration; it is the assurance that the Lord remains with us when the worship *comes to an end* and when the world of the deadline, the telephone, and the motor surrounds us with its curtains of noise. It is to give us the certainty that he rules this world, too; that he gives us tasks of love in waiting rooms, in laboratories, and in our own homes, and that he has a greeting ready for us along every road, assuring us that he remembers us.

— HELMUT THIELICKE, *I Believe: The Christian's Creed*

The Lord's Supper service has room for some ethereal images like that of the "thrice-holy" that faced Isaiah in the temple. But at the most personal point the sacrament is very physical. Just as God is revealed in the bad grammar of the well-preached word, so now you have to think in rather crass terms about another mode of the presence. The same kind of bread you will eat at home this noon is on this table. The wine here is similar to what you can have at dinner. You pass them through the same mouth. They carry the same germs. One may harden, the other turns sour, like any other bread and wine. People with bad breath and cavities receive them past droopy mustaches or elegantly tinted lips. Keep the crude images in mind, since no other ones will keep to the forefront the offense and the scandal. This food will pass through the body and be digested and excreted through natural processes. Jesus knew all about that when he pointed to bread and said "This — my body!" and when he lifted a cup and gave it with "This — my blood!"

— MARTIN E. MARTY, *The Lord's Supper*

A Pope in majestic vestments intones the words — *Take, eat; this is my body . . . Drink ye all of [this]; for this is my blood* — at his High Altar in St. Peter's, its cavernous space overflowing with accompanying music which expresses the same mystical joy in the sacrifice of Calvary, in the Lamb of God that takes away the sins of the world. Thus, too, in his own austere style, a stern Presbyterian minister in a black gown with stony reverence offers bread and unfermented wine to his flock in remembrance of that gathering in Jerusalem when Jesus made his final dispositions before submitting himself to the laws of men and the Cross. Innumerable variations in the commemoration, but always the same event and the same words recalled.

The worshippers wait at the altar rails, like famished dossers at a soup-kitchen, their mouths open, their hands outspread; then return to their places visibly revived. *"Heureux les invités au repas du Seigneur! Voici l' Agneau de Dieu qui enlève le péché du monde,"* the priest says in the French Mass as he dispenses the consecrated bread, *Le Corps du Christ.* Happy, indeed, the guests at this feast.

— MALCOLM MUGGERIDGE, *Jesus The Man Who Lives*

When the bread of the Eucharist was broken we were reminded that in "the body of Christ crushed for you" the bodies of those who had been crushed in the [Guatemalan civil war] were gathered, and that in the blood of Christ was mingled the blood of all those who had fallen. In that moment, as each one broke a bit of bread from the loaf and drank from the cup, it seemed as if some strange and mysterious power was grasping us and holding us, as if in that single instant all the people who were being dehumanized and debased around the world were being lifted up in God's hand. We look at our own lives of course, and the life of our own church and our own country and it fills us with a certain emptiness. Suddenly, in the mirror of the lives of these Guatemalans gathered beneath the cross of Christ we become exposed for what we really are. But in the passing of the peace, the praying of the "Our Father" and the hearing of the words of benediction, we also felt a surge of that renewing power out of which real joy is born.

> — H. MCKENNIE GOODPASTURE,
> *Cross and Sword*

Daily Scripture Readings

KEY TEXT: EPHESIANS 5:29-30
Sunday: John 6:25-40
Monday: John 6:40-59

Tuesday: Acts 2:42-47
Wednesday: 1 John 4:7-21
Thursday: Luke 24:13-27
Friday: Luke 24:28-35
Saturday: Matthew 18:15-20

Questions for Reflection and Discussion

Some Christians believe that the bread and cup literally become Jesus' body and blood in the celebration of communion. Others hold that the bread and wine or juice are a remembrance of his sacrifice. Still others have recognized in the Lord's Supper his spiritual, though not physical, presence, to strengthen and encourage our faith. What truths do these various perspectives point to?

When have you felt God's presence or power in the celebration of the Lord's Supper?

Closing Prayer

God, show me how to enjoy fellowship with you. Make my life a sacrament that points to your power and presence. In Jesus' name.

WEEK TWENTY-NINE:

HIS SPIRITUAL PRESENCE

Opening Prayer

Help me to grow in grace, Father, and in the knowledge of Jesus Christ. In his name, I pray. Amen.

Heidelberg Questions

QUESTION 78: Are the bread and wine changed into the real body and blood of Christ?

No. Just as the water of baptism is not changed into Christ's blood and does not itself wash away sins but is simply God's sign and assurance,[1] so too the bread of the Lord's Supper is not changed into the actual body of Christ[2] even though it is called the body of Christ[3] in keeping with the nature and language of sacraments.[4]

(*[1]Ephesians 5:26; Titus 3:5; [2]Matthew 26:26-29; [3]1 Corinthians 10:16-17; 11:26-28; [4]Genesis 17:10-11; Exodus 12:11,13; 1 Corinthians 10:1-4*)

QUESTION 79: Why then does Christ call the bread his body and the cup his blood, or the new covenant in his blood? (Paul uses the words, a participation in Christ's body and blood.)

Christ has good reason for these words. He wants to teach us that as bread and wine nourish our temporal life, so too his crucified body and poured-out blood truly nourish our souls for eternal life.[1]

But more important, he wants to assure us, by this visible sign and pledge, that we, through the Holy Spirit's work, share in his true body and blood as surely as our mouths receive these holy signs in his remembrance,[2] and that all of his suffering and obedience are as definitely ours as if we personally had suffered and paid for our sins.[3]

(*[1]John 6:51,55; [2]1 Corinthians 10:16-17; 11:26; [3]Romans 6:5-11*)

Exposition

The Reformation was a revolutionary era, a time of violent conflict both outside the church and within. The years from 1517, when Martin Luther posted his 95 theses on the church door at Wittenberg, to 1563, when the Heidelberg Catechism was published, were filled with religious, political, and economic turmoil. The cities were moving toward economic dominance. The Ottoman Empire had conquered Constantinople and Egypt, and was threatening eastern Europe and the Balkans. The Roman Catholic Church had become scandalously corrupt and was desperately in need of renewal. During the first years of the Protestant Reformation, ecclesiastical matters took on a life-and-death importance. Persecutions flared into open flame, and thousands of evangelical Christians were burnt at the stake. The Wars of Religion broke out in 1562 and continued intermittently for some thirty years. One of the most famous incidents of those years profoundly shocked the Protestant world: the brutal massacre of St. Bartholomew's day in Paris on August 24, 1572. Protestant leaders had streamed into the city for the marriage of Henri of Navarre, leader of the Huguenots and later King Henry IV of France, to Margaret of Valois. Assassins sent by the queen, Catherine of Medici, incited the killings, and the populace joined in. Thousands of Huguenots were dragged from their beds that night and killed in the streets of the capital.

Given the supercharged climate, people tended to hold tenaciously to their views. In Protestant districts and independent cities, these were heady days of newfound freedom from papal control. Men and women felt deeply the theological debates of the day. Much controversy swirled around Holy Communion: What was the nature and significance of the sacrament? Who should administer it? Who was welcome at the Lord's Table? How could teaching, discipline, and pastoral care be done effectively so that Christians would understand their meaning and grow into maturity in Christ? Even among the Protestants there was disagreement on the sacrament. Luther maintained that Christ is physically present in the elements of the Lord's Supper — "in, with, and under" the bread and wine, he is eaten physically by the mouth. Calvin said this was impossible, for Christ is seated at the right hand of the Father. Instead, Jesus is eaten spiritually by faith through the bread and wine. Baptists would come to see the supper not as the presence of Christ in the means of grace, but as a solemn memorial of Christ's death for our sins.

Still the Reformers all stood in opposition to the Roman Catholic doctrine of "transubstantiation," that is, that the elements of the sacrament of communion actually become the body and blood of Jesus. Roman Catholic doctrine held that the Lord's Supper conferred forgiveness as Christ was re-sacrificed by his people and offered up to God for sin. To the Reformers this was outrageous. To genuflect before the bread and wine as if they were the Lord himself was akin to idolatry and was condemned as a pagan superstition. But both Roman Catholic and

Lutheran had this in common — that a change takes place in the bread and wine. The Reformed framers of the Heidelberg Catechism taught that the bread and wine were unchanged as bread and wine and were set aside from ordinary bread and wine only by their holy use. The apostle Paul makes this clear when he refers to the "bread" of the Lord's Supper.

The catechism seeks to explain the simplicity and power of what takes place in communion. The power is in the recollection of the sacrifice of Christ, confirmed in believers by the Holy Spirit. Jesus' disciples could only eat of his body and blood *spiritually*. When the Lord consecrated the elements at the table in giving thanks, he was still physically reclining before the table. His blood still coursed through his veins. His words indicated that his body and blood would be offered for them in his death. The bread and cup were for his disciples a potent symbol of his impending sacrifice. No other mystical change in the bread and cup needed to take place to increase the meaning of his death or to apply it to his disciples. His words alone were enough when he said *"for you."* He promised that his death would mean forgiveness of sins. All that the disciples had to do was to share in him and to remain in fellowship with him.

Signs and seals offered by God in the sacraments are indeed means of grace, because through them God strengthens his people and keeps them close to his heart. Circumcision was a sign of the covenant the Lord made with Israel. The Passover lamb was a sign that the Lord passed over the houses of the Hebrews. The water of baptism is a sign that believers are cleansed from sin and brought into the church. And bread and wine are called the body and blood of Jesus because they are signs of his sacrifice that makes possible our fellowship with him. The signs are distinct from the mystery they point to. Each of these serves as a vehicle for God's blessing when entered into by faith.

Bread and wine are two of the most basic foods that sustain our bodies. In putting into place these tokens of his presence, Jesus reminds us that his crucified body and shed blood are the best food and drink to sustain our souls. It is not our eating that makes it so, but the Holy Spirit working in us. He is the one who seals us to our Lord and the one who makes the gifts of God in Jesus our own.

Lausanne, Switzerland, perched among the vineyards above the azure crescent of Lake Geneva, was one of the cities that embraced the Reformation. In that time and in the centuries following, the city became a haven for persecuted evangelical Christians. Outside the walls of its cathedral church there is a weathered bronze plaque. It reads, *"In memory of the French Seminary of Lausanne, 1729-1812. The seminary was founded through the efforts of Antoine Court and Benjamin Duplan. It gave the persecuted Reformed churches of France over 400 pastors, many of whom died for their faith."*[8] During a time of tremendous oppression, these Christians found courage and nurture to be disciples through the sustaining presence of God in the preaching of the Word and in the fellowship of communion.

Other Voices

Let us engrave this useful lesson upon our hearts, that we should consider it the great end of our existence to be found numbered among the worshipers of God; and that we should avail ourselves of the inestimable privilege of the stated assemblies of the church, which are necessary helps to our infirmity and means of mutual excitement and encouragement. By these, and our common sacraments, the Lord who is one God, and who designed that we should be one in him, is training us up together in the hope of eternal life, and in the united celebration of his holy name.

— JOHN CALVIN, *Commentary on Psalm 52*

Death can't be killed with death.

So, sow life.
Kill death with life.
But to reap life — full, infinite, unceasing —
the death must by yours,
Loving all you can.

For only with life can you sow life
Which, like love, is stronger than death.

To share with friends from time to time
A little bread, a little wine,
Shares our life and work.

To share that same bread
With the wounded Christ
Shares struggle, death, and resurrection.

— JULIA ESQUIVEL, "Sowing Life"

Hope arises out of the hard truth of how things are. Christians will always live carrying in one hand the promise of how it will be and in the other the hard reality of how it is. To deny either is to hold only half of the gospel. . . .

In worshiping God we realize we were never created to be whole. God will not restore what we were never intended to have. What we were created to enjoy is fellowship with God, who alone is whole and complete.

Nowhere in the Bible are we told that God wants to give us wholeness. What God wants to give us is himself. If we really believed that, it would be enough. In fact, it would be more than enough. It would overwhelm us.

The effect of our fascination with wholeness is that it embarks us on a journey for which there is no end, a journey that takes us further away from God. He invites us to journey in a different direction.

— M. CRAIG BARNES, *Yearning: Living Between How It Is & How It Ought to Be*

I believe that in the Holy Eucharist (that is, the supper of thanksgiving) the true body of Christ is present by the contemplation of faith. In other words, those who thank the Lord for the kindness conferred on us in his Son acknowledge that he assumed true flesh and in it truly suffered and truly washed away our sins by his own blood. Thus everything done by Christ becomes present to them by the contemplation of faith. But that the body of Christ, that is his natural body in essence and reality, is either present in the Supper or eaten with our mouth and teeth, as is asserted by the papists and by some who long for the flesh pots of Egypt [Lutherans], we not only deny but firmly maintain to be an error opposed to God's word. . . . The natural body of Christ is not eaten with our mouth as he himself showed when he said to the Jews who were disputing about the corporeal eating of his flesh, "The flesh counts for nothing" (John 6:63). . . . The words "This is my body" should be received not literally, but figuratively, just as the words "This is the Passover" (Exodus 12:11).

— ULRICH ZWINGLI, *Confession of Faith*

Daily Scripture Readings

KEY TEXT: JOB 38:4-7
    Sunday: Mark 14:12-26
    Monday: Luke 22:7-32
    Tuesday: Romans 6:1-14

Wednesday: Ephesians 5:25-32
Thursday: Exodus 12:1-14
Friday: 2 Corinthians 5:11-21
Saturday: Titus 3:3-8

Questions for Reflection and Discussion

How do you explain the power of communion? Can it be explained? Why or why not?

Why is it important not to confuse the sign with the mystery it points to?

What does it mean to you to partake in the flesh and blood of Jesus?

Closing Prayer

Dear Father, you are good to give yourself in your Son, once and for all and yet continually. Help me to respond in love, in service, and in praise.

Week Thirty:

If You Love Jesus and Hate Your Sin

Opening Prayer

Lord, take this little time I have and use it for your purpose. Take what little understanding I have and use it to teach me. Take the problems I have, but not before you use them to accomplish in me what needs to be done. In the merit of Jesus, I pray this.

Heidelberg Questions

Question 80: How does the Lord's Supper differ from the Roman Catholic Mass?

The Lord's Supper declares to us that our sins have been completely forgiven through the one sacrifice of Jesus Christ which he himself finished on the cross once for all.[1] It also declares to us that the Holy Spirit grafts us into Christ,[2] who with his very body is now in heaven at the right hand of the Father[3] where he wants us to worship him.[4]

([1]John 19:30; Hebrews 7:27; 9:12,25-26; 10:10-18; [2]1 Corinthians 6:17; 10:16-17; [3]Acts 7:55-56; Hebrews 1:3; 8:1; [4]Matthew 6:20-21; John 4:21-24; Philippians 3:20; Colossians 3:1-3)

Question 81: Who are to come to the Lord's Table?

Those who are displeased with themselves because of their sins, but who nevertheless trust that their sins are pardoned and that their continuing weakness is covered by the suffering and death of Christ, and who also desire more and more to strengthen their faith and to lead a better life.

Hypocrites and those who are unrepentant, however, eat and drink judgment on themselves.[1]

([1]1 Corinthians 10:19-22; 11:26-32)

QUESTION 82: Are those to be admitted to the Lord's Supper who show by what they say and do that they are unbelieving and ungodly?

No, that would dishonor God's covenant and bring down God's anger upon the entire congregation.[1] Therefore, according to the instruction of Christ and his apostles, the Christian church is duty-bound to exclude such people, by the official use of the keys of the kingdom, until they reform their lives.

([1] *1 Corinthians 11:17-32; Psalm 50:14-16; Isaiah 1:11-17*)

Exposition

It is here, Karl Barth wrote, that "the full wrath of the Reformation against the [Catholic] Counter-Reformation breaks out." Question 80 negates the Roman Catholic doctrine that the Reformers held had corrupted the church.

Here the catechism declares "No!" to two challenges. First, it rejects the idea that the Lord's Supper brings forgiveness of sins. It cannot. To see the supper as an offering that propitiates for sin is to make the witness of the saving event into the saving event itself. The catechism protests that Jesus' sacrifice on the cross was unique; the church cannot repeat it again, as if that were needed to bring about our salvation. The sacrifice of God's own Son was a once-for-all event and cannot be duplicated. The doctrine of salvation by grace alone through faith alone was the central biblical rediscovery of the sixteenth century. If the mass were a human attempt to get right with God, then it was a challenge to the gospel of Christ.

Second, the catechism also rejects that the bread and wine are transformed to become the same as Christ's body and blood. (A later version of the catechism starkly calls this a "condemnable — or *accursed* — idolatry." Luther voices the criticism even more harshly, writing that "the mass of the papacy" was "the greatest and most monstrous abomination" and "the extreme of all papal idolatries.") There is only one sacrifice, one authority, one Lord of the church. The Reformers were keenly aware of the human propensity to add to the gospel of Christ. They were acutely concerned that nothing obscure what God had done in Christ; to add is to take away, to undo, to put the creature in the place of the Creator, the redeemed in the place of the Redeemer.

Ursinus and Olevianus, the framers of the catechism, saw that the gospel ministry followed in the prophetic office of the proclamation of God's Word. The minister of the gospel of Christ does not offer a priestly sacrifice, but feeds the people by the exposition of Scripture. The church of today inherits this prophetic tradition. There is no longer any place for a sacrificing priesthood, but for teachers of the Word of God, those who equip all of God's people for the common priesthood. Mere attendance at the Lord's Supper is not enough to save us. Simply eating the bread and sharing in the cup do not magically transform us. It is the Word of God that *informs* us of the ways of God and *transforms* us into the likeness of Christ. We must appropriate the benefits of Christ through faith in him — through heart and mind.

This is why for the Reformers of the sixteenth century, the mass constituted an attack on the lordship of Christ. Evangelical faith trusts in Christ alone as Savior. The Lord's Supper not only remembers what he has done, but looks forward to what he will do in bringing his people to the table in the wedding feast to come.

What is it, then, to be ready to receive the supper? It is to love Jesus a little and to desire to love him more. Since communion with the Lord is not just outer form but inward reality, there are naturally conditions for coming to the table. The apostle Paul tells us, "Examine yourselves, and only then eat of the bread and drink of the cup" (1 Corinthians 11:28, NRSV). Jesus died to deliver sinners from their sins, and by the power of his death we are to put to death all that is displeasing to him. That is not to say that a person comes to the table because of his or her deserving. But we have to want to let Christ have his way in us.

Children of God are invited to be transformed and to embark on a journey toward holiness. Jesus is the Priest who offered the sacrifice of his blood; he is also the King who calls us to a lifestyle of righteousness now made possible by his Spirit. Holiness is more a process than a destination in this life, and yet we must manifest signs that we're in the process. We have to let him begin the transformation. Thus it is that the first needed thing in coming to the table of the Lord is to be sorry for one's sins. We need to trust that in Christ our sins are forgiven, covered by his suffering and death. And we need to desire to be delivered of the burden of our sins, to live a life worthy of God's calling. Renunciation of evil is the flip side of embracing God's will for us.

We do better when we reflectively prepare for the service of communion by taking a moral inventory of ourselves ahead of time. In earlier days, many churches would hold services of preparation for the Lord's Supper, often on the day before. Some Reformed churches still close the Lord's Day service of worship with a benediction, allowing those so inclined to leave, before continuing with the Lord's Supper. Worship is the highest calling of the people of God, and our communion with him is in response to his overtures of love. When we contemplate the meaning of his body broken for us, his blood poured out for us, we are looking into the heart of the Father who longs to welcome us home. Neither the purity of our liturgy nor the excellence of our preaching will accomplish what God intends until we worship him in "spirit and in truth." When that takes place, there is a quality of deep fellowship with God and with one another that flows out of and responds to the eternal fellowship of love between Father, Son, and Spirit. This is the reality that the New Testament calls *koinonia*.

Other Voices

Christianity comes from Christ, and Christ comes not for "the righteous, but [for] sinners" (Matthew 9:13).

Those who don't know *that* are not yet

in the market for Christianity, even though they may sit in church every Sunday. Those who don't know that sit in church as art students would sit in a hospital, enjoying its architecture, but not as its patients. The church is not a museum for saints but a hospital for sinners. To publicly profess to the world that you are a Christian, by going to church every Sunday, is not to say to the world that you are better than they are but that you are desperately ill.

The church is a lot like Alcoholics Anonymous. The very first thing you have to admit and never forget in AA is that "I am an alcoholic." A Christian is one who knows he is a sinaholic, and he has accepted God's cure. The stupidest of all reasons for not going to church is one of the commonest ones: "I'm not good enough." The only qualification is to be *bad* enough. Does anyone refuse to go to the hospital because they're not healthy enough?

— PETER KREEFT, *Making Choices: Practical Wisdom for Everyday Moral Decisions*

A broken altar, Lord, your servant rears,
Made of a heart, and cemented with tears:
Whose parts are as your hand did frame;
No workman's tool has touched the same.

A heart alone
Is such a stone,
As nothing but
Your power does cut.

Wherefore each part
Of my hard heart

Meets in this frame,
To praise your name;

That, if I chance to hold my peace,
These stones to praise you may not cease.
O let your blessed sacrifice be mine,
And sanctify this altar to be thine.

— GEORGE HERBERT, "The Altar,"
from *The Temple*

My God, my Father, I lift up my heart to thee. Give me thy Holy Spirit.

Grant me the grace to approach this table with humble repentance and ardent desire in Jesus Christ our Lord.

Grant me to receive this holy sacrament with firm faith in thy word, that in receiving these visible signs from thy hand I may receive by faith the body and blood of Jesus Christ, who died for me as the nourishment of eternal life.

May I take from it the peace and spiritual joy proper to thy children with ardent love for thee, my God, and a firm resolve henceforth to consecrate my life to thy service, until I see thy face and my soul is received by Jesus Christ my Savior, who has redeemed it by his death.

— PIERRE DU MOULIN,
On Approaching Thy Holy Table

Christians, too, [like Jews] live under obligation to remember because they live under the shadow of the cross. When they celebrate the Lord's Supper they echo the words of Jesus Christ: "This is my body that is for you. Do this in *remembrance* of me. . . . This cup is the new covenant in my blood. Do this, as often as you drink it, in *remembrance* of me." (1 Corinthians 11:23ff.) The Lord's Supper is the ritual time in which we remember the broken body and spilled blood of our Savior. As we partake of it, we remember that night in which the "Lord of Glory" was betrayed, humiliated, subjected to a mock trial, and brutally murdered; we recall why Jesus Christ was crucified and what the consequences were. There can be no Christian faith without *that* memory; *everything* in Christian faith depends on it.

— MIROSLAV VOLF, *Exclusion and Embrace: A Theological Exploration of Identity, Otherness, and Reconciliation*

Daily Scripture Readings

KEY TEXT: JOHN 19:30
    Sunday: Hebrews 7:18-28
    Monday: Hebrews 9:1-10
    Tuesday: Hebrews 9:11-28
    Wednesday: Hebrews 10:1-18
    Thursday: John 4:1-24
    Friday: Isaiah 1:11-17
    Saturday: Psalm 50

Questions for Reflection and Discussion

According to the catechism, who is welcome at the Lord's Table? Should we put up any barriers to who may come? If so, what are they? What qualifies someone to receive communion?

Given the perspective of the catechism, should Christians be free to share communion in denominational traditions different from their own? Why? How does one show integrity to one's own theological convictions when it comes to the Lord's Table?

Through the years the Lord's Supper has sometimes divided Christians as much as it has united them. What is the basis for our unity across the Christian community? How can we better demonstrate that unity to a world rife with divisions between gender, family, tribe, and nation?

Closing Prayer

Lord, what you have intended as a gracious gift, we have often allowed to divide your body. Overcome my sins and brokenness, and help me to love you and others. I ask this in Jesus' name.

Week Thirty-one:
Keys of the Kingdom

Opening Prayer

Let me not fear your reproach, gracious Father, but accept your discipline that I might grow stronger. Purify your church, beginning with me. Amen.

Heidelberg Questions

Question 83: What are the keys of the kingdom?

The preaching of the holy gospel and Christian discipline toward repentance. Both preaching and discipline open the kingdom of heaven to believers and close it to unbelievers.[1]

([1]*Matthew 16:19; John 20:22-23*)

Question 84: How does preaching the gospel open and close the kingdom of heaven?

According to the command of Christ:

The kingdom of heaven is opened by proclaiming and publicly declaring to all believers, each and every one, that, as often as they accept the gospel promise in true faith, God, because of what Christ has done, truly forgives all their sins.

The kingdom of heaven is closed, however, by proclaiming and publicly declaring to unbelievers and hypocrites that, as long as they do not repent, the anger of God and eternal condemnation rest on them.

God's judgment, both in this life and in the life to come, is based on this gospel testimony.[1]

([1]*Matthew 16:19; John 3:31-36; 20:21-23*)

QUESTION 85: How is the kingdom of heaven closed and opened by Christian discipline?

According to the command of Christ:

Those who, though called Christians, profess unchristian teachings or live unchristian lives, and after repeated and loving counsel refuse to abandon their errors and wickedness, and after being reported to the church, that is, to its officers, fail to respond also to their admonition — such persons the officers exclude from the Christian fellowship by withholding the sacraments from them, and God himself excludes them from the kingdom of Christ.[1]

Such persons, when promising and demonstrating genuine reform, are received again as members of Christ and of his church.[2]

([1]*Matthew 18:15-20; 1 Corinthians 5:3-5,11-13; 2 Thessalonians 3:14-15;* [2]*Luke 15:20-24; 2 Corinthians 2:6-11*)

Exposition

The church distinguishes itself not only by the proclamation of the gospel for salvation, not only by being a beacon of hope and a sign of God's kingdom in a darkening world, not only by the bread and cup of communion, not only by the gifts of the Holy Spirit at work in the fellowship, it is also known by the exercise of discipline. The church with no discipline is a church with no standards.

Discipline has fallen on hard times these days. There is a negative assessment all around us about it, because we believe there is not authority for it. When I was in college, I had a T-shirt that declared, "Question Authority." (It blew away one night as it hung on a balcony to dry in Paris.) I still believe there's a sense in which questioning authority is needed in a world filled with counterfeit authorities. But if a culture rejects *all* authority, if it lifts up tolerance as the supreme virtue and proclaims the relativity of all truth, there are no limits of any kind. Technology and bioengineering tell us that what we cannot do today, we will do tomorrow. Seldom is the ethical question asked: because we *can* do a thing, *should* we do such a thing? It is the same in the realm of personal freedom. We have prided ourselves on coloring outside the lines, on being able to "think outside the box." It scarcely enters into our thinking that there should be limits imposed on what we can do. Discipline is seen as intrusive and even arbitrary.

Discipline is essential for human development. Discipline is fundamentally instruction, or correction. Without it, the child would never learn to talk, the student master a multiplication table, or a congregation of Christians learn the depth of community or the nature of the mission to which they are invited. Without it, our physical and mental muscles would atrophy. Our own experience and the history of the church confirm the positive results that take place when discipline is rightly exercised.

True, the church has at times been too confining and authoritarian, exercising a kind of judgmental discipline that is incompatible with grace. In this as perhaps no other area of corporate life there is the possibility of abuse. People can be deeply hurt when discipline is done badly or for wrong reasons. The church must take care to act by the Spirit of God and not by the spirit of the world. Yet because discipline has been wrongly exercised is no reason to refuse it. That would make no more sense than refusing to take medicine for the flu because of possible misdiagnosis, or refusing to open the Bible because it is sometimes taught irresponsibly. The church incapable of discipline is incapable of being the church. The author of the epistle to the Hebrews exhorts, "Discipline always seems painful rather than pleasant at the time, but later it yields the peaceful fruit of righteousness to those who have been trained by it" (Hebrews 12:11, NRSV).

To discipline is to rebuke, to admonish, and to correct with a view toward restoration of the offender. Seen in this light, no society can hold together without discipline; no family can survive without it — how much less the church. If the gospel message is the soul of the church, then, says Calvin, the discipline is the sinews. Like the cords that hold together the body, godly discipline maintains order, keeping each member in its place. If each member acted autonomously, the result would be chaos. We call it anarchy when that takes place on the larger scale.

The key is in the intent. The Christian community has no room for punitive discipline. The object is not to punish, but to restore; not to humiliate, but to bring healing out of hurtful circumstances rather than allow the cancer of sin to eat away until there is little to restore in the soul of a believer or in the soul of a congregation. The purpose is to rein in evil and to nourish the community. The authority of Christ has been given to the church and finds expression in discipline given in his Spirit. Christ is honored by the purity of his body; the body is build up, not destroyed, when correction is applied in love. From one stage to another, there is a series of appropriate actions that remedy the threats to the well-being of the church.

Those stages echo the sequence of Matthew 18. The first step is private admonition. "If your brother sins against you," teaches Jesus, "go and show him his fault, just between the two of you. If he listens to you, you have won your brother over" (18:15). Today's church would be a healthier and happier place if we demonstrated this kind of mutual accountability rather than let grievances fester. Much of the time we prefer to tell ourselves, "It's no big deal, anyway," and continue to harbor resentment against the person who has hurt us. When we do that, we multiply the damage.

If the brother or sister continues in immoral behavior, the church is to take two or three witnesses to confront the offender. If the person persists, they are to be brought before the elders. There is always the hope that the person will turn away from the destructive behavior and submit to authority. In this way, the teaching of the church becomes forceful as the congregation sees there are consequences for hurtful and unbiblical patterns.

If anyone continues by refusing to listen to the church, then the Lord commands that that person be removed from the believers' fellowship in order to maintain its peace and purity.

The scriptural warrant for the function of discipline is seen in the "keys of the kingdom." This is a metaphor for the administration of a trust, just as a person knows they really have been hired for a job when he or she is given the keys and the alarm code to the office. This authority was given to Peter and by extension to all the apostles, based on their confession of faith in Christ, and to their successors in the governance of the church. Spiritual in character, the discipline of the church is unlike that of any other authority. It is not to kill life, but to bring it. It is not the discipline of civil authority, and it is only binding as the church member submits to it. It is not to snuff out joy, but to enable health and to liberate men and women from everything that would poison us.

The catechism goes on to reflect that the kingdom of heaven is opened to people by the sharing of the good news of Jesus Christ. Those who receive the offered love of God discover the expansive horizons of new life. Everyone who believes is assured of forgiveness and acceptance into the loving heart of God, just as if the Father spoke personally to each one.

In the same way, the preaching of the gospel closes the kingdom of heaven to those who do not believe. Those who turn away from the offered love of God find a life that closes in on itself and becomes a pinched, narrow existence. Everyone who dies in unbelief is under the condemnation of the righteous judge of heaven. That is not a popular view to hold in our age of anything-goes tolerance. It is not one that the church should wield as a weapon toward others. But for the church to remain healthy and to retain a sense of urgency about its work, we must be able to bring the hard word of judgment on evil as well as the soft word of promise. The gospel message can do no less.

Other Voices

Holy obedience is the single eye that bathes the entire personality in light. It is the purity of heart that can desire only one thing — the good. It is a God-intoxicated life that can embrace wealth or poverty, hunger or plenty, crucifixion or acclaim with equal ease at the word of Christ.

Dr. Graham Scroggie, a gifted preacher of another generation, preached on the Lordship of Christ at a huge Keswick Convention in England. A great orator, he spoke powerfully. After the crowd had left, he saw a young college student seated alone. He went to her, asking if he could help. "Oh, Dr. Scroggie," she blurted out, "your message was so compelling but I am afraid to truly make Christ Lord, afraid of what he will ask of me!" Wisely, Graham Scroggie turned his worn Bible to the story of Peter at Joppa, where God had taught him about his racial and cultural discrimination. Three times God brought down a sheet laden with animals unclean to orthodox Judaism and said, "Rise, Peter; kill and eat." Three times Peter responded, "No, Lord." Tenderly, Dr. Scroggie said, "You know it is possible to say 'No,' and it is possible to say 'Lord,' but it is not really possible to say, 'No, Lord.' I'm going to leave my Bible with you and this pen and go into another room and pray for you, and I want you to cross out either the word 'No' or the word 'Lord.'" He did so, and when in prayer he felt that the matter had been settled he slipped back into the auditorium. The young woman was weeping quietly, and peering over her shoulder he saw the word "No" crossed out. Softly she was saying, "He's Lord, He's Lord, He's Lord." Such is the stuff of holy obedience.

— RICHARD J. FOSTER, *Freedom of Simplicity*

The hope of eternal life, however, does not, as Marx charged, have the effect of an opiate. Because it is based on love it cannot but create love. . . . Here let me mention one very widespread misunderstanding. Many people, trained in the doctrine of progress, have the idea that it is only the belief in progress that can stimulate man to activity, especially to social activity. What nonsense! As though the people of the Reformation period were inactive because none of them had the idea of progress. That is one of the fairy tales of our age — that men need the idea of progress to make them active. What we really need to make us active is love, and if we have love we need no other stimulus. . . . The future for which the Christian hopes is not made by man but by God. But man is called by Christ to share in God's work, to become a coworker with him for the Kingdom of God — and this call is sufficient to activate man's total effort.

— EMIL BRUNNER, *Faith, Hope, and Love*

We have a strange illusion that mere time cancels sin . . . [but] all times are eternally present to God. Is it not at least possible that along some one line of His multi-dimensional eternity He sees you forever in the nursery, pulling the wings off a fly, forever toadying, lying, and lusting as a schoolboy, forever in that moment of cowardice or insolence as a subaltern? It may be that salvation consists not in the canceling of these eternal moments but in the perfected humility that bears the shame forever, rejoicing in the occasion which it furnished to God's compassion and glad that it should be common knowledge to the universe. Perhaps in that eternal moment St. Peter — he will forgive me if am wrong — forever denies his Master. If so, it would indeed be true that the joys of Heaven are for most of us, in our present condition, "an acquired taste" — and certain ways of life may render the taste impossible of acquisition. Perhaps the lost are those who dare not go to such a *public* place. Of course I do not know that this is true; but I think the possibility is worth keeping in mind.

— C. S. LEWIS, *The Problem of Pain*

Honor and praise be unto you, O Lord our God, for all your tender mercies again bestowed upon us throughout another week.

Continual thanks be unto you for creating us in your own likeness; for redeeming us by the precious blood of your dear Son when we were lost; and for sanctifying us with the Holy Spirit.

For your help and succor in our necessities, your protection in many dangers of body and soul; your comfort in our sorrows, and for sparing us in life, and giving us so large a time to repent. For all the benefits, O most merciful Father, that we have received of your goodness alone, we thank you; and we beseech you to grant us always your Holy Spirit, that we may grow in grace, in steadfast faith, and perseverance in all good works, through Jesus Christ our Lord.

— JOHN KNOX, *A Sabbath Prayer of Thanksgiving*

Daily Scripture Readings

KEY TEXT: MATTHEW 16:19
  Sunday: John 20:1-23
  Monday: John 3:25-36
  Tuesday: Matthew 18:15-20
  Wednesday: 1 Corinthians 5:1-13
  Thursday: 2 Thessalonians 3:6-15
  Friday: Luke 15:11-20
  Saturday: Luke 15:20-32

Questions for Reflection and Discussion

What do you remember about your parents' discipline when you were growing up? Looking back, do you see that discipline as positive or negative? Why or why not?

Why is it important for the church to maintain spiritual and ethical standards? What is the place of forgiveness in the church?

What is the difference between reprisal and discipline? Why does the church have the responsibility to discipline its members? How can we help ensure that its discipline is positive and restorative, not punitive?

Closing Prayer

Lord, you are the righteous Father who disciplines the children you love. Let me be open to your discipline and to submit to the righteous authority of the church. As that takes place, please make me and make your church more what you have in mind for us to be. In Jesus' name, amen.

Part Three

OUR LIVING SACRIFICE

Week Thirty-two:
Blessed to Be a Blessing

Opening Prayer

Father, your mercies are new every morning. I know you have called me to be a blessing to others. With your help, I commit myself to doing that today. Amen.

Heidelberg Questions

QUESTION 86: We have been delivered from our misery by God's grace alone through Christ and not because we have earned it: why then must we still do good?

To be sure, Christ has redeemed us by his blood. But we do good because Christ by his Spirit is also renewing us to be like himself, so that in all our living we may show that we are thankful to God for all he has done for us,[1] and so that he may be praised through us.[2]

And we do good so that we may be assured of our faith by its fruits,[3] and so that by our godly living our neighbors may be won over to Christ.[4]

([1]*Romans 6:13; 12:1-2; 1 Peter 2:5-10;* [2]*Matthew 5:16; 1 Corinthians 6:19-20;* [3]*Matthew 7:17-18; Galatians 5:22-24; 2 Peter 2:12; 3:1;* [4]*Matthew 5:14-16; Romans 14:17-19; 1 Peter 2:12; 3:1-2)*

QUESTION 87: Can those be saved who do not turn to God from their ungrateful and impenitent ways?

By no means. Scripture tells us that no unchaste person, no idolater, adulterer, thief, no covetous person, no drunkard, slanderer, robber, or the like is going to inherit the kingdom of God.[1]

([1]*1 Corinthians 6:9-10; Galatians 5:19-21; Ephesians 5:1-20; 1 John 3:14)*

Exposition

These questions inaugurate the third section of the catechism, which unpacks the meaning of thankfulness in the Christian's life. The material has now completed the circle begun in the first two questions; the first introduces and the second frames the themes of guilt, grace, and gratitude. Theologians have used the terms "justification" and "sanctification," that is, we're made right with God through his free gift of grace by faith; then, we're made more and more into what God desires us to be. God has saved us in order that we might serve him in the world.

That is why the church emphasizes "holiness" — not that we should ever forget we are broken sinners who need help, nor that we should ever convey a "holier than thou" image to others; the church emphasizes holiness because faith has to make a difference in the life of the believer. We need to do good works. We need to make a difference if our faith is real. Christians are invited into a new lifestyle marked by the law of God because that law expresses what is good and what leads to wholeness. The essential thing is the placement of the teaching on good works in the catechism. The teaching on good works did not appear in the beginning of the catechism, as if to suggest that in doing them we make ourselves deserving of salvation. They come at the end, to demonstrate that only those whom God has made new are able to do works that are really pleasing to God. Our works do not earn salvation. They do not even bring about the change God is effecting in our lives — only he can do that. Instead, they are the manner in which we declare our thankfulness to God.

What does the Christian have to be grateful for? For life, for redemption and the hope of heaven, for God's Spirit that is making us better than we were, no longer bound by the sin and fear of our past. How do we show gratitude? We do it in many ways: we tell others what Jesus means to us and what he has done for us. We truly desire to give up the patterns of pride, envy, lust, gluttony, all those things that offend God, and conform our lives according to his will. We exercise faith that we will receive from God everything we can possibly need. We show our thanks in living by God's commands and by faithfully bringing our petitions and praises to God in prayer. That is why the last section has two parts: the Law and the Lord's Prayer.

Gratitude is what moves us from pinched existence into expansive living. People with an over-developed sense of entitlement are unhappy people because someone is always doing something to offend them. But people who see in Jesus the undeserved renewal of our relationship with God are filled with wonder, delighted by God's goodness and generosity toward them. If God has redeemed us, then our sins are removed from us, we are being made new in the midst of a world that is decaying, and we're given new purpose and power in life. Gratitude is a natural response to all God has done. The Holy Spirit in us is active; more than merely the one who saves us, he is the one who transforms us into the likeness of God. His benefits are given to the grateful, and his work generates gratitude.

Along with some good times of growth, I remember struggles with my parents during my junior high school years. I wanted to exert my independence from their suzerainty and to assert my own will. At the same time, I wanted their guidance and support; my longing for independence was not entirely consistent.

Once when I was about thirteen, my parents and I had been having a hard week. It seemed that we were constantly bickering, and we were weary of it. By Saturday, I was in no mood for submitting when my mom scolded me for some infraction. Instead of finishing my chores, I sneaked out the back of the house, got on my Stingray bike, and pedaled to my friend Doug's house a mile away.

I knew full well my parents would be looking for me. Still, I laid low the whole morning and into the afternoon, playing with model cars and board games at Doug's house. The longer I stayed, the more I worried I was going to be in trouble when I got home, and the less I cared to venture home. Finally about five o'clock, I mustered the courage to get on my bike and head home to face the inevitable "grounding." I headed down the street, weaving distractedly up and down driveways and between parked cars.

That's when I heard my dad's voice, "Randy, let's load your bike into the back. I'll drive you home." His voice made me jump, but as he craned his neck out the window of the station wagon, his face looked kind. He'd been driving around looking for me. He pulled over to the curb, moved the lever to put the engine into park, and swung out of the driver's side door to come around and open the tailgate for me. He loaded my bike into the back end, shut the gate, and then turned to me. "Son, Mom and I had two tickets to go see the musical *The Sound of Music* at the Music Center downtown. We thought maybe you'd like to go with me tonight. Would you like that?"

"Uh, sure," I squeaked, uncertain whether I was going to be in trouble.

"Well, we've got to hurry. Let's go home and get changed," he said.

He didn't say another word about my having disappeared all day. By the time we were in our best clothes, driving downtown for a quick supper before the musical, I felt reassured that his intentions were benevolent.

They were. When I expected punishment, my father and mother saw that the relationship needed restoration. My sheepish relief was immense, but so was my appreciation for their reaching out in love. Next time it was my turn to do the dishes, I did it without a word of objection. What no sense of duty could conjure up for me, thankfulness did.

God has reached out to us in surprising love in the person of his Son, Jesus. The only authentic way we can respond is with gratitude.

Other Voices

Just as worship begins in holy expectancy, it ends in holy obedience. If worship does not propel us into greater obedience, it has not been worship. To stand before the Holy One of eternity is to change. Resentments cannot be held with the same tenacity when we enter his gracious light. As Jesus says, we need to leave our gift at the altar and go set the matter straight (Matthew 5:23, 24). In worship an increased power steals its way into the heart sanctuary, an increased compassion grows in the soul. To worship is to change.

— RICHARD J. FOSTER, *Celebration of Discipline: The Path to Spiritual Growth*

I said, "Let me walk in the fields."
   He said, "Nay, walk in the town."
I said, "There are no flowers there."
   He said, "No flowers, but a crown."

∾

I said, "But the sky is black,
   There is nothing but noise and din."
But he wept as he sent me back —
   "There is more," he said, "there is sin."

— GEORGE MACDONALD,
"Acceptance of God's Will"

Daily Scripture Readings

KEY TEXT: 1 PETER 2:12
   Sunday: 1 Peter 2:5-10
   Monday: Matthew 5:13-16
   Tuesday: Matthew 7:15-20
   Wednesday: 1 Timothy 6:17-19
   Thursday: 1 Peter 4:1-11
   Friday: 1 John 3:11-21
   Saturday: James 2:14-26

Questions for Reflection and Discussion

What, to you, are actions of a person who is a genuine Christian? What kind of behaviors would make you question whether a person really is a believer?

The Protestant Reformers took utmost care to teach the church that we are saved by faith not works. Is this notion in conflict with the Christian's responsibility to care for others, to do justice, and to show mercy? Why or why not?

A nonChristian friend asks you, "How can Christians in places like Northern Ireland or the former Yugoslav republics be killing each other?" What do you say in response? What perspective does question 87 bring to those who claim to be Christian but continue in acts of brutality or oppression? How might this challenge cultural Christians in our own setting?

What is one action you have done because of the difference Christ has made in your life? Is there anything God is calling you to do now?

*Closing Prayer*_____

Help me to believe in you and to believe in what you can do through me. Gracious God, I want to please you with my life, beginning here, beginning now, in the strength of your Spirit and in the name of Jesus. Amen.

Week Thirty-three:
Into New Life

Opening Prayer

Gracious God, I have come to understand a little more of the meaning of your claim on me. I need to allow you to be more to me than simply Savior. I now invite you to be my Lord indeed, master over every part of my life. In so doing, I will discover the fullness of the life available in you. In your name I pray. Amen.

Heidelberg Questions

QUESTION 88: What is involved in genuine repentance or conversion?
Two things: the dying-away of the old self, and the coming-to-life of the new.[1]
(*[1]Romans 6:1-11; 2 Corinthians 5:17; Ephesians 4:22-24; Colossians 3:5-10*)

QUESTION 89: What is the dying-away of the old self?
It is to be genuinely sorry for sin, to hate it more and more, and to run away from it.[1]
(*[1]Psalm 51:3-4,17; Joel 2:12-13; Romans 8:12-13; 2 Corinthians 7:10*)

QUESTION 90: What is the coming-to-life of the new self?
It is wholehearted joy in God through Christ[1] and a delight to do every kind of good, as God wants us to.[2]
(*[1]Psalm 51:8,12; Isaiah 57:15; Romans 5:1; 14:17; [2]Romans 6:10-11; Galatians 2:20*)

QUESTION 91: What do we do that is good?

Only that which arises out of true faith,[1] conforms to God's law,[2] and is done for his glory;[3] and not that which is based on what we think is right or on established human tradition.[4]

(*[1]John 15:5; Hebrews 11:6; [2]Leviticus 18:4; 1 Samuel 15:22; Ephesians 2:10; [3]1 Corinthians 10:31; [4]Deuteronomy 12:32; Isaiah 29:13; Ezekiel 20:18-19; Matthew 15:7-9*)

Exposition

People who have grown up in the church often feel reluctant to talk about conversion. That is especially true in the Reformed tradition, where more emphasis is placed on a lifestyle of responsible discipleship and stewardship than on the experience of the believer. There is a nervousness that stems perhaps from a distaste of emotionalism and a desire for the Christian commitment to be deeper and longer lasting. It's worth remembering that Calvin himself talked of his conversion as the decisive moment when God claimed him for himself. True, he was reticent about the experience — he didn't even pen one line about the *nature* of the experience. There is no description of his "heart strangely warmed." Nonetheless, the *fact* of his conversion is the touchstone of his faith, because it demonstrated God's faithfulness for him.

In a sense, it is healthy not to dwell too heavily on one's experience in the Christian faith. Faith is more than feelings — the catechism has taught us that faith entails repentance, commitment, and engagement with the purposes of God. Faith is a reality that goes far beyond our subjective experience.

Yet faith is also profoundly experiential. To be a Christian is to be converted. Some in the body of Christ are there because of a deep-rooted faith that grew up so gradually they can never say when they first knew they belonged to Christ. Others are there because they can pinpoint a dramatic experience of God that won them over, maybe in a time of crisis. Whatever the case, Christians are those able to declare, "I have made a decision for Christ." That decision is always based upon and made possible by God's prior decision on behalf of the Christian, on those he has called to belong to him. But God's decision is consciously ratified by the individual believer.

Question 88 scrutinizes what makes up a true conversion. It is a twofold procedure that includes both giving-up and taking-on. First is repentance. It entails both feeling and decision. One word for "repent" in the Old Testament, *naham*, implies difficulty in breathing, meaning to pant or groan. It came to mean to lament, or to regret. It is a visceral word that when applied to the act of repentance suggests grief over one's sins. Repentance is to weep over one's damaged condition apart from God. Another word translated "repent" from the Old Testament is *shubh*, to turn, or return. This is often the word spoken by the prophets to the people, to come back to right worship of the Lord. Repentance is not only to feel bad, but to actually turn away from evil. The New Testament terms translated "repent," *metanoeo* and *epistrepho,* mean to change the mind, to make a change of direction toward God. The early church reflected that understanding by asking adult converts questions like, "Do you renounce the ways of sin and the power of the evil one in your life?" Repentance is to decide to leave the old life behind. It results with a radical change that has to do with the whole person. If it is real, repentance always produces good works, or "fruits" consistent with its character.

All through the Bible, repentance is the beginning of renewal, from Isaiah seeing his own sinfulness in light of God's glory to Daniel's prayer for the restoration of Israel during exile. Godly sorrow and turning back start the wheels turning again toward revived destiny. This is what Paul refers to in 2 Corinthians 7:10: "Godly sorrow brings repentance that leads to salvation and leaves no regret."

Conversion is also a positive, a taking-on, an affirmation of Christ's claim on one's life. Paul makes this twofold movement clear in his letter to the church at Colossae:

> Put to death, therefore, whatever belongs to your earthly nature. . . . You must rid yourselves of all such things as these. . . . You have taken off your old self with its practices and have put on the new self. . . . Therefore, as God's chosen people, holy and dearly loved, clothe yourselves with compassion. (Colossians 3:5,8,9,12)

This is a work only possible in us by the Holy Spirit. The work of the Spirit is what makes the Christian feel sorrow and repugnance over his or her sins. It is also what enables that person to joyfully embrace God's will, to move more and more toward it with confidence and thanks. The starting point is with God, not with us. People convert to Christ not because they are spiritually astute or are looking for a new life. People convert because God calls them to turn around. When God gets ahold of people's lives, there is always change — it launches a lifelong process of conversion as God makes his people more and more into the likeness of his Son, Jesus.

Other Voices

"Have I your permission [to kill the lizard that lives on your shoulder]?" said the Angel to the Ghost.

"I know it will kill me."

"It won't. But supposing it did?"

"You're right. It would be better to be dead than to live with this creature."

"Then I may?"

"Damn and blast you! Go on can't you? Get it over. Do what you like," bellowed the Ghost: but ended, whimpering, "God help me. God help me."

Next moment the Ghost gave a scream of agony such as I never heard on Earth. The Burning One closed his crimson grip on the reptile: twisted it, while it bit and writhed, and then flung it, broken backed, on the turf.

"Ow! That's done for me," gasped the Ghost, reeling backwards.

For a moment I could make out nothing distinctly. Then I saw, between me and the nearest bush, unmistakably solid but growing every moment solider, the upper arm and the shoulder of a man. Then, brighter still and stronger, the legs and hands. The neck and golden head materialized while I watched, and if my attention had not wavered I should have seen the actual completing of a man — an immense man, naked not much smaller than the Angel.

— C. S. LEWIS, *The Great Divorce*

[M]ere improvement is no redemption, though redemption always improves people even here and now and will, in the end, improve them to a degree we cannot yet imagine. God became man to turn creatures into sons: not simply to produce better men of the old kind but to produce a new kind of man. It is not like in teaching a horse to jump better and better but like turning a horse into a winged creature. Of course, once it has got its wings, it will soar over fences which could never have been jumped and thus beat the natural horse at is own game. But there may be a period, while the wings are just beginning to grow, when it cannot do so: and at that stage the lumps on the shoulders — no one could tell by looking at them that they are going to be wings — may even give it an awkward appearance.

— C. S. LEWIS, *Mere Christianity*

Deliverance from sin is not deliverance from human nature. . . . God does not make us holy in the sense of character; He makes us holy in the sense of innocence, and we have to turn that innocence into holy character by a series of moral choices.

— OSWALD CHAMBERS, *My Utmost for His Highest*

I was traveling by camel along the track between Geriville and El Abiod, heading for a desert area to spend some days in solitude.

At a certain point along the track I came to a work detail. About fifty natives, under the direction of a minor official of the Engineer Corps, were toiling to repair the road, ruined by the winter rain.

No machines, no technology under the Saharan sun; only the toil of wielding the shovel and pick all day in the heat and the dust. I passed up the line of workmen scattered on the track, replying to their greetings and offering the liters of water in my *gherba* for their thirst.

At a certain point, among the mouths approaching the *gherba* to drink, I saw a smile break out which I shall never forget.

Poor, ragged, sweating, dirty: it was Brother Paul, a Little Brother who had chosen that detail in which to live out his Calvary, to be a kind of leaven there.

Nobody would have detected the

European underneath those clothes, that beard and that turban, yellow from the dust and the sun.

I knew Brother Paul well, because we had been novices together.

A Parisian engineer, he had been working on the Reganna atomic bomb when he heard the Lord's call.

He left everything, and became a Little Brother. Now he was there. Nobody knew he was an engineer. He was a poor man like the others.

I remember his mother when she came to the novitiate on the occasion of him making his vows.

"Brother Charles," she had said, "help me understand my son's vocation! I have made him an engineer; you have made him a manual laborer. Why? You might at least have used my son for what he is worth! Wouldn't it be more advantageous, more useful for the Church to have him work as an intellectual?"

"There are things," I replied, "we cannot understand by mere intellect and common sense. Only faith can enlighten us. Why did Jesus wish to be poor? Why did he wish to hide his divinity and power and live among us as the least of us? Why the defeat of the cross, the scandal of Calvary, the ignominy of death for him who was life? No, the Church doesn't need one more engineer; she needs a grain of wheat to die in the furrows."

So many things cannot be understood on this earth. Isn't everything around us a mystery?

I can understand why Paul had to give up everything — his way of life, his career — for love of God and love of his brethren. But I also understood the reactions of his mother. Indeed, many would say: "What a pity! Such an intelligent person going to work in the Sahara! He could have built a printing press for making available good literature. He could have . . ." And they would be right too.

— CARLO CARRETTO, *Letters from the Desert*

Daily Scripture Readings

KEY TEXT: MICAH 6:8
    Sunday: Amos 5:18-25
    Monday: Psalm 51
    Tuesday: Joel 2:12-29
    Wednesday: John 3:1-21
    Thursday: John 15:1-17
    Friday: 2 Corinthians 7:5-13
    Saturday: Ezekiel 37:1-14

Questions for Reflection and Discussion

Have you ever experienced a dramatic change of direction in your life, whether of values, time commitment, a new relationship, or use of your money? What brought it about?

What do you think Jesus meant when he said to Nicodemus in John 3, "You must be born again"?

How do you think God convinces people of their need for leaving the past behind them and entering into a new life? Has this ever happened to you?

Closing Prayer

Dear Lord, I want to take the time right now to thank you for the new life you've given me. Please help me to live in ways consistent with the new reality about who I am. Let my life radiate with your presence and power. In the merit of Jesus, I pray. Amen.

Week Thirty-four:

A New Way to Live

Opening Prayer

Lord, I commit myself anew this day to live for your purposes in the world. Teach me what it is to live authentically, joyfully, obediently, witnessing to you in everything I do. Amen.

Heidelberg Questions

QUESTION 92: What does the Lord say in his law?

God spoke all these words:

The First Commandment

I am the LORD your God, who brought you out of Egypt, out of the land of slavery. You shall have no other gods before me.

The Second Commandment

You shall not make for yourself an idol in the form of anything in heaven above or on the earth beneath or in the waters below. You shall not bow down to them or worship them; for I, the LORD your God, am a jealous God, punishing the children for the sin of the fathers to the third and fourth generation of those who hate me, but showing love to a thousand generations of those who love me and keep my commandments.

The Third Commandment

You shall not misuse the name of the LORD your God, for the LORD will not hold anyone guiltless who misuses his name.

The Fourth Commandment

Remember the Sabbath day by keeping it holy. Six days you shall labor and do all your work, but the seventh day is a Sabbath to the LORD your God. On it you shall not do any work, neither you, nor your son or daughter, nor your manservant or maidservant, nor your animals, nor the alien within your gates. For in six days the LORD made the heavens and earth, the sea, and all that is in them, but he rested on the seventh day. Therefore the LORD blessed the Sabbath day and made it holy.

The Fifth Commandment

Honor your father and your mother, so that you may live long in the land the LORD your God is giving you.

The Sixth Commandment

You shall not murder.

The Seventh Commandment

You shall not commit adultery.

The Eighth Commandment

You shall not steal.

The Ninth Commandment

You shall not give false testimony against your neighbor.

The Tenth Commandment

You shall not covet your neighbor's house. You shall not covet your neighbor's wife, or his manservant or maidservant, his ox or donkey, or anything that belongs to your neighbor.[1]

(*[1]Exodus 20:1-17; Deuteronomy 5:6-21*)

QUESTION 93: How are these commandments divided?

Into two tables. The first has four commandments, teaching us what our relation to God should be. The second has six commandments, teaching us what we owe our neighbor.[1]

(*[1]Matthew 22:37-39*)

QUESTION 94: What does the Lord require in the first commandment?

That I, not wanting to endanger my very salvation, avoid and shun all idolatry,[1] magic, superstitious rites,[2] and prayer to saints or to other creatures.[3]

That I sincerely acknowledge the only true God,[4] trust him alone,[5] look to him for every good thing[6] humbly[7] and patiently,[8] love him,[9] fear him,[10] and honor him[11] with all my heart.

In short, that I give up anything rather than go against his will in any way.[12]

(*[1]1 Corinthians 6:9-10; 10:5-14; 1 John 5:21; [2]Leviticus 19:31; Deuteronomy 18:9-12; [3]Matthew 4:10; Revelation 19:10; 22:8-9; [4]John 17:3; [5]Jeremiah 17:5,7; [6]Psalm 104:27-28; James 1:17; [7]1 Peter 5:5-6; [8]Colossians 1:11; Hebrews 10:36; [9]Matthew 27:37 (Deuteronomy 6:5); [10]Proverbs 9:10; 1 Peter 1:17; [11]Matthew 4:10 (Deuteronomy 6:13); [12]Matthew 5:29-30; 10:37-39*)

QUESTION 95: What is idolatry?

Idolatry is having or inventing something in which one trusts in place of or alongside of the only true God, who has revealed himself in his Word.[1]

(*[1] 1 Chronicles 16:26; Galatians 4:8-9; Ephesians 5:5; Philippians 3:19*)

Exposition

I leaned over the rail with the sign that read, "KEEP BACK FROM CAGE." With my head against the bars of the cage, I could gain a better vantage point to watch the spider monkeys, and besides, the cool metal felt good against my cheeks. My dad and mom weren't saying anything. They had enough distractions with my three brothers tugging at their arms, tired after a day at the San Diego Zoo.

Without any warning, something snatched the glasses from my face. Surprised and angry, I blurted, "Hey!"

My younger brother Jay was laughing and pointing. "Look, the monkey took Randy's glasses!" There it was, the wretched animal swinging from the rafters of its atrium, prattling excitedly over its prize. Others tried to swoop in and take my glasses from it, eliciting indignant snarls from the thief.

Dad ran and got a zookeeper, who came back in a moment with a hose. "Got your glasses, did he? How did that happen — did you give them to him?" I looked at him through a haze. "No, he just took them." The monkey had swung down to the stained, concrete floor and was clenching the frames in leathery fists, grinding the lenses against the ground. "Now, Coco, give the glasses back. They don't belong to you." The monkey, impervious, continued to grind. I grew frantic.

The zookeeper turned on the water and fixed the spray on the monkey. Water exploded off the bars of the cage and splattered on my T-shirt. Coco seemed shocked at the treatment. He tried to hold on but lost the glasses as they went tumbling across the cage in a jet of water. Another monkey picked them up and skipped over to hand them to the zookeeper. "Good girl, Chloe. But, Coco, you're a naughty monkey." Coco scolded Chloe for her good deed, his chattering joining with the laughter of my brothers.

I held my glasses. The lenses were scratched opaque in the center, growing translucent at the outer edges. They wouldn't be much help for seeing now. But I could read Mom's exasperated expression before me. "Didn't you see the sign to keep back from the cage?"

The sign could have kept me from trouble if I had chosen to be instructed by it. In the same way, the Ten Commandments are a sign that will keep us from woe if we let them. When we pay attention to the sign, we show that we trust the one who put it up, that that person knew what was important for our well-being and intended to communicate it.

It is important to note once again the placement of the Ten Commandments, or the Decalogue, in the catechism. They are not placed in the beginning to show us our sin. Nor are they placed in the middle, as if to suggest we participate in our salvation by living up to them. Instead, they are placed in the final section on gratitude. It is here that they assume their positive place for the child of God as a way to present ourselves as living sacrifices to God.

Further, the biblical accounts of the giving of the Law to Moses tell us that "God spoke all these words" (Exodus 20:1). It is the living God who gives this word to his people. Is there any ultimate measure for right and wrong in our world? Many would say no, but God's Word confronts that notion with a grand affirmation. This stands in contradiction to the relativism of our age, because the first — and last — word belongs to God not to humanity. God's Word is our measure of holiness, of health, of wholeness. God's intentions for his people always have to do with putting away, or dying to sin, and to do with putting on, or embracing new values. Both the positive and the negative are a part of our proper response as disciples. Both together compose an overarching positive for us.

Next we must note the opening words to the Ten Commandments. This section too begins not with *law* but with *grace*. The first words are the preamble, which states "I am the LORD your God, who brought you out of Egypt, out of the land of slavery" (Exodus 20:2). This is no tentative engagement with God's people; there are no qualifiers, no "what ifs." God speaks decisively in the affirmation, "I am your God." Not I will be, if you live up to the provisions of the new lifestyle I'm calling you to. Not I will be, if you prove yourselves worthy of the covenant promises. But "I *am*." Everything else that follows by way of command or prohibition is based on that declaration.

The first of the commandments begins with the demand to worship God alone. Everything in life flows from a right posture toward our Creator. The second shows God's jealousy, not a self-centered jealously of the human kind, but the passion to be loved by his beloved. Indifference on God's part would only indicate that he did not have a heart of love for his people. The third concerns the honor of the Lord's name, which is how he communicates his essence to creation. The fourth commandment is in regard to the Sabbath, the principle of communion with God by which Christians worship and enjoy rest on the Lord's Day, the first day of the week. Six commandments follow that bring order and justice to relationship with neighbor, the last summing up God's will that is in the heart of each of the six: "You shall not covet . . . anything that belongs to your neighbor." Thus the commandments are divided into two tables; the first concerns our relationship with God and the second concerns our relationship with our neighbor. Together they provide order that encompasses the whole of human life. They form the basis for Christian ethics and demonstrate the strong moral imperative of our faith. The aspect of prohibition and of command for each together form the signpost that can keep us out of trouble and enable us to express our thanks to God for the salvation we enjoy.

Question 94 asks what God calls us to in the first command. The catechism discerns four sins that Christians need to guard against: idolatry, magic, superstition, and prayers to saints. It may be that Christians in the West today overlook these temptations as being of lesser danger. Christians in the developing world, however, know that these are vivid perils. In many cultures, foreign elements have been incorporated into Christian orthodoxy. In the West, the danger may be more subtle but just as pernicious. Certainly, our culture has seen over the last two generations a tremendous increase of interest in "new age," paganism, witchcraft, tarot, fortune-telling, Eastern religions, and other nontraditional spiritualities. The church needs to confront these value systems in the discourse of ideas, while reaching out in love and service to the people involved in them. But idolatry? The definition of an idol, after all, is anything that takes the place of God in one's admiration and devotion. Seen this way, traditional North American culture too is clearly burdened by the idolatry of greed, consumerism, and individualism. Idolatry is serious business. If the catechism is correct, then it is a salvation issue that needs all of our vigilance to keep away from idolatry, magic, superstition, and false prayer.

Like all the commandments, the first commandment prohibits a particular sin and it gives a positive instruction for God's people. It is not enough to *not* do wrong, but to do the good God calls us to. The heart of the first commandment is childlike trust. We can live our lives on the foundation that the God who has committed himself to us is the one who knows what we need in order to be whole. More than avoiding idolatry, the child of God places humble confidence in God to provide everything we need, out of reverence, confidence, and love.

Other Voices

The first means [of acquiring the presence of God] is leading a very pure life.

The *second* is remaining very faithful to the practice of this presence and to the interior awareness of God in ourselves. We ought always to do this gently, humbly, and lovingly, without allowing ourselves to be troubled or worried.

We must take care to glance inwardly toward God, even for a moment, before proceeding with our outward actions. Then, as we go about our duties, we must continue to gaze upon God from time to time. And finally, we must finish all our actions looking to God. As time and much labor are necessary to acquire this practice, we must not be discouraged when we fail in it, because the habit is formed only with difficulty; but when it is formed, everything we do we will do with pleasure.

Is it not right that the heart, which is the first member to be quickened to life in us, and which dominates over the *other* members of our body, should be the first and the last part of us to love and worship God, as we begin or end our spiritual and bodily actions? It is in the heart that we should carefully produce this brief interior glance, which we must do, as I have said before, without struggling or studying to make it easier.

— BROTHER LAWRENCE,
The Practice of the Presence of God

Resentment and gratitude cannot coexist, since resentment blocks the perception and experience of life as a gift. My resentment tells me that I don't receive what I deserve. It always manifests itself in envy.

Gratitude, *however*, goes beyond the "mine" and "thine" and claims the truth that all of life is a pure gift. In the past I always thought of gratitude as a spontaneous response to the awareness of gifts received, but now I realize that gratitude can also be lived as a discipline. The discipline of gratitude is the explicit effort to acknowledge that all I am and have is given to me as a gift of love, a gift to be celebrated with joy.

Gratitude as a discipline involves a conscious choice. I can choose to be grateful even when my emotions and *feelings* are still steeped in hurt and resentment. . . .

There is always the choice between resentment and gratitude because God has appeared in my darkness, urged me to *come* home, and declared in a voice filled with affection: "You are with me always, and all I have is yours."

— HENRI J. M. NOUWEN, *The Return of the Prodigal Son: A Story of Homecoming*

To a person of sensitive conscience, a world without this resource of divine forgiveness would be a sheer hell of self-condemnation: how little we did compared to what was needed . . . how only in retrospect did we see issues crying for attention that we ignored . . . how destructive were some of our attempts to be constructive. . . . We know such litanies by heart, and can only be grateful that the mercy of God is more powerful than our attempts at self-justification and self-depreciation.

The good news is that such judgments are not finally in our hands. We are to work, measuring what we do not by the factor of our success but only by the factor of God's faithfulness to us. At the end of our days, the decisive matter will not be that we succeeded, but that we tried. And until that time, we are invited to share in God's concern for creating a more just world, and to recognize, beyond all slogans and theological constructions, that our bottom line is a recognition that "to know God is to do justice," and that "the mercies of God are fresh every morning."

— ROBERT MCAFEE BROWN, *Speaking of Christianity: Practical Compassion, Social Justice, and Other Wonders*

There you have a sure basis for judgment, one that cannot deceive you, when Christ teaches you to know them by their fruit. In my reading about all the heretics and schismatics I have discovered that without fail they all set out to do something different from what God had required and commanded, one in this teaching and another in that. One forbade the eating of certain food, another forbade marriage, a third condemned the civil government, and each set forth something all his own. Thus they all fall into this pattern. It all depends, therefore, on really knowing and maintaining the definition of what Christ calls good works or fruits: a good work is one that is required or commanded by the Word of God and proceeds on the basis of that commandment.

— MARTIN LUTHER, *Luther's Works, vol. 21:
The Sermon on the Mount
and the Magnificat*

Let them go —
the things that have
accumulated through the years.
If they be only things
Then
let them go.
As barnacles
they but impede the ship
and slow
it down when it should go
full speed ahead.
Why dread
the disentangling?
Does the snake
Regret the shedding
of its skin?
When the butterfly eludes
its chrysalis, does regret
set in?

— Ruth Bell Graham, *Legacy of a Packrat*

Daily Scripture Readings

KEY TEXT: EXODUS 20:2 - 3
Sunday: Exodus 19:16-25
Monday: Exodus 20:1-21; 34:29-35

Tuesday: Deuteronomy 5:1-21
Wednesday: Deuteronomy 5:22-33
Thursday: Matthew 22:34-40
Friday: Jeremiah 16:10-15; 17:5-8
Saturday: Ephesians 5:1-5

Questions for Reflection and Discussion

Does a person's motive make a difference to you, as long as they do what they're supposed to? Why or why not? Can you think of a time when somebody encouraged you because you had good motives, even if the results weren't impressive?

What do you think is the image most people have of the Ten Commandments — as positive, negative, or somewhere in the middle? Explain your answer.

What would happen if everybody followed the Ten Commandments? How would the world be a better place?

Why are there two sections, or "tables," of the commandments? What does it say about God's place in our life that the first portion focuses on our responsibility to God? What does it say about ethics that the second portion focuses on our relationships with others?

*Closing Prayer*_____

Dear God, it would be so much easier in life if I could simply worry about myself. But how can I do that when you have changed me from the inside out? There's nothing I can do but to submit to you, to show my gratitude, to bear witness to the reality of your reign in the world. Lead me into the good works you have in mind for me to do and give me the courage to live a life in the adventure of your service. In Christ, I pray this. Amen.

WEEK THIRTY-FIVE: WORSHIP IN SPIRIT AND IN TRUTH

Heidelberg Questions

QUESTION 96: What is God's will for us in the second commandment?

That we in no way make any image of God[1] nor worship him in any other way than he has commanded in his Word.[2]

(*[1]Deuteronomy 4:15-19; Isaiah 40:18-25; Acts 17:29; Romans 1:22-23; [2]Leviticus 10:1-7; 1 Samuel 15:22-23; John 4:23-24*)

QUESTION 97: May we then not make any image at all?

God cannot and may not be visibly portrayed in any way.

Although creatures may be portrayed, yet God forbids making or having such images if one's intention is to worship them or to serve God through them.[1]

(*[1]Exodus 34:13-14,17; 2 Kings 18:4-5*)

QUESTION 98: But may not images be permitted in the churches as teaching aids for the unlearned?

No, we shouldn't try to be wiser than God. He wants his people instructed by the living preaching of his Word[1] — not by idols that cannot even talk.[2]

(*[1]Romans 10:14-15,17; 2 Timothy 3:16-17; 2 Peter 1:19; [2]Jeremiah 10:8; Habakkuk 2:18-20*)

Exposition

In the 1980s, American artist Julian Schnabel rose to the top of a hot art market with his provocative, visceral, eclectic style of painting. One painting, titled "A Portrait of God," caused quite a stir. It featured shattered pieces of crockery stuck on a large canvas that was slathered with bondo and oil paint. Many Christians viewed with suspicion any endeavor with such a title. How can one *portray* God, who is spirit? A best-selling book in our own day is titled "A History of God."[9] How can one write a *history* of God, who is without beginning or end? To some believers, provocative titles such as these practically announce the painter's or writer's intention of alienating believers.

The same concerns prevailed in New Testament times. Contemporary historians tell us that riots broke out in Jerusalem when troops carried the imperial eagle of Rome into the city, because devout Jews saw the likeness as idolatrous.

The first commandment focuses on whom we worship; the second is concerned with how we worship. The first demands that we worship the one true God, and God alone, and acknowledge no other gods beside him. In the second commandment, God instructs that we should not worship him with images or pictures.

Biblical faith worries about the possibility of image-worship, whether of tangible idols or of false mental images of God. The problem with images is that they are a human construct, an expression of the drive to create God in one's own image. To the biblical faith, it is as wrong to make an image of God as it is to deny the existence of God. The faith of Israel and of the church through the ages has not been based on sight or image, but on hearing and obeying the spoken Word of God. Still, people have always been prone to idolatry, from ancient Israel's fascination with pagan deities, to the medieval obsession with relics, to the contemporary syncretistic practices when Christianity merges with indigenous cultures. The second commandment is concerned with explicitly making images to be venerated, but the catechism rightly understands the larger principle to be any wrong worship of the living God.

By implication, then, the second commandment has to do with false ways of worshiping, like devoting one's self to works in order to win salvation and paying empty lip service to God without heartfelt worship. Our worship is to be focused on God, Father, Son, and Holy Spirit. It is to be regular, in public and in private life, by prayer and meditation on Scripture. The invisible God has appeared in visible form through the burning bush, through angelic beings, through pillars of cloud and fire. God has disclosed the divine self through wind and dove and tongues of fire. But these were all of God's own doing. We are not free to depict God through images.

However, in no way does Scripture condemn the visual arts as such. All created things can be depicted by picture. The tabernacle and the temple of the Old Testament were filled with designs and images that enhanced the emotional and the aesthetic satisfaction of the experience of worship. The Lord describes Bezalel as chosen, "filled . . . with the Spirit of God, with skill, ability and knowledge in all kinds of crafts — to make artistic designs" (Exodus 31:1-11). God himself was the one who gifted and commissioned the artist to create objects of beauty. It could be said that this is an indication that artistic ability is a spiritual gift!

The main thing is that such objects are not to be worshiped. That is a dilemma in our time, when the museum has in many ways become the temple of our culture. We are not to worship pictures or to serve God by them. Like everything else in the human experience, the arts are to be subjugated to the reign of God and brought under control of his Spirit. We are free to find joy in the contemplation of a Georgia O'Keefe painting or a Lipchitz sculpture, or in reflection on a musical composition by the Beatles. By the same token, we must be discerning as believers. In everything there is the danger of hero worship, of distorting the gift, and of putting it in the place of the divine giver. There is always the potential that sin can poison the imagination through covetousness or lust. Who knows how much pornography has been justified in the name of art?

The churches of Switzerland form an unmistakable contrast today. The Catholic parishes tend toward the ornate, even in tiny village churches. Yet across the city, and sometimes only across the street, the Protestant churches stand clear and unadorned: no pictures, crucifixes, or shrines. Walls are whitewashed, and in the older churches the windows may be of leaded glass. No means of instruction was to be used in the churches aside from the Word of God. These churches may appear bare to our eyes. To Reformed Christians, though, the beauty of the church is in the lively preaching of the gospel and a vital congregation.

To some, Swiss Reformer Zwingli was an iconoclast; it was his followers who smashed out the windows of the Cathedral church in Zurich, ripping paintings from the walls and statues from their niches. They were sorely troubled that images had taken the place of biblical faith in the members of the churches. Yet it was Zwingli who wrote, "Pictures which are not used for worship . . . I do not reject; on the contrary, I recognize painting and sculpture as gifts of God."

May the Lord of the church help us as we seek to worship him rightly!

Other Voices

And yet I am not gripped by the superstition of thinking absolutely no images permissible. But because sculpture and painting are gifts of God, I seek a pure and legitimate use of each, lest those things which the Lord has conferred upon us for his glory and our good be not only polluted by perverse misuse but also turned to our destruction. We believe it wrong that God should be represented by a visible appearance, because he himself has forbidden it [Exodus 20:4] and it cannot be done without some defacing of his glory. And lest they think us alone in this opinion, those who concern themselves with their writings will find that all well-balanced writers have always disapproved of it. If it is not right to represent God by a physical likeness, much less will we be allowed to worship it as God, or God in it. Therefore it remains that only those things are to be sculptured or painted which the eyes are capable of seeing: let not God's majesty, which is far above the perception of the eyes, be debased through unseemly representations.

— JOHN CALVIN, *Institutes of the Christian Religion*

It is said that Eric Liddell had the most awkward running style of any athlete of his time. Ian Charleson, the actor who played Liddell in the film *Chariots of Fire,* said it was difficult to emulate his running style because he ran with his head back. When Charleson attempted it, he kept running off the track or bumping into other runners.

By the sixth day of filming, Charleson said he finally understood what Eric Liddell must have been doing. He recalled that in drama school he and others had engaged in trust exercises. They ran as hard as they could toward a wall, trusting someone to stop them. "I suddenly realized — Liddell must have run like that. He must have run with his head up and literally trusted to get there. He ran with faith. He didn't even look where he was going."

Liddell stepped away from a great athletic career and the promise of a celebrity's lifestyle in England to become a missionary to China. Once there, he ended up in a Japanese concentration camp where he died at a relatively young age from a brain tumor.

But Eric Liddell lived and died as he ran. With his head up. Trusting. His favorite words were "Absolute surrender" and "Be still, my soul." His final words to his friends were simply "It's complete surrender."

I am quite sure that Liddell would not have chosen to die in a prison camp at a young age. His children were not yet raised, and because of the war, he was away from his family. But he died peacefully, nevertheless. Why? Because he had learned not to ask God questions that arose out of preconceived illusions. Peace came through absolute surrender to the sovereign ways of God.

— GAIL MACDONALD, *A Step Farther & Higher*

When Barth became pastor at Safenwil in 1911, he found the same basic pattern of scant attendance at worship services and disinterest in church religion. In this context Barth began to reconsider the "culture Christianity" in which he had been brought up and in which he had been trained. Sensing the sterility of his own message and his inability to reach his parishioners, Barth struggled to recover an experience with the God who transcends culture but meets us in our culture. From this wrestle came his powerful commentary on *The*

Epistle to the Romans in 1918. From this point Barth's theology was marked by a thoroughgoing theocentricism. In light of the Word of God, he critiqued the idolatry of modern culture and attacked the modern theologies that failed to do the work of exposing it. Barth's later passionate opposition to German National Socialism and his sensitivity to the demonic dimensions of modern culture become intelligible in the light of his personal encounter with the bankruptcy of Christendom at the parish level among the masses.

— WILBERT SHENK, *Write the Vision: The Church Renewed*

What shape is an idol?

I worship Ganesa, brother, god of worldly wisdom, patron of shopkeepers. He is in the shape of a little fat man with an elephant's head; he is made of soapstone and has two small rubies for eyes. What shape do you worship?

I worship a fishtail Cadillac convertible, brother. All my days I give it offerings of oil and polish. Hours of my time are devoted to its ritual; and it brings me luck in all my undertakings; and it establishes me among my fellows as a success in life. What model is your car, brother?

I worship my house beautiful, sister. Long and loving meditation have I spent on it; the chairs contrast with the rug, the curtains harmonize with the woodwork, all of it is perfect and holy. The ashtrays are in exactly the right place, and should some blasphemer drop ashes on the floor, I nearly die of shock. I live only for the service of my house, and it rewards me with the envy of my sisters, who must rise up and call me blessed. Lest my children profane the holiness of my house with dirt and noise, I drive them out of doors. What shape is your idol, sister? Is it your house, or your clothes, or perhaps even your worth-while and cultural club?

I worship the pictures I paint, brother. . . . I worship my job; I'm the best darn publicity expert this side of Hollywood. . . . I worship my golf game, my bridge game. . . . I worship my comfort; after all, isn't enjoyment the goal of life? . . . I worship my church; I want to tell you, the work we've done in missions beats all other denominations in this city, and next year we can afford that new organ, and you won't find a better choir anywhere. . . . I worship myself. . . .

What shape is *your* idol?

— JOY DAVIDMAN, *Smoke on the Mountain: An Interpretation of the Ten Commandments*

Daily Scripture Readings

KEY TEXT: LEVITICUS 10:3
Sunday: Deuteronomy 4:15-31
Monday: Isaiah 40:18-31
Tuesday: Exodus 32:1-35
Wednesday: Jeremiah 10:1-16
Thursday: 2 Kings 18:1-7
Friday: Romans 1:18-23
Saturday: John 4:1-26

Questions for Reflection and Discussion

Is it okay to use an icon while praying? Why or why not?

In what kind of setting are you most comfortable worshiping? Do you like one that seems full or empty? Why? What do you think this says about your understanding and experience of God?

What are ways that the visual arts can enhance our experience in life? Our experience of God? What are some cautions in this regard, lest we fall into idolatry?

Should we use art for teaching purposes in Sunday school? Why or why not? What about a crucifix? An empty cross?

Closing Prayer

God, your Word in Holy Scripture is enough for me. Let me trust you in it and find you in it, ready to instruct me and shape me. I want to be your willing and humble pupil. Amen.

Week Thirty-six:
Honoring God's Good Name

Opening Prayer

Lord, please take this time and meet me here. Open my mind, my heart, and my will to you. Fill me with a reverence for your holy name, because your name is worthy of all honor and praise. In Jesus, I pray. Amen.

Heidelberg Questions

QUESTION 99: What is God's will for us in the third commandment?

That we neither blaspheme nor misuse the name of God by cursing,[1] perjury,[2] or unnecessary oaths,[3] nor share in such horrible sins by being silent bystanders.[4]

In a word, it requires that we use the holy name of God only with reverence and awe,[5] so that we may properly confess him,[6] pray to him,[7] and praise him in everything we do and say.[8]

([1]*Leviticus 24:10-17;* [2]*Leviticus 19:12;* [3]*Matthew 5:37; James 5:12;* [4]*Proverbs 5:1; 29:24;* [5]*Psalm 99:1-5; Jeremiah 4:2;* [6]*Matthew 10:32-33; Romans 10:9-10;* [7]*Psalm 50:14-15; 1 Timothy 2:8;* [8]*Colossians 3:17*)

QUESTION 100: Is blasphemy of God's name by swearing and cursing really such serious sin that God is angry also with those who do not do all they can to help prevent it and forbid it?

Yes, indeed.[1] No sin is greater; no sin makes God angrier than blaspheming his name. That is why he commanded the death penalty for it.[2]

([1]*Leviticus 5:1;* [2]*Leviticus 24:10-17*)

Exposition

In Shakespeare's *Romeo and Juliet,* the young girl Juliet wonders, "What's in a name?" What, indeed? In our day, naming rights are sold to the highest bidder for sports events, stadiums, and civic arenas. In this climate, the intrinsic value of a name has dissipated, and some public personalities apparently give little thought to the integrity of their own names. But to most cultures, a name is what sets people apart and validates them. A person's good name is his or her best endowment. The name, or reputation, says who that person is. It is used to represent the person and his or her perceived worth in the world. Hence the phrase, "to make a name for one's self."

We can hardly conceive of the importance people in Bible times gave to a name. They would almost always accord a symbolic meaning to it. To the people of ancient Israel, a name somehow revealed the essence of a person. Personal names were constructed of words that had their own meaning, and people were very conscious of the importance of names. Somehow, it was believed, a name represented the nature of a person.

The naming of a child had such special importance. The parents would reflect upon their hopes and dreams for the child and their feelings and circumstances at the moment. Often the name they gave their child would express their gratitude to God or the commitment of the new life to God. Sometimes the names described faith convictions, and at times they highlighted physical traits. When he made a covenant with Abram ("exalted father"), God changed his name to Abraham ("father of many"). To show his good intentions toward Abraham's wife, he changed her name from Sarai to Sarah ("princess"). When God granted a baby to the aged Sarah and Abraham, they named the child Isaac, which means "laughter" — his name reflected the joy of his birth. Isaac later named his son Esau, which means "hairy"; he was to name his other son Jacob, the "one who grabs the heel" (the one who deceives). And Moses was the one "drawn out of the water."

Sometimes *El* or *Ja,* the shortened names for God, were added to the beginning or end of a word to make names — thus Elisha, "God is salvation"; Eliam, "God is a kinsman"; Daniel, "God is my judge"; or Eliphalet, "God is deliverance." Hosea was instructed to give prophetic names to his children: Lo-Ammi, "not my people," for his son, and Lo-Ruhama, "no mercy," for his daughter.

We see the expressive nature of names, and the importance the Lord gave them, when he told Peter, "You are Simon; you will be called Peter ('rock')." Jesus saw how a name can express the transforming power of God in a person's life and call them into a new reality.

Place names similarly reflected the character or meaning of a place. Bethel was one of the important early shrines for worshiping God. Its name means "house of God." Beersheba is "well of the oath"; Bethlehem is "the house of bread." En-Gedi ("kid spring") gets its name from the goats that inhabited the high rocky peaks around the oasis. Jerusalem means "foundation of peace."

As nowhere else, there is with God a powerful connection between the name and the person it represents. God's names reveal the divine character. Consider the names for the Father: the Almighty, the Lord of lords, Judge, the living God, Our Strength, Fortress, the Father of Lights, Yahweh, the Eternal One, the I AM, the Holy One of Israel. When God spoke to Moses at the burning bush, he revealed his name as "I am who I am," the One who is present for his people, the One who binds himself to his people in his promise "I am with you." The writer of Psalm 75 declares, "Your wondrous works declare that Your name is near" (75:1, NKJV). The name of God is the presence and power of God with us and for us. Yet today, most have become so casual about God that we have forgotten how to reverence his name.

Christians are those who have been given a new identity by God. We have taken on the name of Christ, living in his likeness — he in us to correct and complete our character, and we in him to be guarded and kept. Compelled by his love, we have submitted to his rule in our life. His name is the one that saves, the one that symbolizes everything we live for. At his birth, the angel told Joseph, "You are to give him the name Jesus, because he will save his people from their sins" (Matthew 1:21). The naming was a consecration and a dedication to God's purposes. His name is "the name that is above every name, that at the name of Jesus every knee should bow, . . . and every tongue confess that Jesus Christ is Lord" (Philippians 2:9-11), "for there is no other name under heaven . . . by which we must be saved" (Acts 4:12).

That is why it is such a grievous sin to take the name of the Lord in vain. God's name is sacred because it symbolizes his person. Therefore cursing, blasphemy, and profanely using God's name are anomalies for the believer. Instead, we are to fear and reverence God's name. Like the prophet Isaiah foresaw, "he will be called Wonderful Counselor, Mighty God, Everlasting Father, Prince of Peace" (Isaiah 9:6). When his beautiful name is on our lips, it must be uttered with reverence. Whether we talk with fellow Christian or curious atheist, our words should clearly show that God is our God and that we are his children.

Other Voices

God is known only where He Himself makes His Name known. Apart from this self-manifestation He is unknowable; from our point of view He is remote, inaccessible. The "Name" is that which is peculiar to Himself, it is that which distinguishes Him from all else. . . . We cannot discover it by the exercise of our own faculty of reason; it is a knowledge which — in the strict sense of the word — can only be *given*. . . .

Secondly, the concept, the "Name" of God, suggests further that God is Person: He is not an "It"; He is our primary "Thou." That which we can think and know by our own efforts is always an object. . . . Even the human person is never truly "person" to us so long as we merely "think" it; the human being only becomes "person" to us when he speaks to us himself, when he manifests the mystery of his being as a "thou," in the very act of addressing us. . . .

Therefore I cannot myself unconditionally think of God as this unconditioned "Thou," but I can only know Him in so far as He Himself, by His own action, makes Himself known to me.

— EMIL BRUNNER,
Dogmatics

What God is is perhaps above human understanding, but not *that* God is. For many of the wise have got so far as to have no doubt of the existence of God, though there have been some who attributed divinity to many beings — through their limited understanding, no doubt, which did not venture to attribute to one and only one being the great power and majesty that they saw must belong to divinity. . . .

Furthermore, *what* God is, we have just as little knowledge of from ourselves as a beetle has of what man is. Nay, this infinite and eternal divine is much farther separated from man than man is from the beetle because a comparison between any kinds of created things can more properly be made than between any created thing and the Creator, and all perishable things are nearer and more closely related to each other than to the eternal and unbounded divine, however much you may find in them a likeness and footprints, as they say, of that divine.

Since, then, we can in no way attain of our own effort to a knowledge of what God is, it must be admitted that only by God Himself can we be taught what He is.

— ULRICH ZWINGLI, *Commentary on True and False Religion*

The premise of all that God has ordained, however, is deity, God's freedom and majesty. What good is all our zeal toward God, or with God, or even for God, if we do not consider at all who and what God is, if there is no basic interruption of our zeal by the recollection that God's thoughts are not our thoughts nor his ways ours?

— KARL BARTH, *The Theology of John Calvin*

God will have all, or none; serve Him, or fall
Down before Baal, Bel, or Belial:
Either be hot, or cold: God doth despise,
Abhor, and spew out all Neutralities.

— ROBERT HERRICK, "Neutrality Loathesome"

Daily Scripture Readings

KEY TEXT: PROVERBS 18:10
  Sunday: Nehemiah 9:5-38
  Monday: Psalm 113
  Tuesday: Isaiah 29:13-24
  Wednesday: Isaiah 50:1-10
  Thursday: 1 Peter 1:13-21
  Friday: Psalm 50:1-15
  Saturday: James 5:7-12

Questions for Reflection and Discussion

Why do you think using God's name as a curse has become so common in our culture, whether in conversation, movies, radio, television, or print?

What does it mean to really esteem and honor God? What are some ways you can take God's name more seriously?

Closing Prayer

The world around me resonates with words that puff up self, that injure others, that obscure truth, and that manipulate the weak. Let me speak authentically, letting my "yes be yes" and my "no be no." Help me to recognize and honor the sacredness of your name. In Jesus, I pray this. Amen.

Week Thirty-seven:
Allegiance to Whom?

Opening Prayer

God of truth and justice, let your voice be heard in the world. Let me hear you and respond in ways that please you. And let me speak clearly, congruently, and with consideration. In Jesus' name, amen.

Heidelberg Questions

QUESTION 101: But may we swear an oath in God's name if we do it reverently?

Yes, when the government demands it, or when necessity required it, in order to maintain and promote truth and trustworthiness for God's glory and our neighbor's good.

Such oaths are approved in God's Word[1] and were rightly used by Old and New Testament believers.[2]

([1]*Deuteronomy 6:13; 10:20; Jeremiah 4:1-2; Hebrews 6:16;* [2]*Genesis 21:24; Joshua 9:15; 1 Kings 1:29-30; Romans 1:9; 2 Corinthians 1:23*)

QUESTION 102: May we swear by saints or other creatures?

No. A legitimate oath means calling upon God as the one who knows my heart to witness to my truthfulness and to punish me if I swear falsely.[1] No creature is worthy of such honor.[2]

([1]*Romans 9:1; 2 Corinthians 1:23;* [2]*Matthew 5:34-37; 23:16-22; James 5:12*)

Exposition

My second-grade classmate looked at me with intense fire in his eyes. He wanted assurance that if I borrowed his new baseball bat, I would bring it back. "Do you swear on the *Dog Star*?" he demanded. He would only give in upon receiving my solemn oath.

These two questions of the catechism deal with the taking of oaths. We have already been admonished to take care with God's name. Using his name vainly is a grievous wrong. But these questions and answers teach us that swearing an oath in God's name is not the same as the blasphemous use of God's name, and that it is legitimate for the Christian to make such a pledge. What makes the difference is the purpose and the object of the oath.

In olden times, to speak an oath was to invoke a curse on one's self if one failed to speak the truth or to keep a promise. Oaths were a part of lawsuits and court proceedings, in public dealings and in everyday life. It was common in the ancient Middle East to swear by myriad gods, by the life of the person addressed, by the king, by one's own head, by heaven, by the earth, and by angels. The laws of the Old Testament were not intended so much to limit the common practice of making oaths as to teach the sacredness of an oath, keeping persons from swearing frivolously and from swearing by false gods. The prophets speak against this false swearing. Swearing in the name of the Lord was seen as a sign of loyalty to him. Oaths are an explicit promise, calling on God as witness, as to the truthfulness of a promise made.

Abraham, Isaac, Jacob, David — each of these men swore solemn oaths at one time or another. The apostle Paul likewise swore oaths, recorded in his epistles (2 Corinthians 1:23 and Galatians 1:20), to underscore the integrity of his ministry. Jesus also made a vow when required to by the high priest at his trial before the Sanhedrin (Matthew 26:63). God himself, according to the writer of Hebrews, swore an oath by his own name when making the covenant with Abraham (Hebrews 6:13).

The oath that is permitted is one that calls on God as the one to whom we must make account. The purpose must be to maintain truth, to sustain the good of neighbor, and to uphold the glory of God. He will bear witness to the truth of a promise and will help us uphold it as well. The apostle Paul makes clear that we need to obey secular authorities, as long as they do not demand allegiance contrary to Christian morality. They have been instituted by God in order to maintain order and to hold back lawlessness in human society. Sometimes the Christian is required by a secular state to swear an oath. Taking an oath is allowed when the civil government requires us or when it is necessary in order to tell the truth.

God is the only one who knows the heart. We need to make ourselves accountable, in a broken world filled with falsehood, to the God who upholds the truth. Jesus says in his Sermon on the Mount in Matthew that we are to let our "yes be yes" and our "no be no." He says that anything beyond that comes from the evil one. Not that an oath itself is evil, but that its necessity comes from having to live in a world filled with evil and rife with moral ambiguity. It would not be so if the world were Christian. When Jesus said, "Do not swear at all," he was teaching that the Christian must have at all times an absolute commitment to truth, that every word must be treated with the same reverence for truth as a sacred oath. Yes, oaths may be taken in this broken world, but they are irrelevant according to the standards of God's kingdom.

Other Voices

The Ten Commandments, we have said, are also Ten Promises. And if the sins here are great ones, the promises are equally great.

"I promise," says the Lord, "that among my covenant people there will be no more careless, empty swearing, cursing, and profanity. No, there will be great silences. And when the name of God is spoken out of silence it will be heavy, weighty, full of awe, and full of blessing." I like to think that as the name of God receives its true weight once again, all our other words will be weightier. The world is full of talk that doesn't mean anything; it's only talk, empty sound filling up empty minutes and hours, light as a feather. But if out of reverence for the name of God there is less talk and more silence among us, maybe even our ordinary language will regain weight and meaning and worth.

You shall not take that Name in vain. A solemn commandment. You will not take that Name in vain. A glorious promise!

— ALBERT CURRY WINN, *A Christian Primer: The Prayer, the Creed, and the Commandments*

Too readily, the churches have accepted [the role of chaplain to the culture] as their proper place. At the same time, the churches become so accommodated to the American way of life that they are now domesticated, and it is no longer obvious what justifies their existence as particular communities. The religious loyalties that churches seem to claim and the social functions that they actually perform are at odds with each other. Discipleship has been absorbed into citizenship.

The churches have a great opportunity in these circumstances, however. The same pressures that threaten the continued survival of some churches, disturb the confidence of others, and devalue the meaning of them all can actually be helpful in providing an opening for new possibilities. Emerging into view on the far side of the church's long experience of Christendom is a wide vista of potential for the people of God in the postmodern and post-Christian world of North America. The present is a wildly opportune moment for churches to find themselves and to put on the garments of their calling, their vocation.

— DARRELL L. GUDER, *Missional Church: A Vision for the Sending of the Church in North America*

One stranger way of misusing the name of God is the modern trick of not using it at all. Many, though their hearts may ache for a faith, have so many painful associations connected with the very *word* "God" that they cannot bear the sound of it. The too stern father, the too fatuous Sunday school teacher, the too simpering religious picture, the too dull sermon — all have combined to give the divine name overtones of boredom, disgust, and disbelief. "One word is too often profaned for me to profane it!" some moderns might say, as Shelley said of the word "love." And so they substitute for the Name all manner of evasive phrases — First Cause, Life Force, Cosmic Oversoul, Universal Law. A dangerous attraction of such phrases is that Causes and Forces and the like aren't gods of *justice* — they may have made you, but once that's done, they forget all about you and don't keep tabs on your little habits. Usually, however, the reason for believing in a Life Force rather than a God is less sinful than silly. Question a Force enthusiast, and ten to one he will say, "I can't believe in a God — an old man with white whiskers sitting on a cloud!" As if a Christian above the level of infant or imbecile ever did believe in a God of that sort!

Here we have a new type of word magic — the Name, once tabooed because it was so great, is now tabooed because it is so small. As C. S. Lewis points out, those who think to make their concept of God larger by talking of Ultimate Principles and such are in reality only making it vaguer; they are reducing the good, wise, and loving Being to an abstraction incapable of

goodness, wisdom, or love — and indeed of being too! Offhand it would seem as if there were no harm in a man's inventing his own name for the Almighty, yet in practice rejecting the word almost always leads to rejecting the reality. For words do have one sort of magic — they have a magical power over the operations of our thinking. When we drop the word "God," we are on the way to losing touch with the truth behind it. There is no virtue in not calling upon Him on the ground that he isn't there to answer.

— JOY DAVIDMAN, *Smoke on the Mountain: An Interpretation of the Ten Commandments*

Interestingly, the Essenes (a Jewish sect contemporary with Jesus) had high standards in this matter [of being true to one's word]. Josephus wrote of them: "They are eminent for fidelity and are the ministers of peace. Whatsoever they say also is firmer than an oath. But swearing is avoided by them, and they esteem it worse than perjury, for they say that he now cannot be believed without (swearing by) God, is already condemned." As A. M. Hunter puts it, "Oaths arise because men are so often liars." The same is true of all forms of exaggeration, hyperbole and the use of superlatives. We are not content to say we had an enjoyable time; we have to describe it as "fantastic" or "fabulous" or even "fantabulous" or some other invention. But the more we resort to such expressions, the more we devalue human language and human promises. Christians should say what they mean and mean what they say. Our unadorned word should be enough, "yes" or "no". And when a monosyllable will do, why waste our breath by adding to it?

— JOHN R. W. STOTT, *Christian Counter-Culture*

Daily Scripture Readings

KEY TEXT: DEUTERONOMY 6:13
Sunday: Genesis 21:22-34
Monday: Jeremiah 4:1-4
Tuesday: Romans 1:8-17
Wednesday: 2 Corinthians 1:18-24
Thursday: Matthew 5:33-37
Friday: Matthew 23:16-22
Saturday: Hebrews 6:13-18

Questions for Reflection and Discussion

Can you think of a setting where we may be called upon to take a solemn oath? What is it?

How do you know God is not against the swearing of oaths per se?

What does it mean for the Christian to take God's name seriously and sincerely?

Closing Prayer

Gracious God, no one else in life is worthy of the honor you hold. Help me to reverence you properly with my thoughts, my actions, and my speech. I ask this in Jesus' name. Amen.

Week Thirty-eight:
Keeping God at the Center

Opening Prayer

Almighty God of power and grace, you are the one who makes possible the impossible. Thank you for inviting me to come to you. Help me to make worship the heartbeat of everything I do. In Jesus' name, amen.

Heidelberg Questions

QUESTION 103: What is God's will for you in the fourth commandment?

First, that the gospel ministry and education for it be maintained,[1] and that, especially on the festive day of rest, I regularly attend the assembly of God's people[2] to learn what God's Word teaches,[3] to participate in the sacraments,[4] to pray to God publicly,[5] and to bring Christian offerings for the poor.[6]

Second, that every day of my life I rest from my evil ways, let the Lord work in me through his Spirit, and so begin already in this life the eternal Sabbath.[7]

(*[1]Deuteronomy 6:4-9; 20:25; 1 Corinthians 9:13-14; 2 Timothy 2:2; 3:13-17; Titus 1:5; [2]Deuteronomy 12:5-12; Psalm 40:9-10; 68:26; Acts 2:42-47; Hebrews 10:23-25; [3]Romans 10:14-17; 1 Corinthians 14:31-32; 1 Timothy 4:13; [4]1 Corinthians 11:23-25; [5]Colossians 3:16; 1 Timothy 2:1; [6]Psalm 50:14; 1 Corinthians 16:2; 2 Corinthians 8–9; [7]Isaiah 66:23; Hebrews 4:9-11)*

Exposition

Worship characterizes the church of Jesus Christ like nothing else. No matter what else a church does in its life together, you can be certain that week in and week out, in good times and bad, throughout the years, even when without a pastor, the church will gather on the first day of the week to worship God. I know of a vibrant four-thousand-member church in Seattle whose five Sunday services are usually packed with worshipers. One weekend last year it began to snow, very lightly, and it continued for two days. Seattle is a city where snow is not unheard of, but where there is not a lot of provision for it. By Sunday morning, there was over a foot of snow on the ground, and no cars — including mine — were getting out of their own driveways. I tuned into the radio to listen to the broadcast of the service. Sure enough — even though attendance was but a fraction of its usual number, the service was held. The preacher made reference to many worshipers who had come by cross-country skis; apparently, there were even a few who had tramped to the church in snowshoes.

Worship is the nucleus of life for the child of God. It defines the purpose and mission of the church. In it, we return to God and enter into communion with him and with each other. In it, we are oriented afresh to God's purpose in the world; from the wellspring of faith in worship, we are deployed *into* the world for his service.

Worship is the first task of the people of God. It is where we are encouraged and shaped in our faith. Without it, our words are vacuous and our actions are pointless. Just as the earliest Christians gathered on the first day of the week, so Christians in every time and place since have discovered their identity through the regular corporate act of praising God. The first day of the week had special significance as a way to remember the Lord's resurrection from the dead. His resurrection was a declaration that God had conquered death and the power of darkness. It was a sign of the new creation available in Jesus. Because of that, the first Christian community gathered on Sunday as "the Lord's Day" to celebrate the Resurrection by declaring God's Word and sharing in the Lord's Supper.

The commandment to "remember the Sabbath and keep it holy" is found in two places in Scripture. In the giving of the commandments to Moses, recorded in Exodus 20, this commandment is given with the reason, "on the seventh day . . . God rested from all the work that he had done in creation" (Genesis 2:2, NRSV). God didn't rest because he was tired from the work of creation. God rested so that he could enter into communion with his creation. In so doing, he established the rhythm of creation itself, a choreography of work and play, of talk and silence, of activity and rest.

In the second Scripture passage, Deuteronomy 5, the commandments are reiterated for the people in the wilderness. Here, the fourth commandment is given with the reason, "you were a slave in the land of Egypt" (Deuteronomy 5:15, NRSV). This lets us know that our humanity consists of more than merely what we can produce. Slavery, or unrelenting toil, dehumanizes people. To be what God created us to be, we have to be able to rest and to enter into fellowship with God and with one another. The important thing is not the seventh day mandated in the commandment, but regular ministry of the gospel, attending to God's Word, and public gathering to equip God's people for service. The community had assembled again for divine worship.

With an activity so foundational to our identity as Christians, one where God takes the initiative and calls us to himself, the church needs to do everything in its power to worship thoughtfully and with care. The apostle Paul admonished the church to allow for freedom in a service and yet to conduct its worship "decently and in order" (1 Corinthians 14:40, NRSV). The church has structured its service, then, around a four-part movement that includes gathering in God's name, proclaiming the Word of God, giving thanks to God, and going in God's name.

Every service of worship should begin with the summons to enter into the presence of the holy God. The call to worship is an invitation to be changed. We worship by leaving behind the world and its agenda, by denying ourselves and our priorities, and by lifting God to his throne on our praises. This is the essence of the fourth commandment. John Calvin says in his *Institutes of the Christian Religion,* "The purpose of this commandment is that, being dead to our own inclinations and works, we should meditate on the Kingdom of God — and that we should practice that meditation in the ways established by him." That is, we place ourselves in a position to be transformed by God by leaving behind our self-oriented way of living. We come before him ready to receive what he has for us. Every worship service starts with praise to God offered in words, prayer, or song. For biblically grounded Christians, worshiping God as he directs is of critical concern.

The service of worship centers in the proclamation of God's Word. That is when the Bible is read and explained as God's own declaration of himself and his good intervention into humanity. The church itself is created by the Word of God. The good news is God's offer of Jesus Christ for us, and Scripture is the unique and authoritative witness to him. The service must be anchored in Scripture. If it is not, it will drift into trouble and will cease to have any saving relevance for people. Thus, the tradition of reading from the Old Testament, the Gospels, and the Epistles. After the reading, there is an interpretation of the Scripture in sermon.

The service then moves to the thanksgiving. This is done with prayers and with the singing of praise. In the early years of the Reformed movement in the church, many congregations only sang from the Psalter, or the collection of psalms from the Old Testament. It was felt that that was the form of worship instituted in the Bible; even the apostle Paul, it was felt, endorsed this when he referred to the singing of "psalms, hymns, and spiritual songs," a phrase which itself comes from the Psalms. But to see this is to miss the point. Paul was not emphasizing narrow limitation, but the very opposite: there is a wide freedom to how we appropriately worship God. This is also a time for the congregation to be nourished by the celebration of the sacraments, a thankful remembering of the mighty work of God. Communion prompts believers in their intimate connection with Jesus and with one another. Baptisms help believers renew the meaning of their own baptisms and remind them of their baptismal covenant.

Lastly, the service concludes by sending the members of the church out into service. That is because the core relationships of our lives are worship, community, and mission. They flow out of the three-in-one character of God himself, who is the one worthy of worship, the one who calls us into community as members of his body, and the one who deploys us into mission in his name. This is why Christians need the opportunity to contribute to the needs of the poor, returning a portion of what God has entrusted to their care to show their gratitude to God for his salvation. In a real sense, the Lord's Day service of common (public) worship is concluded only as the people of God get about the work of God in a sinful world and witness to the new life available in him.

The Sabbath principle has to do with more than the church service. The Christian takes that sense of worship into the various areas of life. In the home, Christians are invited to build up their faith by reading Scripture and other devotional materials, singing, praying, and sharing in godly conversation. There are many practicing Christian families, many Christian friends, even Christian married couples who never talk together about their faith. But when we share together in such a way, it turns ordinary time into sanctified time, and conversation opens up to joy and insight into what God is doing in our lives. Too many Christians have neglected the great privilege — and the need — of this glad day of rest. You never know what God might choose to do when you honor the principle of Sabbath that he commands.

Other Voices

We know deep within us that the world is an incredibly busy place — and that our busyness is only getting worse. It wasn't long ago that futurists were predicting that the advent of computers would shorten the average workweek. Instead, people find that on top of the forty-plus hours they work they can continue to be "at work" via cellular phones and laptop PC's. The virtual office of modern technology compels people to take their jobs wherever they go. And go they do — if not physically, then through fax and e-mail. We can close a deal or answer inquiries twenty-four hours a day with instantaneous worldwide communication.

On the home front, the latest laborsaving devices simply raised the standards, as if being a parent weren't enough. Home-baked bread? Sure. Crisply ironed laundry? Sure. Perfectly manicured lawns? Why not? We all *expect* to accomplish more in less time, but instead we wind up with *no* time. A chance to redirect? Use our gifts for God? . . . Gone is a weekly, ever-repeating opportunity to reflect and to reorient our direction. Schedules so dictate our lives that we forget we can choose to change.

— JANE A. G. KISE, *Life Keys: Discovering Who You Are, Why You're Here, and What You Do Best*

Worship is our response to the overtures of love from the heart of the Father. Its central reality is found "in spirit and truth." It is kindled within us only when the Spirit of God touches our human spirit. Forms and rituals do not produce worship, nor does the disuse of forms and rituals. We can use all the right techniques and methods, we can have the best possible liturgy, but we have not worshipped the Lord until Spirit touches spirit.

— RICHARD J. FOSTER, *Celebration of Discipline: The Path to Spiritual Growth*

The clock is my dictator, I shall not rest.
It makes me lie down only when
    exhausted.
It leads me to deep depression.
It hounds my soul.
It leads me in circles of frenzy for activity's
    sake.
Even though I run frantically from task to
    task,
I will never get it all done.
For my "ideal" is with me.
Deadlines and my need for approval, they
    drive me.
They demand performance from me,
    beyond the limits of my schedule.
They anoint my head with migraines.
My in-basket overflows.
Surely fatigue and time pressure shall fol-
    low me all the days of my life,
And I will dwell in the bonds of frustration
    forever.

— MARCIA K. HORNOK,
"Psalm 23, Antithesis"

Madame,

In the midst of your work console yourself with Him as often as you can. During your meals and your conversations, lift your heart towards Him sometimes; the slightest little remembrance will always be very pleasant to Him. To do this you do not need to shout loudly. He is closer to us than we think.

We do not have to be constantly in church to be with God. We can make of our heart a prayer room into which we can retire from time to time to converse with Him gently, humbly and lovingly. Everyone is capable of these familiar conversations with God — some more, some less. He knows what our capabilities are. Let us begin: perhaps He is only waiting a generous resolve on our part.

Take courage: we have little time left to live. You are almost sixty-four years old, and I am approaching eighty. Let us live and die with God! The sufferings will always be sweeter and more pleasant when we are with Him, and the greatest pleasure without Him will be cruel torture. May He be blessed by all. Amen.

— BROTHER LAWRENCE, *The Practice of the Presence of God*

John of Patmos, a pastor of the late first century, has worship on his mind, is pre-eminently concerned with worship. The vision which is The Revelation comes to him while he is at worship on a certain Sunday on the Mediterranean island of Patmos. He is responsible for a certain circuit of churches on the mainland whose primary task is worship. Worship shapes the human community in response to the living God. If worship is neglected or perverted, our communities fall into chaos or under tyranny.

Our times are not propitious for worship. The times never are. The world is hostile to worship. The Devil hates worship. As The Revelation makes clear, worship must be carried out under conditions decidedly uncongenial to it. Some Christians even get killed because they worship.

John's Revelation is not easy reading. Besides being a pastor, John is a poet, fond of metaphor and symbol, image and allusion, passionate in his desire to bring us into the presence of Jesus believing and adoring. But the demands he makes on our intelligence and imagination are well rewarded, for in keeping company with John, our worship of God will almost certainly deepen in urgency and joy.

— EUGENE H. PETERSON, *The Message: The New Testament in Contemporary English*

Daily Scripture Readings

KEY TEXT: DEUTERONOMY 6:4-9
    Sunday: Deuteronomy 12:1-12
    Monday: Psalm 40:1-10
    Tuesday: Nehemiah 10:28-39
    Wednesday: Isaiah 56:1-8

    Thursday: John 5:16-30
    Friday: John 5:31-45
    Saturday: Acts 16:11-15

Questions for Reflection and Discussion

What do you most enjoy doing on a day off? If you could spend tomorrow doing anything and being anywhere you wanted, what would it be?

Describe when corporate worship has been most meaningful for you. What made the difference?

What are some ways a Christian can prepare for the experience of Sunday morning worship?

How are you in keeping Sabbath in your own life?

Closing Prayer

Lord, I long to worship you. When I take the Sabbath principle seriously, I find that I am more healthy and whole, more connected with the ground of my being. Teach me to worship as you command, and help me to make that a consistent priority in my life. Amen.

Week Thirty-nine:
Honoring Our Parents

Opening Prayer

You have given me a great gift, O God, in those who have taught me and cared for me in life. Let me show my gratitude, and to honor them as you want me to. Amen.

Heidelberg Questions

QUESTION 104: What is God's will for you in the fifth commandment?

That I honor, love, and be loyal to my father and mother and all those in authority over me; that I obey and submit to them, as is proper, when they correct and punish me;[1] and also that I be patient with their failings[2] — for through them God chooses to rule us.[3]

([1]*Exodus 21:17; Proverbs 1:8; 4:1; Romans 13:1-2; Ephesians 5:21-22; 6:1-9; Colossians 3:18–4:1; [2]Proverbs 10:10; 23:22; 1 Peter 2:18; [3]Matthew 22:21; Romans 13:1-8; Ephesians 6:1-9; Colossians 3:18-21)*

Exposition

Our three-year-old daughter had angrily thrown her Dr. Seuss books across the living room floor. She screwed her face into a belligerent mask when I told her to pick them up. "You can't make me!" she shouted. Her tiny figure looked so futilely defiant that I had to stifle a laugh. "Oh, yes I can!" Evelyne and I had learned from experience not to teach them that disobedience is cute. There were better, more appropriate ways for a three-year-old to express her individuality.

We spend our lives in the tension between the commandment to honor father and mother and what is expressed in Genesis 2:24: "For this reason a man will leave his father and mother and be united to his wife, and they will become one flesh." In other words, we strive to live with proper respect due to those in authority over us, beginning with our parents, and yet to properly grow into maturity as adults.

This commandment begins what is known as the "second table of the law." The first four commandments focused on our relationship with God. The last six focus on our social relationships, or how allegiance to God is translated into the arena of relationships with others. Not surprisingly, the first commandment of this section addresses our duty to our parents as the primal relationship in life. It has to do with all who fill the role of parent to child, whether grandparents, stepparents, adoptive parents, or other caretaker relatives.

What do we owe the persons who play this role in our lives? The first thing is honor. Perhaps in our culture today, one doesn't often hear of honor, except in the military or in cynical terms. This consists of esteeming someone, of counting them worthy of respect. The Bible tells us that modesty and respect are due older persons from the younger. We are quick to jump in to counter this admonition with mental objections — "What about when a person isn't *worthy* of honor? What about when a parent tells a child to do something against God's commands?" Though cases of bad parenting are easy to find, that doesn't undo our responsibility of showing respect. It is worth noting that the command is not to *obey* parents in all things. God's commands take precedence above all other authority.

We are to show love for our parents. The scriptural understanding of love is not the same as sentiment. It is not necessarily feeling good about the person we love. It is working to bring about the best for another person, recognizing their worth before God. We owe this kind of love toward our parents, partly out of gratitude for the care they have shown us and partly because they represent the order instated by God for human society. We are to show faithfulness, patience, and obedience toward them.

As with many of the commandments, this goes against the grain in our society. We live in a permissive age. Since the social revolution of the 1960s, it has been considered fashionable to rebel against parental authority. A young person today who resists social pressure by saying, "my parents don't allow me to do that," makes him or herself the object of derision.

But the overriding characteristic of Jesus' ministry was doing the will of the Father. He claimed to only do what the Father told him to do: "I do nothing on my own but speak just what the Father has taught me. . . . I always do what pleases him" (John 8:28-29). He submitted to the Father's will even when he had to do it at great personal cost on the cross: "My Father, if it is possible, may this cup be taken from me. Yet not as I will, but as you will" (Matthew 26:39). Knowing that his highest allegiance was owed to the heavenly Father, he nevertheless submitted himself to his earthly father and mother: "Then he went down to Nazareth with them and was obedient to them" (Luke 2:51).

It has pleased God to guide us by the hand of our parents and others in authority over us. Often, people think that growing up means total independence, even overthrow of parental control. The Bible makes clear that with all relationships, the authority and commands of God take precedence. Still, as God's appointed representatives, parents deserve our respect and honor.

Other Voices

The Japanese Haiku probed my heart with particular poignancy:
Seeing my birth cord
Kept at our old
Native place . . .
New Year's day I wept.

Whence these tears? For the security of childhood too long forgotten? Or for the tragedy of being born? It could well be both, for tears are never simple things nor life an open book.

I do know this. We spend the greater part of early life attempting to throw off the cocoon of birth and adolescence. There is an unreasonable urge to escape the influence and structures of our nativity, longing for the bright wings of individuality and unhindered self-expression. I fear that our age has made this urge a privilege, if not a demand. With dispassionate skill, the therapist enters in to probe the agonizing core of one's being until the new self emerges, freed from the traumas of parental love gone awry. Healing from old wounds is necessary, but where is the birth-cord?

The stewardship of life is a gift to us, and if we have despised this birthright, we would do well to weep for the birth-cord of our nativity. These are good tears.

— RAY ANDERSON, *Soulprints:*
Personal Reflections on
Faith, Hope, and Love

We were privileged to have, for ten years, a son who filled our lives with love, excitement, and humor. Jeff died a few days short of his tenth birthday, after a three-month fight with cancer. Although the pain of his death is still with us, the sting of the loss has lessened with time.

One evening, lying on the living room sofa (which had been his bed for a month), Jeff suddenly said to Judy, "Mom, I'm going to die! Mom, I'm going to die!"

Jack sat down on the bed next to him to try to comfort him.

"Dad," Jeff said, "I'm going to die!"

"I know, Jeff," Judy said.

"Is that okay? How long will it take?" he asked.

Throughout his illness, Jeff was very much aware of his closeness to God and totally secure in the love of Jesus Christ as his Savior. We assured him that we were ready to let him go and that he would be in the arms of Jesus, all of us sensing that this would be the last evening we would spend together as a family. Calmed by that reassurance, Jeff's anxiety quickly departed. That night our little boy died, peacefully, in his sleep.

A few days after Jeff's death, we were cleaning out the drawers of his dresser. There we found a little green Gideon New Testament in the back pocket of a pair of his jeans. Inside the front cover he had written, "I LOVE GOD!" When we opened the Bible, we found a note he had written sometime before he became ill. In his childish writing, it said, "I love you, Mom and Dad, even when you get mad at me. I will always love you."

That was a gift of unconditional love from him to us.

Even as we write this, some twenty years later, we still feel the sadness of our loss. And yet we know the healing that has come from our healer. We have learned that surely it takes a special touch of God's grace for us to be able to choose faith over despair when we are caught in the middle of a painful situation. But it is important to hold on to his promises, to know that God cares.

An enduring HOPE DEFEATS the despair of pain,

An enduring FORGIVENESS DEFLATES the power of pain,

An enduring PATIENCE DISCLAIMS the permanence of pain,

An enduring FAITH DISTILLS the potency of pain,

An enduring PEACE DELIVERS from the grip of pain!

— JUDITH AND JACK BALSWICK,
*Families in Pain: Working
Through the Hurts*

Why do I remember with such pain going to sit in Mother's lap one day when she had someone in for tea, and she pushed me down, gently, and said in her quiet, just slightly Southern voice, "You're too old to sit on my lap now." . . .

Oh, we had our clashes, Mother and I, we're both temperamental enough for that. During school or college holidays I wanted to write or read or paint or play the piano when Mother wanted me to be social. I could not be for her the gracious and graceful young woman she dreamed of. Nevertheless, I often heard her say that one belief in which she never faltered was that I had been born for a special purpose, and this belief led her to set up impossible standards for me, and when I failed to live up to them she would scold. It sounds as though her expectations put an intolerable burden on me, but somehow she managed to keep them from doing so, and it has been only in the past years that she has referred to them frequently.

— MADELEINE L'ENGLE, *The Summer of the Great-Grandmother*

[The musical *Fiddler on the Roof*] raises the issue of honor and reverence for parents. Yente, the village *shadkhan* ("matchmaker"), tells Golde, "Ah, children, children! They are your blessing in your old age." Though, as the story turns out, this was somewhat wishful thinking on Yente's part, nevertheless the importance of honoring father and mother is as old as Moses and the Moral Law itself. An inspired Hebrew sage once wrote, "Children's children are a crown to the aged, and parents are the pride of their children" (Proverbs 17:6). Building on this theme, the rabbis of old taught, "Whoever hears a section of the Torah from his grandson is considered as hearing it at Mount Sinai on the day of Revelation" (Jerusalem Talmud, Shabbat 1:2).

— MARVIN R. WILSON, *Our Father Abraham: Jewish Roots of the Christian Faith*

It should be obvious by now that your daughter can tell what is real and what isn't. You can't hide from such a relationally intuitive machine as an adolescent girl who

cares for you. How we fathers deal with our inner lives reveals the core honesty of our faith. Your daughter knows you well, and she loves you anyway. She can tell if you play at faith or if you really mean it. She can see if your prayers, your involvement in Christian activities, and your convictions flow from a soul that has been taken captive by the overwhelming grace of God. As author and speaker Brennan Manning has said, she will take notice if your heart has been "seized by the power of a great affection."

To live an authentic life means that you strive to live as one set free. Fear and failure can be your most strident adversaries when you empower them by concealment and denial. To live out authentic faith, you must consistently dredge the depths of your heart, experiences, values, and relationships. You must willingly present whatever you find to the God who quietly waits with healing compassion and fierce mercy.

— CHAP AND DEE CLARK, *Daughters and Dads: Building a Lasting Relationship*

Daily Scripture Readings

KEY TEXT: EXODUS 20:12
  Sunday: Proverbs 1:1-19
  Monday: 1 Peter 2:13-25
  Tuesday: Proverbs 31:1-9
  Wednesday: 1 Samuel 3:10-21
  Thursday: Ephesians 6:1-4
  Friday: Matthew 15:1-9
  Saturday: Luke 15:11-32

Questions for Reflection and Discussion

Tell about your parents, whether biological or adoptive. When you were very young, when was it easiest to obey them? When was it hardest?

What are some of the authority figures in our society? How do these impact your life?

What advice would you give a Christian young person who wants to honor his or her nonChristian parents, but who can see them making bad personal choices?

What do you see as the primary duty of children to parents? Of parents to children?

Closing Prayer

Lord, bless and keep my parents and brothers and sisters and children in the faith. Keep them in your love and give them many years of blessing. In Jesus' name, amen.

Week Forty:
Loving My Neighbor

Opening Prayer

Gracious God, the world is so much in need of love. As far as the world is from your ways, you still love it. Please fill me so much with your love that showing care for others becomes second nature with me. I won't be able to do it without you!

Heidelberg Questions

Question 105: What is God's will for you in the sixth commandment?

I am not to belittle, insult, hate, or kill my neighbor — not by my thoughts, my words, my look or gesture, and certainly not by actual deeds — and I am not to be party to this in others;[1] rather, I am to put away all desire for revenge.[2]

I am not to harm or recklessly endanger myself either.[3]

Prevention of murder is also why government is armed with the sword.[4]

([1]*Genesis 9:6; Leviticus 19:17-18; Matthew 5:21-22; 26:52;* [2]*Proverbs 25:21-22; Matthew 18:35; Romans 12:19; Ephesians 4:26;* [3]*Matthew 4:7; 26:52; Romans 13:11-14;* [4]*Genesis 9:6; Exodus 21:14; Romans 13:4*)

Question 106: Does this commandment refer only to killing?

By forbidding murder God teaches us that he hates the root of murder: envy, hatred, anger, vindictiveness.[1]

In God's sight all such are murder.[2]

([1]*Proverbs 14:30; Romans 1:29; 12:19; Galatians 5:19-21; 1 John 2:9-11;* [2]*1 John 3:15*)

Question 107: Is it enough then that we do not kill our neighbor in any such way?

No. By condemning envy, hatred, and anger God tells us to love our neighbors as ourselves,[1] to be patient, peace-loving, gentle, merciful, and friendly to them,[2] to protect them from harm as much as we can, and to do good even to our enemies.[3]

[[1]*Matthew 7:12; 22:39; Romans 12:10;* [2]*Matthew 5:3-12; Luke 6:36; Romans 12:10,18; Galatians 6:1-2; Ephesians 4:2; Colossians 3:12; 1 Peter 3:8;* [3]*Exodus 23:4-5; Matthew 5:44-45; Romans 12:20-21 (Proverbs 25:21-22)]*

Exposition

Notice the order of commandments 6 through 9: they have to do with protecting, respectively, our neighbor's life, family, property, and good name. Yet, more than merely being concerned with our *rights,* these commandments help us to live in right *relationship.* Relationship shapes our ethics, or our way of dealing with each other.

Christians have wrestled with the issues of the death penalty, with justifiable war, and with self-defense. The commandment does not explicitly deal with any of these, but only with murder, the taking of another's life. There are many ways of destroying a life. Not only is that done by direct violence, but also by more subtle means, by the subterfuge that overlooks another's needs. When Jesus spoke to this commandment, when he taught his disciples in what we call his "Sermon on the Mount," he made explicit what was already implicit in the command. He told them, "You have heard that it was said . . . 'Do not murder.' . . . But I tell you that anyone who is angry with his brother will be subject to judgment" (Matthew 5:21-22). Murder grows out of speaking evil against our neighbor, of hatred, of insult, of vengefulness.

This commandment tells of God's concern not only for others, but also for us. God is against injury to self as well as to another, as a violation against the intrinsic value of each life. We are not to withhold from others or from ourselves rest, shelter, food, or anything else we need for life and health. We are not to overindulge or mutilate our bodies. Scripture does not name suicide as an unforgivable sin. When despair or mental imbalance drives a person to take his or her own life, that person is to be pitied. Still, suicide is not ever a valid option for the Christian, for our lives are not our own. They belong to God.

We live in a world of conflict, ready to boil over at any moment, from Northern Ireland to Guatemala, from East Timor to Bosnia. We see violence not only on a global scale, but also on the personal level, in our own inner cities and civic centers and in prosperous suburbs, on our freeways and on our school playgrounds. Why should it surprise us? We engender a language of confrontation, calling disputes over values in the public arena "cultural wars." We talk about corporate "headhunters," or about "going for the kill." Our children watch hundreds of televised murders a year and revel in the thrill of slaughtering opponents in computerized games. In the midst of this insanity, the bracing, simple Word of God still stands as a touchstone: "You shall not kill."

Killing is committed not just with physical weapons. It is done by thought, by words of contempt, by mocking and belittling. It is done by inciting violence toward another. Its root is unrighteous anger, hatred, envy, and desire for revenge. God hates all of these unholy desires and sees them on a par with secret murder. But the commandment goes further than the prohibition against murder, claims the catechism.

It is not enough merely to not injure our neighbor. We have the responsibility to actively care for our neighbor's needs, to behave toward him in accordance with the will of God, regardless of that person's nationality, religion, moral standards, or any other distinction. We are to "love our neighbor as ourselves," demonstrating patience, peace, meekness, mercy, and kindness. We are to do good even to our enemies. This kind of brave, costly stance toward those unable or unwilling to repay us is the measure of our Christian obedience. Love toward our enemies is more than simply holding back from paying back.

Other Voices

It is my task to discuss the gift of freedom, and to do so with the foundation of evangelical ethics in view. Let me anticipate the solution to the problem inherent in this theme in three summary propositions. This first describes the freedom which *God* Himself possesses; the second delineates it as the gift bestowed by God upon *man*; the third relates the consequences of these two to the problem of the foundation of evangelical *ethics*.

First: *God's* freedom *is His very own*. It is the sovereign grace wherein God chooses to commit Himself to man. Thereby God is Lord as *man's* God.

Secondly: *Man's freedom is his as the gift of God*. It is the joy wherein man appropriates God's election. Thereby man is God's creature, His partner, and His child as *God's* man.

Thirdly: Evangelical ethics is the reflection upon the *divine call to human action* which is implied by the gift of freedom.

— KARL BARTH, *The Humanity of God*

As money and power produce more competent forms of violence against human beings in the world, Christians need to reflect anew on the meaning of the cross for their identity in the world. The cross points to the violence of human beings and of their social institutions. North American churches must find God on the cross — the symbol of divine nearness to places of pain and violent rejection. Mainline churches that rediscover their identity in the cross willingly surrender their lives by taking on the burdens and struggles of suffering and abandoned people. Christians who seek the Crucified Lord in society will find him with the socially abused, the murdered, the racially hated, and the economically destitute of an ever more familiar global context.

— HAROLD J. RECINOS, *Who Comes in the Name of the Lord?*

One member of our group decided to try an experiment. He found an old Bible and a pair of scissors, and he cut out of that Bible every single reference to the poor. It took him a very long time. When he came to Amos and read, "Let justice roll down like waters, and righteousness like an ever-flowing stream," he cut it out. When he came to Isaiah, and he heard the prophet say, "Is not this the fast that I choose . . . to let the oppressed go free . . . ?" he cut it right out. All of the Psalms in which God is seen as the deliverer of the poor just disappeared.

In the New Testament, when he came to the Song of Mary — which promised, "The mighty will be put down from their thrones, the lowly exalted, the poor filled with good things, and the rich sent empty away" — he cut it out. You can imagine what happened to Matthew 25. He cut out Jesus' Nazareth manifesto in Luke 4: "The Spirit of the Lord is upon me, because he has anointed me to preach good news to the poor. He has sent me to proclaim release to the captives and recovery of sight to the blind, to set at liberty all those who are oppressed, and to proclaim the acceptable year of the Lord." It was all cut out. "Blessed are the poor" and "Blessed are the poor in spirit" — they were gone, too. All the beatitudes had to go.

When he was all through, the Bible was literally in shreds. It wouldn't hold together; it was falling apart in our hands.

I used to take that old Bible with me to preach. I'd hold it high above American congregations and say, "My friends, this is the American Bible — full of holes from all that we have cut out." Evangelicals and liberals, Protestants and Catholics in America — all have Bibles full of holes. The poor have been cut out of the word of God.

What we must begin to do in our day is put our Bibles back together again, restore the integrity of the word of God in our lives, in our faith communities, and in our world. Our fidelity to scripture will not be tested by our dogma and doctrine, but by how our lives demonstrate that we believe in the word of God.

The good news is that it is already happening. It's already going on. Our Bibles are being put back together. The word of God is being restored in our time.

— JIM WALLIS, "The Second Reformation Has Begun," from *Envisioning the New City: A Reader on Urban Ministry* by Eleanor Scott Meyers, ed.

There is a sense in which [compassion] makes no sense. It is not cost-effective. It does not respond satisfactorily to the administration of goals and strategies, so fondly embraced today by church administrators. In compassion we may march to the beat of a fairly non-institutional drummer. That can make compassion dangerous. We may catch a whiff of anarchy as we draw near to compassion. And yet, as we see time and again in the history of the church, this is precisely what ministry to the marginalized persons will often demand of us.

. . . Compassion is an evangelical ministry. The notion of evangelicalism is something of a religious red flag, of course. It can be a badge of orthodoxy or carry theological associations that mark it as unacceptably conservative. Yet the fundamental image of evangelicalism, that of bringing persons to Christ where they may "taste and see that the Lord is good" and so arrive at their own decisions in the matter of faith, is, without a doubt, integral to the life of the church. It is hard to conceive of a Christian church that would not want to spread the good news of God's compassion in Jesus Christ.

— ANDREW PURVES, *The Search for Compassion: Spirituality and Ministry*

If I cannot see evidence of incarnation in a printing of a bridge in the rain by Hokusai, a book by Chaim Potok or Isaac Bashevis Singer, in music by Bloch or Bernstein, then I will miss its significance in an Annunciation by Franciabigio, the final chorus of the St. Matthew Passion, the words of a sermon by John Donne.

One of the most profoundly moving moments at Ayia Napa came for me when Jesse, a student from Zimbabwe, told me, "I am a good Seventh Day Adventist, but you have shown me God." Jesse will continue to be a good Seventh Day Adventist as he returns to Africa to his family; I will struggle with my own way of belief; neither of us felt the need or desire to change the other's Christian frame of reference. For that moment, at least, all our doors and windows were wide open; we were not carefully shutting out God's purifying light, in order to feel safe and secure; we were bathed in the same light that burned and yet did not consume the bush. We walked barefoot on holy ground.

— MADELEINE L'ENGLE, *Walking on Water: Reflections on Faith and Art*

Daily Scripture Readings

KEY TEXT: EXODUS 20:17
Sunday: Genesis 9:1-17
Monday: Matthew 5:21-26
Tuesday: Matthew 5:38-48
Wednesday: Romans 13:8-14
Thursday: Luke 10:25-37
Friday: Matthew 25:31-46
Saturday: Hebrews 13:1-3

Questions for Reflection and Discussion

Do you think the violence in movies or TV should be a problem for the Christian? Why or why not? What does our fascination with violence say about us, if anything?

Do you think the world is becoming an angrier place than before? What is your evidence for your answer?

What might the Holy Spirit be asking you to do to counter the violence of our culture? What can you do, beginning at the personal level?

Closing Prayer

Thank you, Father, for your grace in my life. I want to express my thanks by living ethically and with integrity in all my relationships. Let me make a difference in your world, I pray. In Jesus, amen.

Week Forty-one:
Seeking a Pure Heart

Opening Prayer

Holy God, I live in the midst of a distorted world. We are all, me included, so far from where you want us to be. Thank you for your grace that can transform my life and keep me in purity of heart, thought, and action. In Jesus' name, amen.

Heidelberg Questions

QUESTION 108: What is God's will for us in the seventh commandment?

God condemns all unchastity.[1] We should therefore thoroughly detest it[2] and, married or single, live decent and chaste lives.[3]

([1]Leviticus 18:30; Ephesians 5:3-5; [2]Jude 22-23; [3]1 Corinthians 7:1-9; 1 Thessalonians 4:3-8; Hebrews 13:4)

QUESTION 109: Does God, in this commandment, forbid only such scandalous sins as adultery?

We are temples of the Holy Spirit, body and soul, and God wants both to be kept clean and holy. That is why he forbids everything, which incites unchastity,[1] whether it be actions, looks, talk, thoughts, or desires.[2]

([1]1 Corinthians 15:33; Ephesians 5:18; [2]Matthew 5:27-29; 1 Corinthians 6:18-20; Ephesians 5:3-4)

Exposition

Most of my growing-up years were spent in Southern California. I went to junior high and high school in the San Fernando Valley north of Los Angeles. We were about a four-hour drive north of the Mexican border between San Diego and Tijuana. My family and I used to drive down to the small town of Rosarita Beach, just a little south of the border on the Baja California peninsula, and spend the weekend in a little trailer resort there. The town had its boom time in the 1920s, when U. S. citizens would visit to buy the liquor they couldn't get back home during the Prohibition years. In the decades since then the former glory had faded. Aside from the old resort hotel, the town was mostly a strip of curio stands clinging to a mile of highway that rumbled with the roar of big trucks using compression brakes.

At nearly eight hundred miles long, the Baja California peninsula is the longest in the world, and its climate is among the world's most arid. During my visits there, I was excited by its limitless scale and exotic allure, and amazed by the forlornness of the landscape. It was so bleak and sun-bleached that it seemed to absorb the poverty of the small farmers and shack-dwelling shark fishermen. I was amazed by the erosion, by the endless empty beaches, and by the sheer number of rusted-out cars that dotted the countryside. It looked to me like a wasteland.

I have since come to see our North-American culture as a desert of another kind, a vast wasteland of sexual brokenness. It seems that all of the areas of public debate on morality have to do with sex, or the consequences of sex unleashed from God's intentions for humanity. AIDS, abortion, pornography, homosexuality, unwed mothers, deadbeat fathers — every one of these is a manifestation of our disregard for the seventh commandment. Countless wrecked lives mark the landscape like the abandoned cars that broke down and never got fixed or hauled away. Since the seventh commandment has to do with our sexual lives, it represents an aspect of life that is uniquely vulnerable in the human person. This commandment is intended to safeguard our personal and family lives.

God created us as sexual persons. Our Creator gave sex as a good gift, a part of ourselves that is able to bring great fulfillment, intimacy, and joy. At the same time, when sex is used wrongly, it has the capacity to destroy something precious in us. God designed sexual expression for the context of marriage.

Marriage is for the union of a man and a woman, of body and soul for life. It is ordained of God, as the Genesis creation accounts make clear, and blessed by Jesus (Matthew 19:4-6). His first public miracle recorded by the beloved disciple John is the changing of water into wine at Cana. Though that miracle was a sign of Jesus' identity as the Messiah, it also affirmed the honor of the institution of marriage (John 2:1-11).

God made us as sexual beings, created male and female. He gave us marriage so that a man and a woman could live together in the assurance of promised love, helping each other and comforting each other through the challenges of life and celebrating through its joys. God made marriage as the context for the most intimate human relationships and as the setting where love can grow to its fullest. He made marriage for the birth and care of children so that they may grow to know their heavenly Father. And in some mysterious way, marriage echoes the deep connection between Christ and his church.

The basis of any marriage is trust, showing each other love, honor, and faithfulness. It is to "bear one another's burdens, and in this way you will fulfill the law of Christ" (Galatians 6:2, NRSV). Its bonds are intended to last. There are circumstances where divorce is morally permissible, and even necessary for the safety of one party of the marriage; but divorce is not God's intention for his children. This commandment, then, is an assertion of the value of marriage and family life. It forbids any impurity in married or in single life. Every person is called to a life of faithfulness in marriage between a man and a woman, or chastity in singleness.

Adultery is getting involved sexually with a person who is not one's spouse. The Bible speaks not only against unchaste actions but also unchaste thoughts and desires. The Lord in the Sermon on the Mount says, "You have heard that it was said, 'Do not commit adultery.' But I tell you that anyone who looks at a woman lustfully has already committed adultery with her in his heart" (Matthew 5:27-28). Jesus is saying that the heart is the source of the problem, not simply outer acts. Why is this of such concern? Because sexual activity outside marriage hurts body and soul. As Christians we are temples of the Holy Spirit, and we need to live according to that reality.

I recently saw in an antique store a fundamentalist poster with 1940s graphics and type. There was a stern warning: "Dancing leads to impure thoughts; which leads to kissing; which leads to adultery; which leads to unwed pregnancy; which leads to shame; which leads to despair." Clearly, the poster was displayed for its "camp" value — it seemed laughably prudish and out of date. Yet, it gave me pause to think. It's easy for our jaded culture to scoff, but who's to say the old fundamentalists didn't understand something important about living the Christian life in a licentious society. It is true that the commandment against adultery implies a positive view of marriage. It is also true that the Christian is defined by more than the list of what we *don't* do ("no smoking, no drinking, no dancing, no movies"). But unless Christians understand that we are *not* at home in this world and that our values *do* fly in the face of what the world says is good, then we are going to get into moral trouble. Is it any wonder our land is such a wilderness?

So what do we do? It is of no help to berate ourselves or shame ourselves for the ways we have failed sexually. Instead, we can see this area of need as an opportunity for God to show his grace and power in us. If we confess our sins; if we establish good disciplines and fill our hearts with the presence of God; if we get involved with a same-sex group of believers who can get to know us and encourage us and hold us accountable in our Christian walk — if we do these things, then we will have healing and strength to be who God is calling us to be.

Other Voices

We are incomparably stupid when we do
    not strive to know who we are,
but limit ourselves to considering only
    roughly these bodies.
We have heard and, because faith tells us
    that we have souls, we know.
But seldom do we consider the precious
    things that can be found in this soul
or Who dwells in it or its high value.
Consequently, little effort is made to pre-
    serve its beauty.

↜

All our attention is taken up with the
    plainness of the diamond's setting
or the outer walls of the castle; that is, with
    these bodies of ours.
We must consider our very souls to be like
    a castle made out of a diamond
or of very clear-cut crystal in which there
    are many dwellings.
The soul of the just person is nothing else
    but a paradise where God finds delight.

↜

It is like a castle with many dwellings
    places; some up above,
others down below, others to the side.
In the center and middle are the dwelling
    places where
the very sweet exchanges
of love between God and the soul take place.

↜

The door of entry to this castle is prayer
    and reflection.
O God, take into account the things we suf-
    fer on our path for lack of knowledge!

The trouble is that since we do not think
    there is anything to know
other than what we must think of You,
we do not even know how to ask those
    whom we know,
nor do we understand what there is to ask!
    We suffer terrible trials because we don't
    understand ourselves,
and that which isn't bad at all, but good,
    we think is a serious fault.
        — TERESA OF ÁVILA, *Interior Castle*

The struggle for sexual identity is answered
not by becoming sexually perfected, but by
becoming sexually mature. And a mature
sexual identity is born of a mature self-
perception.

    You are not simply a homosexual, het-
erosexual, ex-gay, or whatever. You are a
child of God, bearing His image and
indwelt by His Spirit. You have imperfec-
tions in all aspects of life, but they do not
define you, nor do they rule you. If they
exist, they exist as minor nuisances, not
major bondages.

    And with that understanding came
acceptance. Acceptance is not approval,
but a calm realization that there are parts
of life you cannot change, including your
past, your wounds, your present struggles.
You work on them, to be sure, because
your identity as a child of God gives you a
hunger for freedom from any sort of
bondage. But you don't worry about
them. They've lost their control over you,

including their ability to bring stress and sadness into your life. . . .

And you've learned that the discipline He requires of you is enforced to insure that you do indeed experience nothing less than the best. With that knowledge comes assurance and, at long last, peace.

— JOE DALLAS, *Desires in Conflict: Answering the Struggle for Sexual Identity*

Lord, why should I doubt any more, when you have given me such assured pledges of your love? First, you are my creator, I your creature, you my master, I your servant. But hence arises not my comfort: you are my Father, I your child. "You shall be my sons and daughters," says the Lord almighty. Christ is my brother: "I ascend to my Father and your Father, to my God and your God; but, lest this should not be enough, your maker is your husband." Nay, more, I am a member of his body, he my head. Such privileges — had not the Word of truth made them known, who or where is the man that dared in his heart have presumed to have thought it? So wonderful are these thoughts that my spirit fails in me at their consideration, and I am confounded to think that God, who has done so much for me, should have so little from me. But this is my comfort, that when I come to heaven, I shall understand perfectly what he has done for me, and then I shall be able to praise him as I ought. Lord, having this hope let me purify myself as you are pure, and let me be no more afraid of death, but even desire to be dissolved and be with you, which is best of all.

— ANN BRADSTREET, *Prayer*

Liberal churches pose as more enlightened than the rest of us, adjusting the categories of sin under the delusional lure of being theologically *avant garde*. Sadly, many conservative and many fundamentalist churches either remain silent on the topic of sex or else condemn sexual sins publicly but practice them secretly. Charismatic and noncharismatic churches seem equally vulnerable. We quarrel about the existence of charismatic gifts, but neither side displays (in the sexual area) the sanctifying graces.

The world is not fooled. Embarrassing disclosures of the sexual failings of prominent Christians add to the world's cynicism, not just cynicism about God's church — which would be bad enough — but about the gospel his church preaches, which is far worse. Underlying our failures is the subtle but widespread acceptance by church members of many of the world's views and sexual standards. . . . Inevitably, the world's views impact the private feelings of church members. And it is the secret feelings of ordinary members that matter and that determine their behavior, not public statements of official bodies. As for public statements, a number of churches have now sold out to the world.

— JOHN WHITE, *Eros Redeemed*

Daily Scripture Readings

KEY TEXT: HEBREWS 13:4
Sunday: Proverbs 5:1-23
Monday: Song of Solomon
Tuesday: Malachi 2:10-16
Wednesday: Ephesians 5:22-33
Thursday: 1 Peter 3:1-12
Friday: 1 Corinthians 6:12-20
Saturday: 1 Corinthians 7:1-14

Questions for Reflection and Discussion

Agree or disagree: "Our culture has a seriously distorted idea of human sexuality." Why or why not?

Has the church's view of sex been more often positive or negative? How have you seen this?

Some marriage services ask the congregation to answer a vow of support like this: "Will all of you witnessing these vows promise to do everything in your power to uphold [John] and [Mary] in their marriage?" What are ways you can uphold your friends in their marriages? What are ways you can encourage your single friends to remain chaste in their singleness?

Closing Prayer

Lord, thank you for having made me to be a sexual person. I need your help to submit my whole being to you, so that I might please you in the conduct of my life. Teach me what it is to be pure. And thank you for the example I have in Jesus, and the power I have in the Holy Spirit. Amen.

Week Forty-two:
Content with What I Have

Opening Prayer

Lord, why is it so easy for me to want what I don't have? Let me be satisfied with what you give me and be more concerned with others' needs than my own. Be my teacher today, I pray for Jesus' sake. Amen.

Heidelberg Questions

QUESTION 110: What does God forbid in the eighth commandment?

He forbids not only outright theft and robbery, punishable by law.[1]

But in God's sight theft also includes cheating and swindling our neighbor by schemes made to appear legitimate,[2] such as: inaccurate measurements of weight, size, or volume; fraudulent merchandising; counterfeit money; excessive interest; or any other means forbidden by God.[3]

In addition he forbids all greed[4] and pointless squandering of his gifts.[5]

(*[1]Exodus 22:1; 1 Corinthians 5:9-10; 6:9-10; [2]Micah 6:9-11; Luke 3:14; James 5:1-6; [3]Deuteronomy 25:13-16; Psalm 15:5; Proverbs 11:1; 12:22; Ezekiel 45:9-12; Luke 6:35; [4]Luke 12:15; Ephesians 5:5; [5]Proverbs 21:20; 23:20-21; Luke 16:10-13*)

QUESTION 111: What does God require of you in this commandment?

That I do whatever I can for my neighbor's good, that I treat others as I would like them to treat me, and that I work faithfully so that I may share with those in need.[1]

(*[1]Isaiah 58:5-10; Matthew 7:12; Galatians 6:9-10; Ephesians 4:28*)

Exposition

The eighth commandment is about the integrity of possessions. It is God's Word on the relationship we have with *things*. Behind each of the commandments in the second "table" of the law — the section that includes the fifth through the tenth commandments — is a concern for our neighbor. God cares about justice. He cares about basic fairness in all of our relationships. Now we see that there is a human dimension to *possessions* as well. Christian ethicist Lewis Smedes writes in his book *Mere Morality,* "Between persons and things is a bond we call ownership, and God tells all people to respect that bond."[10]

The first statement of the catechism in this, as with each of the commandments, concerns that which is forbidden. God's Word always includes both a *no* and a *yes.* It always judges the world's wrong standards and it always brings good news of God's grace. The negative word is that we shall not steal, and it has a more expansive scope than we might like to think. Yes, it does have to do with "outright theft and robbery," those things that society has identified as crimes and says are "punishable by law." Stealing is perverse because it infringes on ownership. It potentially robs people not only of objects, but also of identity and power. If you swindle a retired couple of their savings, you bilk them of their future. If you burglarize a woman's CD player, perhaps you're taking a gift from her daughter, which is especially precious to her. If you steal a man's car, maybe you're depriving him of his means of getting to work and providing for his family. But God is against all the ways in which we fail to respect the bond of ownership, no matter how subtle, no matter if society winks at it. Dishonesty has so seeped into the watershed of our values as a society that we no longer are clear what constitutes stealing. Smedes says:

> The commandment confronts a modern culture which accepts greed as a style of self-affirmation and whose systems of exchanging property are so complex that recognizing the difference between stealing and dealing is a lost art. We still know that when a thug snatches a woman's purse, he is stealing; we are not sure whether or not a creative ad writer who woos money from people by seductive lies is stealing.[11]

In other words, we are no longer clear in our own mind what stealing means. The catechism rightly says that God is concerned with whatever breaks the integrity of ownership. This is not to say that we are to unquestioningly endorse existing patterns of have and have-not. God does not justify whatever we happen to possess. If that were the case, there would be no reason to question anything but flagrant robbery. Conversely, there would be no impetus to better the living conditions of the poor. On the contrary, the commandment addresses not only those who steal by breaking the law, but also those who by cheating and twisting the law rob others of their property. The commandment "do not steal" casts the moral net wide: it prohibits cheating, embezzlement, fraud, false advertising, exorbitant interest rates, and any other ways people try to get what belongs to somebody else by manipulation of the weak and unwary. And if the catechism is right, the concern of the commandment is broader still. It is against greed and against the "pointless squandering of gifts." Now we see that it encompasses the notion of stewardship. All that we have is an endowment of God, a trust, and we are accountable to God for how we use it. And yet, we waste natural resources and we mismanage public lands. We pollute our environment as if there is no tomorrow, and we fail to put to use the gifts God has given us. We think we have what we have because of our own intelligence or work or good looks — when we do these things we violate the intention of the eighth command. It speaks against all forms of dishonesty and economic injustice.

The critically acclaimed movie *Dances with Wolves* came out in 1990. It is the story of John Dunbar, a disillusioned Army officer who is sent out West in the 1860s. Over the course of time he finds friendship and renewal with a band of Lakota Sioux Indians he encounters. At one point in the film, scouts from the band picked up and followed the tracks of a great herd of bison. Dunbar is invited to come with his new friends to hunt the animals. He watched the atmosphere of great excitement as the whole band dismantled their lodges, packed their belongings onto the travois pulled behind their horses, and headed out in pursuit of the herd. It wasn't long before the people saw vultures circling overhead. Rounding a hillock, they descended upon a desolate scene: scores of carcasses of bison, slaughtered by white hunters for their hides and tongues. A hush fell upon the shocked Indians. Dunbar's voiceover asks the question, "Who would do such a thing?" It was evidence to the Lakota of a soulless people who cared nothing for them.

According to the eighth commandment, the white hide hunters robbed the Indians of their livelihood. Killing great animals only for their tongues was brazen misuse of a natural resource; all the more so because it was in Indian territory and the main food source for another people. When we deprive people of what they need, we steal from them. We are not to take what belongs to someone else. We are to respect the "bonds of ownership." That is the principle behind such Old Testament instructions like that of Deuteronomy 23:24: "If you enter your neighbor's vineyard, you may eat all the grapes you want, but do not put any in your basket."

That word on stealing and on care for neighbor is critical in an era when the division between have and have-nots is widening. The United Nations tells us that the richest one-fifth of the world accounts for 86 percent of all private consumption.[12] We eat 45 percent of all meat and fish; we use 58 percent of total energy; we use 84 percent of all paper; we own 74 percent of all telephone lines; we own 87 percent of the world's vehicles. It is essential that we become aware of the needs of our neighbors.

What is the positive aspect of this commandment? What are we to do in order to fulfill its intention? Again, the Scripture makes it clear: "He who has been stealing must steal no longer, *but must work, doing something useful with his own hands, that he may have something to share with those in need*" (Ephesians 4:28, italics added). The apostle Paul is saying to the church at Ephesus that the attitude of the Christian is to be more than refraining from evil. We are to make a positive difference, to be industrious in order to help our neighbors. It's not enough to "live and let live." God wants us to do all we can to ensure that our neighbors receive what belongs to them.

Part of the way we do that is through a lifestyle of simplicity. Christians in the Reformed tradition, as well as in some other movements within the Christian family, have held the value of simplicity. They have believed faithfulness entails shunning ostentation. Calvin himself was not opposed to pleasure, in spite of his sometimes dour reputation. (In this way he differed from Augustine, who *did* take a dim view of pleasure. Augustine's position stemmed more from the sexual excesses of his unconverted youth than from a reading of the Bible.) Calvin saw that pleasure was a part of a good creation and that it could appropriately be enjoyed when it came the Christian's way, if enjoyed in moderation. The greed of our culture drives us to excess and compulsive consumption. Richard Foster points out in his book *Celebration of Discipline* that simplicity comes from the heart and expresses itself in outward lifestyle.[13] Purity of the heart is to be uncluttered by worry, anxiety, and complexity. David saw this when he wrote, "Delight yourself in the LORD and he will give you the desires of your heart" (Psalm 37:4). When we help people get what they need to sustain life or grow as persons, we are fulfilling the will of God expressed in the eighth commandment. We act as good stewards who are fruitful and who are faithful with what he has entrusted us.

Other Voices

"To have no opinion of ourselves, and to think always well and highly of others, is great wisdom and perfection" (Thomas à Kempis). "Be not wise in your own conceits" (Rom. 12:16).

Only he who lives by the forgiveness of his sin in Jesus Christ will rightly think little of himself. He will know that his own wisdom reached the end of its tether when Jesus forgave him. He remembers the ambition of the first man who wanted to know what is good and evil and perished in his wisdom. That first man who was born on this earth was Cain, the fratricide. His crime is the fruit of man's wisdom. Because the Christian can no longer fancy that he is wise he will also have no high opinion of his own schemes and plans. He will know that it is good for his own will to be broken in the encounter with his neighbor. He will be ready to consider his neighbor's will more important and urgent than his own. What does it matter if our own plans are frustrated? Is it not better to serve our neighbor than to have our own way?

— DIETRICH BONHOEFFER, *Life Together*

It may seem a quite extraordinary thing that the Bible should take up so much space to speak about weights and measures, and the accuracy of scales and containers and units of measurement. It is intensely significant that the assumption is that God is interested in these things, and that careful justice and meticulous honesty in these things is the natural and essential expression of true religion.

The Bible lays it down that there is something badly wrong with the religion of the man who will worship on the Sunday and who will then go out to be a careless or a dishonest tradesman, robbing others by offering less than his best, or a man in any kind of business indulging in smart practice to make a quick profit, or a clever opportunist using someone's need as a chance to make more for himself, or an employer who is blind and unsympathetic to his employees' needs.

Perhaps we regarded the commandment which forbids stealing as having no relevance to us in our respectability. Perhaps now we may have to open our eyes to the fact that it applies to us too.

— WILLIAM BARCLAY, *The Ten Commandments*

Does your faith make you obedient? . . . Now, sirs, I bear my testimony this morning as God's minister, too honest to alter a word to please any man that lives, you are no Christian if you can act in business beneath the dignity of an honest man. If God has not made you honest, he has not saved your soul. Rest assured that if you can go on, disobedient to the moral laws of God, if your life is inconsistent and lascivious, if your conversation is mixed up with things which even a worldling might reject, the love of God is not in you. I do not plead for perfection, but I do plead for honesty, and if your religion has not made you careful and prayerful in common life, if you are not in fact made a new creature in Christ Jesus — your faith is but an empty name, as sounding brass, or a tinkling cymbal.

— HELMUT THIELICKE, *Encounter with Spurgeon*

Christian service differs from humanitarian work by virtue of its motivation and goal. The Christian is motivated by the love that descends into the depths of human depravity; the humanitarian is motivated by the hope of reclaiming people for a meaningful role in society. The Christian is intent above all on bringing people into a right relationship with God; the humanitarian seeks to instill a sense of self-worth and social grace. Christian service is not simply social service but spiritual care. The care of souls means much more than feeding the hungry and clothing the naked; it involves introducing people to the living Christ who alone saves from sin, death, and hell. The ultimate aim in our service to the poor and needy is to make them aware of their

absolute dependence on God. Teresa of Ávila summed it up in one memorable sentence: "The soul of the care of the poor is the care of the poor soul."
— DONALD BLOESCH, *Freedom for Obedience: Evangelical Ethics for Contemporary Times*

Likewise, we cannot be sent ones unless we are willing to be vulnerable to the ones to whom we are sent. To be in mission means to be in the position of being vulnerable to what others are vulnerable to. It means to be willing to suffer what another suffers and to go with another in his or her own suffering. The words *equality* and *justice* take on their deepest meaning in this context. Mission demands equality and justice. It renounces self protection against the powers that threaten the ones to whom we are sent.
— CRAIG DYKSTRA, *Growing in the Life of Faith: Education and Christian Practices*

Daily Scripture Readings

KEY TEXT: EPHESIANS 4:28
  Sunday: Micah 6:1-8
  Monday: Exodus 22:1-15
  Tuesday: Matthew 25:14-30
  Wednesday: 2 Corinthians 9:1-15
  Thursday: Luke 12:13-21

Friday: Ezekiel 18:1-17
Saturday: Titus 2:9-15

Questions for Reflection and Discussion

Can you think of a time when you lost a valuable possession? How did you deal with that loss? Did anything make up for that loss? If so, what?

Why does the Bible place importance on ownership and the use of property? Aren't people more important?

What are ways that stealing takes place in our culture? What are ways that Christians can better take care of the rights and needs of the most vulnerable in our culture? What might God be asking you to do?

Closing Prayer

Dear God, you have given me all I need. You have told us it is acceptable to enjoy your gifts. With your help, I commit to an honest, responsible lifestyle, one where I look to the needs of others. Amen.

Week Forty-three:
Telling the Truth

Opening Prayer

Lord, I want to be truthful, because you are the Truth. Please lead me in your way this day. Amen.

Heidelberg Questions

QUESTION 112: What is God's will for you in the ninth commandment?

God's will is that I never give false testimony against anyone, twist no one's words, not gossip or slander, nor join in condemning anyone without a hearing or without a just cause.[1]

Rather, in court and everywhere else, I should avoid lying and deceit of every kind; these are devices the devil himself uses, and they would call down on me God's intense anger.[2] I should love the truth, speak it candidly, and openly acknowledge it.[3] And I should do what I can to guard and advance my neighbor's good name.[4]

([1]*Psalm 15; Proverbs 19:5; Matthew 7:1; Luke 6:37; Romans 1:28-32;* [2]*Leviticus 19:11-12; Proverbs 12:22; 13:5; John 8:44; Revelation 21:8;* [3]*1 Corinthians 13:6; Ephesians 4:25;* [4]*1 Peter 3:8-9; 4:8)*

Exposition

The commandments have given us a life-map for navigating relationships. They do more than reflect to us our sinfulness. They do more than maintain social order or restrain evil. They also show Christ's body, the church, how to live with God and with one another. In the first table, comprised of commandments 1 through 4, we see the marks of a right relationship with the God who created and redeemed us. In the second table, which includes commandments 5 through 10, we are shown how to care for one another. They demonstrate the ways we are to preserve *authority, life, marriage and chastity, possessions,* and now, *truth.*

Preserving the truth is a way of preserving relationship. Every human interaction depends on one person being able to count on another. Every personal transaction is at the mercy of trust — of *truthfulness.* Without it, we could not promise our love in marriage; we could not buy a car or a house; we could not teach children in school; we could not engage in diplomacy or establish peace between nations. In order for any of these institutions to long endure, there must be truth.

Just as the third commandment protects God's good name, the ninth commandment protects our neighbor's good name. The commandment builds upon each area where we must express love to one another. Not only life and limb, not only mere property, we have the responsibility to care for our neighbor's *honor* as well. And, as with each of the commandments, there is a positive side to its meaning. It's not enough to not lie. We are to tell the truth, to live the truth; to do all we can to live congruently and to uphold the honor and reputation of others.

But we live in a day when truth is given short shrift, when the idea of an absolute standard of telling the truth seems naive. Lying has become so endemic that it might seem a necessary evil, an oil to grease the gears of polite society, a tool to get what we need in a ruthless world, a protection for self-preservation in a workplace where weakness is not tolerated. We've grown profoundly suspicious of our public leaders and of the whole political process after witnessing time and again the spectacle of sordid revelations of politicians' private lives.

The commandment inserts itself into the midst of this cloud of mendacity and says simply, "You shall not lie." In the narrow sense, the command pictures the setting of the courtroom with its plaintiff, accusers, and witnesses. Because of the damage that a lie can do to the honor, the property, or the life of another, this is serious business. Say nothing untrue, nothing that can damage another person.

But like with all the commandments, the scope of this is more expansive than that. It speaks against any and all kinds of lying, deception, stretching the truth, prevarication, falsifying. Its clarity is bracing; its absolutism is startling: it allows no excuses, and it considers no extenuating circumstances. Whether we try to mislead others or God or ourselves, this commandment is all-inclusive. Do not lie.

Truth telling has to do, in part, with being on the outside what we are on the inside. Jesus had harsh criticism for the sin of hypocrisy, for those who attempted to hide inner corruption behind pious masks. "You hypocrites! Isaiah was right when he prophesied about you," he charged. It is written, "These people honor me with their lips, but their hearts are far from me" (Matthew 15:7-8). To others, he said, "You hypocrite, first take the plank out of your eye, and then you will see clearly to remove the speck from your brother's eye" (Luke 6:42). To be persons of integrity, our words have to correspond with outer and inner reality.

What is forbidden in this commandment? Everything that hurts another person's honor. But there is another aspect to it. It speaks against untruth. Our world has been called "postmodern," meaning that we have moved away from the Enlightenment ideal of rationalism. Things no longer have to make sense rationally. Reason is not the highest virtue. The world is no longer seen as a closed system where only what can be verified empirically is real. Many hold that there *is* no one ultimate reality and that what is real is what I create for myself. A radical subjectivism has imposed itself upon contemporary culture.

In consequence, many people have devised an innocuous, malleable "religion" that affirms who they are already and doesn't threaten by demanding real change. It has an aura of authenticity, but nothing substantial. It is basically an expression of wishful thinking: "I think it ought to be this way." In consequence, we are burdened with moral relativism in public schools, in the universities, in the business world, and in the court system. We manipulate the truth and exalt false witnesses to the extent that we're not only confused as to what constitutes the truth, but doubt that it's even possible to know the truth. Society has become profoundly and persistently agnostic about ultimate truth.

The Christian faith stands in contradiction to this kind of agnosticism. God breaks into our empty speculations and sets the truth before us in a way we can understand. We no longer need to grope in the darkness toward the truth. We are freed from vain speculation or wishful thinking, God has given us a glimpse into the truth. Even though we see in part, we do see truly. It is not an exhaustive view we have, but it is sufficient. We can be grounded in reality because God has been pleased to disclose himself to us in truth.

God's nature is truth. God loves truth and cannot tolerate falsehood. Jesus told his disciples at the Last Supper that "when he, the Spirit of truth, comes, he will guide you into all truth" (John 16:13). God has broken into our falsehood and into our vain speculation and has given us a glimpse into reality.

Other Voices

How much harm is done to the Christian fellowship by words which are carelessly spoken — words which hurt, words which are unkind, words which are cruel. When we are tempted to sit in judgment upon our fellow Christian, we must set a seal upon our lips.

Bonhoeffer calls this "the ministry of holding one's tongue":

Often we combat our evil thoughts most effectively if we absolutely refuse to allow them to be expressed in words. . . . He who holds his tongue in check controls both mind and body (James 3:2 ff.). Thus it must be a decisive rule of every Christian fellowship that each individual is prohibited from saying much that occurs to him.

Where this discipline of the tongue is practiced right from the beginning each individual will make a matchless discovery. He will be able to cease from constantly scrutinizing the other person, judging him, condemning him, putting him in his particular place where he can gain ascendancy over him and thus doing violence to him as a person. Now he can allow the brother to exist as a completely free person, as God made him to be.

— ANTHONY A. HOEKEMA, *The Christian Looks at Himself*

The conception of truth proper to the Christian mind is determined by the supernatural orientation of the Christian mind. When we Christians speak of "the great truths" of the Christian Faith, we mean especially those doctrines describing the meeting of the temporal and the eternal, doctrines testifying to a reality beyond our finite order, which has impinged upon that order and still impinges upon it; the doctrines of the Divine Creation, the Incarnation, the Redemption, the work of the Holy Spirit. To start with this illustration of how in practice we Christians use the word *truth* when we are thinking and speaking christianly is to indicate the full breadth of the chasm separating the Christian from the secular mind.

— HARRY BLAMIRES, *The Christian Mind: How Should a Christian Think?*

We cannot overemphasize the value of a good reputation. As an example, a corrupt lobbyist may be tempted to bribe a certain legislator to win his support for a bill being pushed. But because the lobbyist knows the legislator is a man of integrity and cannot be corrupted by a bribe, he will refrain from even approaching the legislator. The reputation of the legislator is well-known: he cannot be bought; he is incorruptible. And his reputation protects him even from being approached by a corrupt lobbyist.

This is the concept Paul had in mind when he wrote about a Christian being girded with the truth. Because of this quality the believer is spared from the attacks of the Evil One, because the Enemy knows that his efforts would be futile directed toward someone who is incorruptible. Because the child of God — by the grace of God and the power of the Holy Spirit — always chooses the way of truth and sincerity, the adversary faces an impenetrable front.

— J. DWIGHT PENTECOST, *Designed to Be Like Him*

In one of the stories of Flannery O'Connor, a black couple, Ruby Turpin and her husband Claud, are in the doctor's waiting room with a crowd of other patients. Mrs. Turpin is a self-opinionated woman. She is never entirely comfortable until she has surveyed those before her, put them mentally in their places and seen herself rise to the top in doing so. She is in the process of doing this with her fellow patients, when her gaze is met with hostility by a fat, pimpled, nineteen- or twenty-year-old girl. The girl scowls as she raises her eyes from her book entitled *Human Development*.

Mrs. Turpin remarks to the woman next to her that she once knew a girl who had everything a child could possibly want, but was still a spoilt, ungrateful brat. At this point, the book flies across the room and hits her. The girl hoarsely whispers: "Go back to hell where you came from, you old wart-hog." After the doctor, nurses and others have rushed to the scene to settle the girl with a syringe and have taken her off in an ambulance, Mrs. Turpin goes home. But she feels dead inside.

Lying on her bed, the vision of herself as a razor-backed hog with warts on its face haunts her. "I am not a wart-hog from hell," she moans. One evening soon after, she goes out to the pig yard and hurls defiance against the Almighty: "Go on, call me a hog! Call me a hog again! From hell!" A garbled echo returns to her. A final surge of fury shakes her and she roars, "Who do you think you are?"

Then the evening sky begins to burn with a transparent intensity. A long purple streak spreads across the sky. As she looks in its direction, she sees in a way she has never seen before:

She saw the streak as a vast swinging bridge extending upward from the earth through a field of living fire. Upon it a vast horde of souls were rumbling towards heaven. There were whole companies of white-trash, clean for the first time in their whole lives, and bands of black niggers in white robes, and battalions of freaks and lunatics shouting and clapping and leaping like frogs. And bringing up the end of the procession was a tribe of people whom she recognized at once as those who, like herself and Claud, had always had a little of everything and the God-given wit to use it right. She leaned forward to observe them closer. They were marching behind the others with great dignity, accountable as they had always been for good order and common sense and respectable behavior. They alone were on key. Yet she could see by their shocked and altered faces that even their virtues were being burned away. She lowered her hands and gripped the rail of the hog pen, her eyes small but fixed unblinkingly on what lay ahead. In a moment the vision faded but she remained where she was, immobile.

The fat, smug ego is the relentless enemy of God and of the happy life. It has to be put in its place. This can only be done by having a transformed imagination, something that can only come about through a "revelation." Mrs. Turpin has to place everybody in her universe within a hierarchy: "nigger", "white trash", "common", "stylish", "good". She compared them all to herself, rather than to God. She was the measure of her own world. She thought she knew herself very well, but faced with God she realized that she knew virtually nothing.

— JAMES HOUSTON, *In Search of Happiness: A Guide to Personal Contentment*

Daily Scripture Readings

KEY TEXT: COLOSSIANS 3:9
  Sunday: Leviticus 19:11-18
  Monday: Psalm 15
  Tuesday: Proverbs 19:1-9
  Wednesday: Ephesians 4:25,29-32
  Thursday: Matthew 7:1-6
  Friday: John 8:31-47
  Saturday: 1 Peter 3:8-22

Questions for Reflection and Discussion

Name some of the ways that lying is tolerated in our culture.

Are there times when lies are justified? Explain your answer.

What does it mean to uphold the honor of your neighbor? What about when that seems different from telling the truth in a strict sense?

How can you help the church be more truthful and more honoring of one another in the ways we communicate?

Closing Prayer

Lord, I am able to be a truthful person only as you help me. Let my words reflect your own character and integrity. For Jesus' sake, amen.

Week Forty-four:
Wanting Nothing but God

Opening Prayer

Almighty God, my Father, only you are worthy of my allegiance and my desire. Help me to seek only you and to take the rest as it comes from your sovereign hand. Purify my mind and heart, because without your work in me, I'm unable to live up to your holy requirements of me. Amen.

Heidelberg Questions

QUESTION 113: What is God's will for you in the tenth commandment?

That not even the slightest thought or desire contrary to any one of God's commandments should ever arise in my heart.

Rather, with all my heart I should always hate sin and take pleasure in whatever is right.[1]

([1]Psalm 19:7-14; 139:23-24; Romans 7:7-8)

QUESTION 114: But can those converted to God obey these commandments perfectly?

In this life even the holiest have only a small beginning of this obedience.[1]

Nevertheless, with all seriousness of purpose, they do begin to live according to all, not only some, of God's commandments.[2]

([1]Ecclesiastes 7:20; Romans 7:14-15; 1 Corinthians 13:9; 1 John 1:8-10; [2]Psalm 1:1-2; Romans 7:22-25; Philippians 3:12-16)

QUESTION 115: No one in this life can obey the Ten Commandments perfectly: why then does God want them preached so pointedly?

First, so that the longer we live the more we may come to know our sinfulness and the more eagerly look to Christ for forgiveness of sins and righteousness.[1]

Second, so that, while praying to God for the grace of the Holy Spirit, we may never stop striving to be renewed more and more after God's image, until after this life we reach our goal: perfection.[2]

([1]*Psalm 32:5; Romans 3:19-26; 7:7; 24:25; 1 John 1:9;* [2]*1 Corinthians 9:24; Philippians 3:12-14; 1 John 3:1-3*)

Exposition

The last commandment, "You shall not covet," is the culmination of the second section of the Ten Commandments. No other ancient laws come near this. Not only is God concerned with the outer comportment, but also he is concerned with inner attitude. In case anyone could read the commandments and think that anything has been omitted, this brings us back to reality. God's claim on us is on the whole person. And even if anyone thinks he or she does well in keeping the other nine, this brings us back to our essential spiritual condition: we need God.

The commandment has to do with desiring our neighbor's property, but it also amplifies the previous nine commandments. Paul reflected this sense of the commandment when he wrote, "Indeed I would not have known what sin was except through the law. For I would not have known what coveting really was if the law had not said, 'Do not covet'" (Romans 7:7). Jesus did a similar thing in his Sermon on the Mount. In Matthew 5 he says, "You have heard that it was said . . . but *I* tell you . . ." Each time he says this, he takes one of the laws — Do not murder, Do not commit adultery — and extends it to become a matter of the heart. He says it is not enough to simply *not* do these things. Rather, our heart has to desire to bring wholeness in each of these aspects of our relationships. In saying this, our Lord was extending the meaning of the tenth commandment to the whole law. All the breaking of the second section of the law traces back to the wrong desire that is addressed in the tenth commandment.

What kind of desire is wrong? Every mean thought, vindictive thought, lustful thought, covetous thought — all these are off limits for us, regardless of where they come from. For example, the media influence on us is far greater than we often realize. Images are communicated into our subconscious and surface unexpectedly, as pictures flit across our mental screen. We may not have chosen to entertain a perverse fantasy or a greedy fancy. But these emanate from a tainted heart that already is prone to sin. They make us vulnerable to a second level of infiltration in our system, when we begin to take pleasure in those desires and yield to them.

Are we the master or the slave of our desires? The tenth commandment warns us not to be enticed by evil. The saying goes, "You can't help a bird flying over your head, but you *can* keep it from building a nest in your hair!" That which tempts us comes from outside stimuli, so we have to be vigilant about the influences in our lives. If you are serious about being sexually pure, for example, don't hang around late in the office when you're alone with a member of the opposite sex. If you are concerned about having integrity, always have another person with you to check the numbers when you count the church offering. If you want to get out of the rat race of accumulation and to cultivate a lifestyle of contentment, then seek first God's kingdom, not your own. Stop watching the television shows and movies that glorify violence, depravity, and acquisitiveness.

Covetousness may seem petty compared with the sins of murder or adultery or robbery or deceit, but it is at the core of each of these. It is what drives us to betray a spouse, to steal, cheat, lie, and kill. It compels us to evil in order to grab money, fame, prestige, and power. An unholy desire for wealth, sex, or power, it is what the medieval monks sought to overcome with their vows of poverty, chastity, and obedience. We need to know the power of God over our desires as in no other area of our lives.

Yet when we see the scope of God's demands and the implications of his call to purity of heart, we must cry out, "Have mercy on me, a sinner!" That is the place God wants us to be; right living is more than not desiring evil, more than spiritual detachment. We must do more than disapprove of evil in the abstract, but we must hate it, struggle against it in ourselves. We learn to do this through self-denial. The world cannot understand this. It is not the same as self-hatred; it is the opposite, because to truly love ourselves we have to seek what we most acutely need, not what we merely crave.

And there are things worth desiring. Paul told the Christians in Corinth to "eagerly desire the *greater* gifts" (1 Corinthians 12:31, italics added). In denying ourselves of what is against God's purpose, we grow to desire the good, to delight in what is pure and true and beautiful. The psalmist tells us, "Delight yourself in the LORD, and he will give you the desires of your heart" (Psalm 37:4). Why? Because the desire of our heart will be God himself, the only one who can satisfy our souls. Jesus told his disciples, "Blessed are those who hunger and thirst for righteousness, for they will be filled" (Matthew 5:6). We should thirst for God like the deer that pants for streams of water. One of the reasons for the spiritual sickness in the church of the West today is a lack of holy desire.

Missionary and pastor David Seamands notes that this notion goes against the detachment of Buddhism, which teaches that desire is the source of all evil in the world. It goes against the Kurt Cobain-coolness and apathy of our culture where it isn't fashionable to be passionate about one's convictions. Seamands writes, "That belief has led even some Christians to a false asceticism and a quest for a sort of glorified nothingness. But Jesus did not come to give us nothing; rather he offers us abundant life."[14]

Christians recognize that only God can transform our hearts and make them conform to his. People who come to know Christ and participate in his life are able to keep God's commandments because his Spirit dwells in them. Nonetheless, we cannot keep them perfectly. We still live in a distorted world, and we still struggle with our own brokenness and inner distortions. The obedience we offer God, no matter how great, is only a small beginning on the road to becoming like Christ. But this does not discourage us from pursuing holiness, from growing in Christ. Our character is being shaped and should conform to greater and greater degree to the standards of God. Even so, even as we make progress in all of God's commands, we still fail. We still fall into sin and have to be restored. Even this failure attests that we don't attain perfection by our own good works. Our sanctification rests only in God's justification through grace. In all of our weakness and frailty we can find comfort in that.

Other Voices

All things are Yours, my God,
Creator of all that exists,
all wisdom, all beauty, and might.
You made me, You own me,
Your glory surrounds me;
I live by your mercy and love.
All things are Yours, and so am I.

All things are Yours, my Lord,
Redeemer of all who have sinned,
new Master of all who repent.
You sought me, You found me,
You call me, You lead me;
now have me live only for You.
All things are Yours, and so am I.

All things are Yours, my Guide,
Renewer and Giver of life,
Transformer of hearts and of minds.
Renew me, transform me,
inspire me, refine me,
and give me the spirit of Christ.
All things are Yours, and so am I.

All things are yours, My child,
so live like the heir that you are,
entrusted with all that you have.
Be faithful, be prudent,
be daring, be caring,

as giving as I am toward you.
All things are yours, and you are Mine.
— Jaroslav Vajda, "All Things Are Yours"

In the days following surgery, I began to discover what it meant that I had not died and would soon recover. . . . I had to face the simple fact that I returned to a world from which I had been released. I was glad to be alive, but on a deeper level I was confused and wondered why it was that Jesus had not yet called me home. . . .

My main question became: "Why am I alive; why wasn't I found ready to enter into the house of God; why was I asked to return to a place where love is so ambiguous, where peace so hard to experience, and joy so deeply hidden in sorrow?" The question came to me in many ways, and I knew that I had to grow slowly into the answer. As I live my life in the years ahead of me, the question will be with me always, and I will never be allowed to let that question go completely. That question brings me to the heart of my vocation: to live with a burning desire to be with God and to be asked to keep proclaiming his love while missing its fulfillment.

— Henri J. M. Nouwen, *Beyond the Mirror*

There is a nice irony in shame: our feelings of inferiority are a sure sign of our superiority, and our feelings of unworthiness testify to our great worth. Only a very noble being can feel shame. The reason is simple: a creature meant to be a little less than God is likely to feel a deep dissatisfaction with herself if she falls a notch below the splendid human being she is meant to be. If we never feel shame, we may have lost contact with the person we most truly are. If we can still feel the pain, it is because we are healthy enough to feel uncomfortable with being less than we ought to be and less than we want to be. This is healthy shame.

Some psychologists seem to assume that all bad feelings we have about ourselves are unhealthy. I believe that they are mistaken. . . . Our shame may be a painful signal that we are failing to be the persons we are meant to be and may therefore be the first hope of healing.

— LEWIS B. SMEDES, *Shame and Grace: Healing the Shame We Don't Deserve*

On this particular day, I was reading in an anthology of documents from the Holocaust, and I came across a short article about a little village in the mountains of southern France. As usual, I was reading the pages with an effort at objectivity; I was trying to sort out the forms and elements of cruelty and of resistance to it in much the same way a veterinarian might sort out ill from healthy cattle. After all, I was doing this work not to torture myself but to understand the indignity and the dignity of man.

About halfway down the third page of the account of this village, I was annoyed by a strange sensation on my cheeks. The story was so simple and so factual that I had found it easy to concentrate upon *it*, not upon my own feelings. And so, still following the story, and thinking about how neatly some of it fit into the old patterns of persecution, I reached up to my cheek to wipe away a bit of dust, and I felt tears upon my fingertips. Not one or two drops; my whole cheek was wet.

"Oh," my sentinel mind told me, "you are losing your grasp on things again. Instead of learning about cruelty, you are becoming one more of its victims. You are doing it again." I was disgusted with myself for daring to intrude.

And so I closed the book and left my college office. When I came home, my operatic Italian wife and my turbulent children, as they have never failed to do, distracted me noisily. I hardly felt the spear that had gone through me. But that night when I lay on my back in bed with my eyes closed, I saw more clearly than ever the images that had made me weep. I saw the two clumsy khaki-colored buses of the Vichy French police pull into the village square. I saw the police captain facing the pastor of the village and warning him that if he did not give up the names of the Jews they had been sheltering in the village, he and his fellow pastor, as well as the families who had been caring for the Jews, would be arrested. I saw the pastor refuse to give up these people who had been strangers in his village, even at the risk of his own destruction.

Then I saw the only Jew the police could find, sitting in an otherwise empty bus. I saw a thirteen-year-old boy, the son of the pastor, pass a piece of his precious chocolate through the window to the prisoner, while twenty gendarmes who were guarding the lone prisoner watched. And then I saw the villagers passing their little gifts through the window until there were gifts all around him — most of them food in those hungry days during the German occupation of France. . . .

To the dismay of my wife, I left the bed unable to say a word, dressed, crossed the dark campus on a starless night and read again those few pages on the village of Le Chambon-sur-Lignon. And to my surprise, again the spear, again the tears, again the frantic, painful pleasure that spills into the mind when a deep, deep need is being satisfied, or when a deep wound is starting to heal.

— PHILIP HALLIE, *Lest Innocent Blood Be Shed*

Daily Scripture Readings

KEY TEXT: 1 JOHN 3:3
   Sunday: Psalm 1
   Monday: Psalm 19:7-14
   Tuesday: Romans 3:19-26
   Wednesday: Romans 7:1-25
   Thursday: 1 Corinthians 9:19-27
   Friday: 1 Corinthians 13
   Saturday: Philippians 4:10-20

Questions for Reflection and Discussion

Why do you think the commandments end on this note — do not "covet"? How realistic is it for God to not only demand that we not sin, but also that we not even desire to sin?

What forces in our lives entice us to covet what we do not have? Do these forces engender peace and contentment in us, or something else? If not the former, then what?

What is an area of your life where you think God would like you to be content with what you already have?

According to the catechism, how much do you think we can expect to live up to God's commandments? If we're not capable of fully living up to them in this life, why bother trying?

Closing Prayer

Jesus, I'm glad you have turned me around and placed me on the road to wholeness. I know that perfection is a process more than a place in this life, but I desire to grow into all that you have for me. Thank you for what you have done and will do in me. Amen.

Week Forty-five:
Talking with the Father

Opening Prayer

Father, something in me aches to be closer to you. Sometimes, though, I just don't know where to start. Please teach me how to talk to you, to show myself to you as I really am. Thank you that you receive me as I am. Thank you that your deepest desire is that your people might know you in all your fullness. In Jesus' name, amen.

Heidelberg Questions

Question 116: Why do Christians need to pray?

Because prayer is the most important part of the thankfulness God requires of us.[1] And also because God gives his grace and Holy Spirit only to those who pray continually and groan inwardly, asking God for these gifts and thanking him for them.[2]

([1]Psalm 50:14-15; 116:12-19; 1 Thessalonians 5:16-18; [2]Matthew 7:7-8; Luke 11:9-13)

Question 117: How does God want us to pray so that he will listen to us?

First, we must pray from the heart to no other than the one true God, who has revealed himself in his Word, asking for everything he has commanded us to ask for.[1]

Second, we must acknowledge our need and misery, hiding nothing, and humble ourselves in his majestic presence.[2]

Third, we must rest on this unshakable foundation: even though we do not deserve it, God will surely listen to our prayer because of Christ our Lord. That is what he promised us in his Word.[3]

([1]Psalm 145:18-20; John 4:22-24; Romans 8:26-27; James 1:5; 1 John 5:14-15; [2]2 Chronicles 7:14; Psalm 2:11; 34:18; 62:8; Isaiah 66:2; Revelation 4; [3]Daniel 9:17-19; Matthew 7:8; John 14:13-14; 16:23; Romans 10:13; James 1:6)

QUESTION 118: What did God command us to pray for?

Everything we need, spiritually and physically,[1] as embraced in the prayer Christ our Lord himself taught us.

([1]*James 1:17; Matthew 6:35*)

QUESTION 119: What is this prayer?

Our Father in heaven, hallowed be your name, your kingdom come, your will be done on earth as it is in heaven. Give us today our daily bread. Forgive us our debts, as we also have forgiven our debtors. And lead us not into temptation, but deliver us from the evil one. For yours is the kingdom and the power and the glory forever. Amen.[1]

([1]*Matthew 6:9-13; Luke 11:2-4*)

Exposition

Why bother to pray? Christians and nonChristians alike have asked the question. If God is in charge of everything, and if God is going to accomplish what he sets out to do, then what difference does it make? Do we need to pray in order to make ourselves acceptable to God? In asking these questions, we need to remember that prayer is a *response* to God's initiative in loving us. That is why the section on prayer comes as it does toward the end of the catechism. It is included in the section on grace; having seen how God has taken care of our sin by his surprising gift of love, we are freed to enjoy friendship with him. That is what prayer is about. Still, we sometimes wonder. What difference will prayers make? Is God actually *changed* by the prayers we offer?

In our day the idea of an immutable and impassible God has fallen into disfavor. He is more often portrayed as vulnerable than all-powerful. But the God of the Bible is the Almighty One. He is eternal, not fickle or prone to moods, "the same yesterday, today, and forever." God does not wind down or deteriorate; he is not subject to entropy. In these senses, he does not change. But that is not to say that God is unfeeling or uncaring. Sometimes, the Bible says, God changes his mind, relenting from judgment. Perhaps one could say God can change his mind, but not his heart. Because he is God, and because he loves us, he is able to help us.

But if prayer does not change God's character, it changes *ours*. As Richard Foster says, "To pray is to change."[15] We cannot but help see things more with God's eyes as we pray. It is an expression of God's grace that he invites us to be participants in what he is doing in the world. He listens to his children and allows himself to be influenced by our pleas. He draws us into the fellowship of Father, Son, and Holy Spirit so that we can bring our needs before him. We pray because in praying we are coming home to the God who made us, who knows us, and who loves us.

To be a Christian is to pray. If we would really follow Jesus, merely adhering to his teaching is not enough. We must also imitate his lifestyle. The defining characteristic of his life on earth was his communion with his Father, sustained by prayer. The heart of the matter is prayer because that is the expression of an intimate relationship with the Father. Prayer, wrote Otto Thelemann, is to be "the native breath of the renewed man."[16] One of the signs that we belong to God is that we desire to be in communication, in *communion,* with him. Prayer nurtures that relationship and expresses it. It is therefore no surprise that Scripture exhorts us to pray "without ceasing" (1 Thessalonians 5:17, NRSV).

How do we do that? What is to be the shape of the Christian's prayer life? We turn to Matthew's gospel to find Jesus' guidelines for prayer.

"And whenever you pray, do not be like the hypocrites; for they love to stand and pray in the synagogues and at the street corners, so that they may be seen by others. Truly I tell you, they have received their reward. But whenever you pray, go into your room and shut the door and pray to your Father who is in secret; and your Father who sees in secret will reward you." (Matthew 6:5-6, NRSV)

At first glance, Jesus might appear in this passage to condemn public prayer. The problem, however, is not public prayer. It is self-focused and ostentatious prayer — prayer that is done to demonstrate one's spiritual stature only distances one from God. Jesus says, don't be like the hypocrites who want to be admired by others in public. Prayer is not a way of gaining points with God or with anybody else. It is to draw on the resources of God, without whom our soul withers. It boils down to this: do not pray for show. Then, Jesus adds this instruction:

"And when you pray, do not keep on babbling like pagans, for they think they will be heard because of their many words. Do not be like them, for your Father knows what you need before you ask him." (Matthew 6:7-8)

But isn't there a place for big prayers? What about when the needs are great? How do we reconcile Jesus' instruction with Paul's admonition to pray constantly?

The point is that we are to cultivate a relationship with God that is authentic and consistent. God is not more inclined to listen when we pray with greater wordiness. It's not as if his children have to clock in enough time before their prayers will work. This would turn conversation with the heavenly Father into drudgery. If the lesson of Matthew 6:6 is, "Not for show," then the lesson of verse 8 is, "Not drawn-out." All the Father requires is the candor of a child.

What kind of prayer is heard by God? Prayer that pleases the Father is *true* (praying from the heart to him alone), *real* (coming to God without putting on airs), and *trusting* (believing that God will hear our prayer).

There is no need for wearing ourselves out trying to impress God. God wants us to bring our true selves to him: our fears, our hurts, our joys, our anger, and our hopes for the future. Our frailties and our foibles do not surprise him. He knows us inside and out and, in spite of aspects of our character that vex us, he loves us just as we are. Don't worry about eloquence when you pray. God listens to the heart, not to impressive-sounding words. (You may help a brother or sister in Christ by your example of how simple and real prayer can be.) In order for prayer to please God it has to come from faith.

My brother Jeff has been burdened by epilepsy most of his life. When he was five years old he had a prolonged high fever that sent him into convulsions and caused some brain damage. In consequence he suffered from multiple seizures throughout his childhood, sometimes as many as ten grand mal seizures a day. At sixteen years of age, he had the opportunity to go to Montreal, Canada, for an operation by a highly regarded team of neurosurgeons. They would remove some scar tissue from his brain in a procedure that they hoped would eliminate many of the seizures. The operation was risky. My parents asked Jeff to pray about whether he should go ahead with it. He asked if he could take a week to consider it.

At the end of the week, Jeff said, "Dad, Mom — I've thought about it, and I've decided I can't lose. I want to go ahead with the surgery."

My mother thought that perhaps Jeff didn't grasp the risk involved. She said, "Jeff, it is a dangerous operation. How can you say you can't lose?"

Jeff responded, "Mom, if I die in the operation, I'll go to be with the Lord, and my problems will be over. And if I don't die but end up in worse condition than I am now, I'll need God even more than now, so I'll love him more. And if I'm better, then I'll spend the rest of my life praising him for my healing. I can't lose."

Jeff went ahead with the operation and has made substantial progress as a result. And he was right about God's help for him. He understood that whatever he prayed *for* flowed out of who he prayed *to* — his heavenly Father who loved him and who would not leave his side.

Other Voices

Let all who pray the prayer Christ taught
    first clear the cluttered heart.
Make room to breathe the living thought
    those well-worn words impart.

‽

Dismiss the fear that this world drifts with
    no one in command.

Your pulse and breath are signs and gifts
    from God's attentive hand.

‽

Refine and test each passing aim against
    this final one:
Has your life hallowed heaven's name and
    has God's will been done?

&

Discard each vengeful hope that's fed the
  dreams of wars you'll win;
Then freely ask for daily bread and pardon
  from your sin.

&

Examine how temptation breeds inside the
  mind's dark maze,
Acknowledging that your life needs deliverance from its ways.

&

By faithful discipline prepare an inward
  holy space
That when you offer Jesus' prayer your
  heart may fill with grace.
— THOMAS H. TROEGER, "Let All Who Pray
            the Prayer Christ Taught"

Genuine prayer is never "good works," an
exercise or a pious attitude, but it is always
the prayer of a child to a Father. Hence it is
never given to self-display, whether before
God, ourselves, or other people. If God
were ignorant of our needs, we should
have to think out beforehand *how* we
should tell him about them, *what* we
should tell him, and *whether* we should tell
him or not. Thus faith, which is the main-
spring of Christian prayer, excludes all
reflection and premeditation.

Prayer is the supreme instance of the
hidden character of the Christian life. It is
the antithesis of self-display. When men
pray, they have ceased to know themselves,
and know only God whom they call upon.
Prayer does not aim at any direct effect on
the world; it is addressed to God alone,
and is therefore the perfect example of
undemonstrative action.
— DIETRICH BONHOEFFER,
        The Cost of Discipleship

Or should we really not pray for ourselves at
all; is the desire for common prayer with our
own lips and in our own words a forbidden
thing? No matter what objections there may
be, the fact simply remains that where
Christians want to live together under the
Word of God they may and they should pray
together to God in their own words. They
have common petitions, common thanks,
common intercessions to bring to God, and
they should do so joyfully and confidently.
Here all fear of one another, all timidity about
praying freely in one's own words in the
presence of others may be put aside where in
all simplicity and soberness the common,
brotherly prayer is lifted to God by one of the
brethren. But likewise all comment and criticism must cease whenever words of prayer
howsoever halting are offered in the name of
Jesus Christ. It is in fact the most normal
thing in the common Christian life to pray
together. Good and profitable as our
restraints may be in order to keep our prayer
pure and Biblical, they must nevertheless not
stifle necessarily free prayer itself, for Jesus
Christ attached a great promise to it.
— DIETRICH BONHOEFFER, *Life Together*

I am at an impasse, and you, O God, have
brought me here. From my earliest days, I
heard of you. From my earliest days, I
believed in you. I shared in the life of your

people: in their prayers, in their work, in their songs, in their listening for your speech and in their watching for your presence. For me your yoke was easy. On me your presence smiled.

Noon has darkened . . .

Will my eyes adjust to this darkness? Will I find you in the dark — not in the streaks of light which remain, but in the darkness? Has anyone ever found you there? Did they love what they saw? Did they see love? And are there songs for singing when the light has gone dim? The songs I learned were all of praise and thanksgiving and repentance. Or in the dark, is it best to wait in silence?

— Nicholas Wolterstorff,
Lament for a Son

Daily Scripture Readings

Key Text: Matthew 6:6
Sunday: 1 Samuel 3:1-10
Monday: 2 Chronicles 7:11-22
Tuesday: Psalm 34
Wednesday: Psalm 42
Thursday: Daniel 9:4-18
Friday: Luke 11:5-13
Saturday: Romans 8:18-26

Questions for Reflection and Discussion

What is the first meaningful experience you remember having in prayer? What was it like?

Do you remember any prayers from your childhood? What were they?

What does it mean to be able to pray well? Is there such a thing? Why or why not?

Closing Prayer

Father, when I think of my experience with you, I know it is in you alone that I can feel happy, interested in life, and fulfilled. So into your hands I place myself. Do with me as you please. Whatever it is, I will thank you. Just keep me close to your heart. Amen.

Week Forty-six:
Teach Us to Pray

Opening Prayer

It's so good to know that you are more than an abstract God, but that you are the intimate God, the one who longs to be known as Father. Be with me today as I come into your presence and try to live in that presence through all my waking hours. In your Son Jesus' name, amen.

Heidelberg Questions

QUESTION 120: Why did Christ command us to call God "our Father"?

At the very beginning of our prayer Christ wants to kindle in us what is basic to our prayer — the childlike awe and trust that God through Christ has become our Father.

Our fathers do not refuse us the things of this life; God our Father will even less refuse to give us what we ask in faith.[1]

(*[1]Matthew 7:9-11; Luke 11:11-13*)

QUESTION 121: Why the words "in heaven"?

These words teach us not to think of God's heavenly majesty as something earthly,[1] and to expect everything for body and soul from his almighty power.[2]

(*[1]Jeremiah 23:23-24; Acts 17:24-25; [2]Matthew 6:25-34; Romans 8:31-32*)

Exposition

Who are we talking to when we pray? We are talking to the God who is "the God and Father of our Lord Jesus Christ." Fatherhood is an essential ingredient of God's nature. This is because there has always been a union of love within the Trinity. "Father" expresses the relationship God has had from eternity with the Son and the Holy Spirit. He has always been the Father, because there has always been the Son.

The Triune God is also *our* Father in heaven — the term is loaded with tender love and grace. God is Father to the world by creation and to the believer by grace. Christians can thereby relate to God with assurance that he has elected us to belong to him, has redeemed us for himself, and has renewed us to share in his life. Without God's work on our behalf, we could only relate to God as judge. Now we can trust him as our Father.

God reaches out in love in order to awaken both childlike confidence and reverence in us. Since the Holy Spirit assures us that we belong to the Father, we can be delivered from dread of God. The apostle Paul sees the freedom that God has in mind for his children: "For you did not receive a spirit of slavery to fall back into fear, but you have received a spirit of adoption. When we cry 'Abba! Father!' it is that very Spirit bearing witness with our spirit that we are children of God" (Romans 8:15-16, NRSV).

Part of that childlike trust is giving up anxiety and resting in him. Just as a little child who knows she can bring all her needs to a loving parent, we know that our God will all the more fulfill what we seek in faith. God's love goes immeasurably beyond human love. Paul's doxology in the letter to the Ephesians expresses this: "Now to him who by the power at work within us is able to accomplish abundantly far more than all we can ask or imagine, to him be glory in the church and in Christ Jesus to all generations, forever and ever. Amen" (Ephesians 3:20-21, NRSV). Paul piles one superlative onto another: God does so much for us — all we need ... in fact, all we can even *ask* ... in fact, all we can *imagine* ... in fact, even *more* ... in fact, *abundantly* more! God is our Father when we are in Christ and in him gives us all things. So "Father" is the starting place for prayer and is the distinguishing characteristic of Christian prayer. All our prayer life grows out of our relationship to the Father.

Another key phrase follows quickly after "Father." When the Lord taught his disciples to pray, he instructed them to add, "in heaven." Those words remind us of the transcendence of God. He is closer to us than the air we breathe. Yet he also stands far above us. He is majestic and exalted, and he rules over all the cosmos. We are to remember that he is holy and not to conceive of him in any earthly form. He is indeed our Father, but he is also our *God*. This is the posture to which Scripture refers when it admonishes us to "fear" God.

Some say that if God is God he cannot be good, and if God is good, he cannot be God. By this, they attempt to come to terms with the problem of evil and the sovereignty of God. It is felt that an all-powerful God would not allow suffering in the world. If God is all-powerful, he must not be good, and vice versa.

But Scripture repudiates this view. The Bible never explains the problem of evil in the world. (God knows that an explanation would never satisfy us.) Instead, we have his comfort and power even in this dark world. This reassurance is echoed in the words "our Father in heaven." Those words remind us that God is both *God* and *good*, and shape the way we "practice the presence of God" in prayer.

So what are the benefits of prayer? Prayer is our communication with God. Prayer is our example from Jesus. Prayer is coming home to the Father. It brings glory to God when he answers prayers offered in Jesus' name.

Prayer changes things. It incorporates us into God's plan in the world. It brings relief to beleaguered people, comfort to the grieving, hope to the despairing, clarity for the confused. It causes the natural course of things to be altered and to come into alignment with God's will.

Sometimes God answers our prayers with a "no." How could it be otherwise? He answers prayer according to what we need and not simply what we crave. God will not be put into a box. He cannot be controlled by our prayers, but is free to act as he will. Remarkably, he preserves our freedom as well. Matthew and Luke record the Lord's Prayer differently, because they see it as a model prayer that shows the essentials of prayer. We can still come to the Father at many times and settings, from private devotions to family or small-group prayer to regular prayers in public worship. We can blurt out our own arrow prayers or read from a book of prayer. We are free to employ various ways of praying. We do this in the confidence that God is the sovereign king of heaven and that he desires to help us because he is our Father.

Other Voices

Our God, our help in ages past,
Our hope for years to come,
Our shelter from the stormy blast,
And our eternal home:

↪

Before the hills in order stood,
Or earth received its frame,
From everlasting Thou art God,
To endless years the same.

↪

A thousand ages in Thy sight
Are like an evening gone;
Short as the watch that ends the night
Before the rising sun.

↪

Time, like an ever rolling stream,
Soon bears us all away;
We fly forgotten, as a dream
Dies at the opening day.

↪

Our God, our help in ages past,
Our hope for years to come,
Be Thou our guard while life shall last,
And our eternal home.

— ISAAC WATTS,
"O God, Our Help in Ages Past"

Prayer is either a sheer illusion or a personal contact between embryonic, incomplete persons (ourselves) and the utterly concrete Person. Prayer in the sense of petition, asking for things, is a small part of it; confession and penitence are its threshold, adoration its sanctuary, the presence and vision and enjoyment of God its bread and wine. In it God shows Himself to us. That He answers prayer is a corollary — not necessarily the most important one — from that revelation. What He does is learned from what He is.

— C. S. LEWIS, "The Efficacy of Prayer,"
from *The World's Last Night and
Other Essays*

"Our Father which art in heaven!" To appreciate this word of adoration correctly, remember that none of the saints in Scripture ever ventured to address God as his Father. This invocation places us at once in the center of the wonderful revelation that Jesus came to make: His Father is our Father, too. It is the essence of redemption: Christ delivers us from the curse so that we can become the children of God. It explains the miracle of regeneration: The Spirit in the new birth gives us new life. And it reveals the mystery of faith: Before the

redemption is accomplished or understood, the disciples speak the word that prepares them for the blessed experience yet to come. The words are the key to the whole prayer and to all prayer. It takes time and life to study them; it will take eternity to understand them fully.

The knowledge of God's Father-love is the first and simplest, but also the last and highest lesson in the school of prayer. Prayer begins in a personal relationship with the living God as well as a personal, conscious fellowship of love with Him. In the knowledge of God's Fatherness revealed by the Holy Spirit, the power of prayer will root and grow. The life of prayer has its joy in the infinite tenderness, care, and patience of an infinite Father Who is ready to hear and to help. *"Our Father which art in heaven."* Wait until the Spirit has made these words spirit and truth to us, filling our hearts and lives. Then we will indeed be within the veil, in the secret place of power where prayer always prevails.

— ANDREW MURRAY, *With Christ in the
School of Prayer*

God our Father means our merciful Father; we ourselves are and always will be prodigal sons who can claim no rights save the one given to us in the person of Jesus Christ.

This does not imply any diminution of what has been said about the divine fatherhood. The splendor and the certainty, the very greatness and majesty of our Father are manifested in the fact that we stand before him without power or worth, without real faith and with empty hands. And yet, in Christ, we are God's children. We can contribute nothing whatever of our own to make the reality of that sonship more certain: divine reality alone is the fullness of all reality.

— KARL BARTH, *Prayer and Preaching*

Daily Scripture Readings

KEY TEXT: JEREMIAH 23:23
Sunday: 1 Kings 8:22-53
Monday: Acts 17:22-31
Tuesday: Matthew 6:25-34
Wednesday: John 17:1-25
Thursday: 1 Thessalonians 5:1-24
Friday: Ephesians 1:15-23
Saturday: 1 John 1:1-10

Questions for Reflection and Discussion

What do you think are indications that a person trusts God? What are some of the signs that you trust him for everything you need?

What good does it do us as Christians to know God as our Father? Is God everybody's Father? Why or why not?

How can you hold together both realities, that God is both immanent and transcendent — that is, that he is both present with us and yet is far above us? What might be different for you if both realities really sank into your consciousness?

Closing Prayer

Heavenly Father, you have spoken to me today. You are the one who holds together the universe and the one who gives me everything I need. Because of that, I am freed to live with peace and with confidence. Thank you!

Week Forty-seven:
To Lift Up God's Name

Opening Prayer

Let my life overflow with praise to you, from my manner of speech to the way I treat people around me, from how I work to the style with which I dress. I want to hallow your name, first and foremost. In Christ, amen.

Heidelberg Questions

QUESTION 122: What does the first request mean?

Hallowed be your name means,

Help us to really know you,[1] to bless, worship, and praise you for all your works and for all that shines forth from them: your almighty power, wisdom, kindness, justice, mercy, and truth.[2]

And it means,

Help us to direct all our living — what we think, say, and do — so that your name will never be blasphemed because of us but always honored and praised.[3]

([1]*Jeremiah 9:23-24; 31:33-34; Matthew 16:17; John 17:3;* [2]*Exodus 34:5-8; Psalm 145; Jeremiah 32:16-20; Luke 1:46-55,68-75; Romans 11:35-36;* [3]*Psalm 115:1; Matthew 5:16*)

Exposition

In 1643, the English Parliament passed a resolution calling for a summary statement of the Christian faith to settle questions of church liturgy and governance. The assembly they gathered in the Westminster Abbey met for more than five years through a turbulent period of English history. By the end of those years, they had produced a directory of worship, a confession of faith, a form of church government, and two catechisms. These standards emphasized the truth of the Scriptures as the authoritative Word of God and would influence three centuries of church life in Scotland and America. The famous first question and answer from the Shorter Catechism gives perspective on the whole of the Christian endeavor:

Q: "What is the chief end of man?"

A: "Man's chief end is to glorify God, and to enjoy him forever."

Bringing glory to God is the main purpose of living. We do this by knowing God and serving him. So it is that the first request of the Lord's Prayer is "hallowed be your name." This petition puts all the other petitions into their proper place, because God's glory is to be our first priority. In order to even come to him in prayer, we have to be impressed with God's goodness and holiness. Praise is our response to him, and it is the first order of life and of prayer. For the Christian, adoring God is more than a conviction. It is a daily experience. It is more than knowing who God is, but is also faith and obedience. It is to praise him for his power, wisdom, kindness, justice, mercy, and truth. We are to give God the honor that is rightly his.

As we pray this petition, we help glorify God's name. We do this not only in our prayer but in all the facets of our life, whether thought, word, or work. Everything we do is to praise God and to show his glory through us. We must live so that God is never blasphemed because of us.

That is why it hurts so much when Christian leaders, caught in some sin, are held up for public ridicule. That is why we flinch to see Christians spewing venom at those with whom they disagree in the civic realm. Anybody who confesses Christ with words must also demonstrate with deeds that he is Lord. This is what brings glory to the Father.

I had the chance to spend some time with Pastor Mario and his poor Nazarene congregation in San Vicente, Mexico. Resources were scarce and buildings were anything but glorious — just a cinderblock sanctuary forty feet long with a tin roof and an outhouse. But these believers were animated by a fervent desire to live for Christ and to make him known. They brought food to widows in their town. They went into squalid agricultural worker camps to witness door-to-door and to show the "Jesus" movie from a beat-up Ford camper, portable speakers blaring from the roof, in the dusty main square. People by the hundreds emerged from the warren of corrugated steel shacks to find out what the excitement was about. Believers prayed for deliverance for those under the power of drugs or violence or black magic, and trusted God for healing. Pastor Mario lived with his wife and three children in a sixteen-by-sixteen-foot house with windows of plastic sheets held in place with bottle caps. The praise services he led in his church would last for hours as he orchestrated the outpouring of emotion and supplication before the Lord. The people were a living testimony that God was alive and that they intended to live for him.

Other Voices

Were we left to ourselves, any praying we did would both start and end with ourselves, for our natural self-centeredness knows no bounds. Indeed, much pagan praying of this kind goes on among supposedly Christian people. But Jesus' pattern prayer, which is both crutch, road, and walking lesson for the spiritually lame like ourselves, tells us to start with God: for God matters infinitely more than we do. So "thy" is the keyword of the opening three petitions, and the first request of all is "hallowed (holy, sanctified) be THY NAME" — which is the biggest and the most basic request of the whole prayer. Understand it and make it your own, and you have unlocked the secret of both prayer and life.

— J. I. PACKER,
God: I Want to Be a Christian

In a world of prayers that indulge the religious ego and cultivate passionate longings, the Psalms stand out with a kind of angular austerity. . . . [They] are acts of obedience, answering the God who has addressed us. God's word precedes these words: these prayers don't seek God, they respond to the God who seeks us. These responses are often ones of surprise, for who expects God to come looking for us? And they are sometimes awkward, for in our religious striving we are usually looking for something quite other than the God who has come looking for us. God comes and speaks — his word catches us in sin, finds us in despair, invades us by grace. The Psalms are our answers. We don't always like what God speaks to us, and we don't always understand it. Left to ourselves, we will pray to some god who speaks what we like hearing, or to the part of God that we manage to understand. But what is critical is that we speak to the God who speaks to us, and to everything that he speaks to us, and in our speaking . . . mature in the great art of conversation with God that is prayer.

— EUGENE H. PETERSON, *Answering God: The Psalms as Tools for Prayer*

Through the discipline of solitude we discover space for God in our innermost being. Through the discipline of community we discover a place for God in our life together. Both disciplines being together precisely because the space within us and the space among us are the same space.

It is that divine space that God's Spirit prays in us. Prayer is first and foremost the active presence of the Holy Spirit in our personal and communal lives. Through the disciplines of solitude and community we try to remove — slowly, gently, yet persistently — the many obstacles which prevent us from listening to God's voice within us. God speaks to us not only once in a while but always. Day and night, during work and during play, in joy and in sorrow, God's Spirit is actively present in us. Our task is to allow that presence to become real for us in all we do, say, or think. Solitude and community are the disciplines by which the space becomes free for us to listen to the presence of God's Spirit and to respond fearlessly and generously.

— HENRI J. M. NOUWEN, *Making All Things New: An Invitation to the Spiritual Life*

In an age when people are pinning their hopes on both politics and technology, it is important that the church resist the temptations of both quietism and utopian activism. George Hunsinger . . . uniting a biblically informed or conservative theology with a progressive politics. The Confessing Church in Nazi Germany tried to maintain a biblical theology but was tempted to ally it with conservative politics. The churches in Holland, Norway, and Britain, on the other hand, were open to a progressive or socialist politics but tried to base this on a liberal theology with the result that Christ was superseded by social concerns. My position is that the people of God may in one situation throw their support behind conservative politics (with its emphasis on family solidarity and moral values in the school system) and in another support progressive politics (with its stress

on equality and human rights). There may even be occasions when church people find that it is God's will for them to be apolitical. The church must always resist alliances with any type of politics or ideology, for only in this way will it be enabled to speak the Word of God with credibility and power.

— DONALD BLOESCH, *Freedom for Obedience: Evangelical Ethics for Contemporary Times*

Daily Scripture Readings

KEY TEXT: REVELATION 7:12
Sunday: Exodus 34:1-14
Monday: Jeremiah 9:23-24; 31:31-37
Tuesday: Psalm 145
Wednesday: Luke 1:46-55,68-75
Thursday: Romans 11:33-36
Friday: Psalm 115
Saturday: Revelation 5:1-14

Questions for Reflection and Discussion

How do we truly get to know God? Is it just as valid to get in touch with God by experience or reason as it is through his personal revelation in Jesus? Why or why not?

The Reformed tradition has held that worship is the first priority of the church. Do you agree? Give reasons for your answer.

Which of God's attributes — such as power, wisdom, justice, mercy, or truth — do you most need right now?

List some ways that the believer can express praise for God, our Creator and Redeemer. Which of these are most meaningful for you?

*Closing Prayer*_____

Gracious God, I'm overwhelmed with how big you are. I praise you for who you are. Thank you for being there for me. Let my life be my way of letting you know what you mean to me. In Jesus, amen.

Week Forty-eight:
Longing for God's Wholeness

Opening Prayer

My greatest desire, Father, is that you might establish your kingdom in all of its fullness. Let me recognize its signs along the way. In Christ, amen.

Heidelberg Questions

QUESTION 123: What does the second request mean?

Your kingdom come means,

Rule us by your Word and Spirit in such a way that more and more we submit to you.[1]

Keep your church strong, and add to it.[2]

Destroy the devil's work; destroy every force that revolts against you and every conspiracy against your Word.[3]

Do this until your kingdom is so complete and perfect that in it you are all in all.[4]

(*[1]Psalm 119:5,105; 143:10; Matthew 6:33; [2]Psalm 122:6-9; Matthew 16:18; Acts 2:42-47; [3]Romans 16:20; 1 John 3:8; [4]Romans 8:22-23; 1 Corinthians 15:28; Revelation 22:17,20)*

Exposition

Jesus summed up what God was doing with the term "the kingdom of heaven." It became the watchword of his ministry. The gospel writers relate that he started his public ministry with this announcement and that it encapsulated the content of his preaching. Matthew says, "Jesus went throughout Galilee, teaching in their synagogues, preaching the good news of the kingdom, and healing every disease and sickness among the people" (Matthew 4:23). Luke states, "After this, Jesus traveled about from one town and village to another, proclaiming the good news of the kingdom of God" (Luke 8:1).

Announcing that news was also the job Jesus gave to his disciples. When he sent into ministry the Twelve, the mission he gave them was "to preach the kingdom of God and to heal the sick" (Luke 9:2). He would call his teaching itself, expressed through parables, "the knowledge of the secrets of the kingdom of heaven" (Matthew 13:11). Again and again, he would open up the heart of God for his people by instructing, "the kingdom of heaven is like . . ."

Then, in his Sermon on the Mount, Jesus says to pray, "Your kingdom come." The gospel writers use the terms "the kingdom of heaven" and "the kingdom of God." They are saying that the kingdom comes when God is here. Heaven breaks into earth when God establishes his way. So it is that Jesus put two phrases side by side: "your kingdom come, your will be done." God's kingdom is manifesting itself when his will is done, when he is recognized as king. Jesus is saying we pray for that reality because it is not earth's reality. Heaven is not yet asserting itself completely in the world. There is brokenness and sadness here, but there *is* a place where God's will is exercised completely and perfectly.

Jesus did not invent the idea of the kingdom. The idea of the kingdom was ingrained in Israel's consciousness since the days of the prophets. Daniel foresaw the coming "kingdom that will . . . crush all those [false] kingdoms and bring them to an end, but it will itself endure forever" (Daniel 2:44). This kingdom was that of the Son of Man: "He was given authority, glory and sovereign power; all peoples, nations and men of every language worshiped him" (Daniel 7:14). In preparation for Jesus, this Son of Man, his cousin John the Baptist would predict the coming of Jesus with the very same words Jesus would use: "Repent, for the kingdom of heaven is near" (Matthew 3:2; 4:17). The difference was in their posture; John was pointing to Jesus in anticipation, and Jesus was pointing to himself in fulfillment.

Jesus' followers were sometimes spoken of as those "waiting for the kingdom." Some longed not for political salvation or military power, but to see the righteousness of God and the joy and peace of the Holy Spirit. But many others did seek a kingdom of earthly power. When they saw his miracle of feeding the five thousand, the crowd wanted to crown him king by force. Even John the Baptist was disappointed in his expectations for his cousin. He sent a message to Jesus from prison after his arrest: "Are you the one who was to come, or should we expect someone else?" (Matthew 11:3). John had expected fire and great drama. But Jesus resisted the temptation to make a kingdom that was impressive by the world's standard of measurement. Instead, Jesus said, the kingdom comes inauspiciously. It didn't come with driving out the Romans and establishing a renewed Jewish king and court. Nor did it come with immediate judgment of evil. The kingdom was like the seed planted that has to grow before its fruits are seen. It was like the wheat that for a time would be indistinguishable from the weeds. It was like the smallest of all the seeds, the mustard seed, and like the unseen leaven in the dough. Jesus said "the kingdom of God does not come with your careful observation, nor will people say, 'Here it is,' or 'There it is,' because the kingdom of God is within you" (Luke 17:20).

Jesus would go on to tell how one day the kingdom would come in power and be recognized by the whole world. But that kingdom would only become reality by his laying down his life in obedience to the Father. Since he humbled himself and subjected himself to death on a cross, he now reigns in power for us.

He is coming again. In the meanwhile, his subjects offer humble prayer that he will be sovereign in our world. We labor to proclaim his Word and to obey it. We declare that his will alone holds ultimate authority. We hope for heaven, our true eternal home. And we live and work in light of the coming kingdom.

Other Voices

Lord, make me an instrument of your peace;
   where there is hatred, let me sow love,
   where there is injury, pardon,
   where there is doubt, faith;
   where there is despair, hope;
   and where there is sadness, joy.

Divine Master, grant that I may not seek so much to be consoled as to console,
   to be understood as to understand,
   to be loved as to love.

For it is in giving that we receive,
   it is in pardoning that we are pardoned,
   and it is in dying that we are born to
     new life.

— FRANCIS OF ASSISI

When men and women are in accord with God in their lives, other people's opposition to God increases. The conflicts spread and become more violent. Things become more and more critical in the world. History itself is nothing other than permanent crisis. That is why so many people dream about "the end of history" — most recently Francis Fukuyama of the State Department in Washington, who sees the end of history dawning in the victory of the liberal democrats and the global marketing of everything. But every anticipated end of history only takes history further and makes it more critical and more dangerous still. We can sum up this paradox of history in two sentences:

"Where there is danger, deliverance grows, too." Those are the consoling words of the German poet Friedrich Hölderlin.

"Where deliverance is near, danger grows." That was the threatening response of German philosopher Ernst Bloch.

Both statements are correct. That is why fear of danger is part of trust for deliverance, and the apocalyptic dread of the world's annihilation belongs to hope for its new creation.

— JÜRGEN MOLTMANN, *Jesus Christ for Today's World*

God, grant me the serenity to accept the things I cannot change, the courage to change the things I can, and the wisdom to know the difference, living one day at a time, enjoying one moment at a time, accepting hardship as a pathway to peace, taking, as Jesus did, this sinful world as it is, not as I would have it, trusting that you will make all things right if I surrender to your will, so that I may be reasonably happy in this life and supremely happy with you forever in the next. Amen.

— REINHOLD NIEBUHR

[If Christ were to appear in person at the Earth Summit in Rio de Janeiro, he would surely condemn the economic model that increases the gap between rich and poor; he would] denounce how this same model of "progress" turns forests into deserts, depletes and destroys soil, disrupts the atmosphere, poisons water, and puts into peril the God-given foundations of life.

And he would say that these are two inseparable sides of one sin — turning away from God as the giver of all life.

But he would also announce good news. He would say again that he came offering abundant life. He would declare God's promises and covenant with all creation. He would ask us to remember the lilies, challenge us not to store up wealth in our barns or banks, and declare that those in bondage are to be set free.

Finally, he would offer to us his redeeming love. A love that draws together Riocentro and Baixada Fluminense. A love that suffers with homeless black children on Rio's streets who fear for their lives. A love that embraces earth, air, fire and water, yearning to bring forth a new creation. A love which calls together a community formed by the Spirit, which lives by the power of the resurrection and testifies to God's faithful embrace of all life in a world that is our common home.

— WESLEY GRANBERG-MICHAELSON, *Redeeming the Creation: The Rio Earth Summit: Challenges for the Churches*

In too many places too many children die of hunger, and too many persons just disappear because they dare to stand up for justice and human rights. Too many are swept away by the tides of war, and too many are tortured in dungeons of death. In too many eyes the years of endless struggle have extinguished the fires of hope and joy, and too many bodies are bowed down by the weight of that peculiarly repugnant death called despair. Too many young persons believe that their youth and their future are already powdered to dust by the threat of nuclear destruction. And even in the face of all this, too many in the Christian church remain silent. We have not yet understood that every act of inhumanity, every unjust law, every untimely death, every utterance of confidence in weapons of mass destruction, every justification of violence and oppression, is a sacrifice on the altar of the false gods of death; it is a denial of the Lord of life. For millions it is true: we are not uplifted by the word of life, we are crushed by the litany of death.

Yet the gospel affirms: Jesus Christ is the life of the world (John 6:35, 48; 10:10; 11:25; 14:6; Revelation 1:17, 18, etc.). This means he is the source of life; he is the giver of the sacred gift of life. He intends for us a life filled with abundance, joy, and meaning. He is the Messiah in whose eyes our lives are precious.

This affirmation is precisely the problem. Dare we believe it? Can we believe it without making of our faith a narrow, spiritual escapism? Can we avoid the cynicism of "reality"? Can we find a way to live with that painful dilemma: "Lord, I believe; please help my unbelief"? And even more painful: can we accept the reality of hope and the call to battle that lie in this affirmation?

— ALLAN BOESAK, *Black and Reformed: Apartheid, Liberation, and the Calvinist Tradition*

Daily Scripture Readings

KEY TEXT: PSALM 119:105
Sunday: Psalm 145
Monday: Daniel 2:24-49
Tuesday: Matthew 6:25-34
Wednesday: Matthew 13:44-52
Thursday: Matthew 16:13-20
Friday: Mark 8:31–9:1
Saturday: Revelation 22:1-27

Questions for Reflection and Discussion

How do you think most people would understand the term "the kingdom of God"? What kind of meaning would it have for them, if any?

Is the "coming kingdom" synonymous with "God's will being done"? Why or why not? Do most Christians think God's kingdom has more to do with this life, or the life to come?

What adjectives come to mind when picturing an earthly kingdom? How are those similar to and different from God's kingdom?

List some ways that you can participate in and exhibit signs of the kingdom God is establishing.

Closing Prayer_____

No amount of work on my part will bring in your kingdom, Lord. Still, you have invited me to participate in the work you are doing, in anticipation of the day when you will make all things new. Thank you that I can live in that purpose and hope.

Week Forty-nine:

Not My Will but Yours

Opening Prayer

Lord, you alone are the ruler of the cosmos. Everything that exists falls down before your power. Still, your mercy is beyond measure. Let me trust today in your perfect will for my life and for your people. In Christ, amen.

Heidelberg Questions

QUESTION 124: What does the third request mean?

Your will be done on earth as it is in heaven means,

Help us and all people to reject our own wills and to obey your will without any back talk. Your will alone is good.[1]

Help us one and all to carry out the work we are called to,[2] as willingly and faithfully as the angels in heaven.[3]

([1]*Matthew 7:21; 16:24-26; Luke 22:42; Romans 12:1-2; Titus 2:11-12;* [2]*1 Corinthians 7:17-24; Ephesians 6:5-9;* [3]*Psalm 103:20-21)*

Exposition

C. S. Lewis, picking a phrase of John Milton, said there are two kinds of people in the world — those who say to God, "Thy will be done," and those to whom God says, "Your will be done." It cannot be otherwise. God gives us the sobering gift of freedom, a freedom to accept his will or put our own will on the throne of our heart. But if we are to pray, "your kingdom come," then we can only cede our will to God's. We cannot have it both ways.

In our culture, we constantly hear the message, "Be true to your heart." But given our nature, romantic platitudes like that will get us into trouble. That sentiment makes personal judgment an ultimate authority. Scripture counters this by teaching that human will is corrupt and turned against God, and that "every inclination of his heart is evil from childhood" (Genesis 8:21). This being the case, wholeness comes by rejecting our own will and submitting to God's will.

This is often a struggle for us. Learning to reject our own inclinations and pursue what God has for us can be agonizing. Medieval Christians described the process of dying to our own will as the *via negativa* and the process of growing in God's will as the *via positiva*. They understood that the Christian life involves a setting aside of ourselves, an emptying of self-will in order that God can fill us with his life and strength. We cannot succeed in our efforts without God's help. Our naturally corrupt will tempts us to doubt that God's design is good. But we can pray that God would give us the strength to overcome sin, and give us the desire to follow his will. We can choose to ignore the inner voice that tells us our way is better. We can submit to God's will "without any back talk" and find peace of mind. The apostle Paul had this twofold tension of negative and positive in mind when he talked of dying to self and living to Christ. Our life's orientation is now that the Lord's will be done.

How do we know his will? The particular plan he has for each of us is to be discerned through prayer, silence, reading of Scripture, and counsel of Christian friends. Often God brings his insights to mind as we journal in our time of reflective meditation. His secret will is sometimes hard to discover so we need to persist in seeking.

His revealed will, however, is clear for us in Scripture. Sometimes Christians rationalize bad behavior when they already know God's will from the Bible. I once heard a man tell me why leaving his wife for another woman was acceptable in his case, overlooking the commandment, "You shall not commit adultery." Given the infinite human capacity for self-deception, we need to guard against the feeling that whatever we want to do is necessarily what God wants for us. Our Lord's example of obedience shows that God's will is to be done both by us and in us. It is not merely in life's decisions we are to do his will, but also in the everyday, ordinary tasks. If we perform our duties as service to God where he has placed us, then we are doing his will. That is how we fulfill our calling into his service.

We must remember that God is not likely to impose his will on us. Ordinarily, he gives us a respectful distance that preserves our freedom to choose his will. Instead of overwhelming us, he woos us into his will.

From the time I was eight years old, my family would spend several weeks a summer on an old farm that began as a homestead in the late 1800s. It was in the Teanaway Valley of the Cascade Mountains, about eighty miles east of Seattle. A cousin bought forty acres and by the river constructed a cabin with gun racks and a stone fireplace and insulation coming out of the walls. The bleached-pink barn stood as a haven for bats and a place to swing from the rafters. We boys would climb three stories of rickety ladder, hearts pounding, to look through a hole in the roof to see miles down the valley. Elk antlers were nailed to tall poplars whose leaves shimmed in the afternoon breezes blowing down the river. Our clan gathered for many reunions there, with trailers in the meadow accommodating overflow guests from the cabin.

Our cousin lived over the mountains but kept horses at the farm. For nine months of the year the horses roamed the property at will. A neighbor two miles down the road regularly fed and watered the horses, but nobody would mount them. Come summer, they would be half-wild; if we wanted to ride horses, we needed to catch them first.

My brother Jay became the best at the task. The rest of us would call the horses and try to entice them with some hay, but would become frustrated after five minutes and end up scaring the nervous animals away again. Not Jay. He would eye one of the horses, usually Buckskin, and start to sweet-talk it, wooing it as he moved almost imperceptibly closer, or backing off and giving it space when it needed, never despairing of his goal. Sometimes it would take hours, but by the time ponderosa shadows stretched across meadow, he would have a halter on the horse and a caressing hand on its muzzle. He understood the need to woo and not overwhelm.

That is God's way with us. In order to grow in fellowship with him, we need to let him overcome our fears, and we need to submit to his will.

Other Voices

Our God is often too small because he is too religious. We imagine that he is chiefly interested in religion — in religious buildings (churches and chapels), religious activities (worship and ritual), and religious books (Bibles and prayer books). Of course he is concerned about these things, but only if they are related to the whole of life. According to the Old Testament prophets and the teaching of Jesus, God is very critical of "religion," if by that is meant religious services divorced from real life, loving service and the moral obedience of the heart.

— JOHN R. W. STOTT, *Issues Facing Christians Today*

Can we believe that each person has a part to play in the great cosmic drama? Can

God's will be done on earth? Can the great eternal purpose of God be fulfilled? Will we seek to glorify God, do God's will on earth as it is done in heaven?

If these questions arouse us, we ask, "How can I discern God's will for my life, for all of my life?"

The meaning of our lives, a quest in which we all engage, must be discovered in a larger context than our personal consciousness; it must be found in the context of God's cosmic purpose for creation and human history. Just as the answer to life is to be found in the larger arena of God's intention for creation, surely our own meanings must derive from this larger understanding of the world.

— BEN CAMPBELL JOHNSON,
Discerning God's Will

God calls us in His sovereign freedom to His work. It is His job to count numbers since He is able to call each of us by name (Isaiah 40:26; John 10:3). "He calls us" — is the mystery of His amazing generosity (Matthew 20:1-16). Is this "His work" equivalent with evangelization of two billion as we conceive it? Or is it something more? Are we Christians to discharge the mission as we define it or as God defines it? Is our understanding always identical with God's understanding? Does God who came to us in Jesus Christ speak of the urgency of mission in terms of two billion people? Is our sense of urgency identical? Is God as impatient with history as we are? In what way does God speak to two bil-

lion? Does he wish for church growth along the same lines as we do?

— KOSUKE KOYOMA, *Fifty Meditations*

The church community is a community of ministry and testimony, with ministry being understood as ministry "for all people": that is, for the world. This ministry also entails the church's political responsibility, insofar as the church must remind the state of the task that God has conferred on it: namely, as a state of law to care for the common good. By its ministry and its testimony the church community corresponds to God, who Jesus Christ elected humanity from all eternity, and who with this promise also lays a might claim on humanity.

— JAN ROHLS, *Reformed Confessions:*
Theology from Zurich to Barmen

There are all different kinds of voices calling you to all different kinds of work, and the problem is to find out which is the voice of God rather than of Society, say, or the Superego, or Self-Interest.

By and large a good rule for finding out is this. The kind of work God usually calls you to is the kind of work (a) that you need most to do and (b) that the world most needs to have done. If you really get a kick out of your work, you've presumably met requirement (a), but if our work is writing TV deodorant commercials, the chances are you've missed requirement (b). On the other hand, if your work is being a doctor in a leper colony, you have probably met requirement (b), but if most of the time you're bored and depressed by it, the chances are you have not only bypassed (a) but probably aren't helping your patients much either.

Neither the hair shirt nor the soft berth will do. The place God calls you to is the place where your deep gladness and the world's deep hunger meet.

— FREDERICK BUECHNER, *Wishful Thinking: A Theological ABC*

Daily Scripture Readings

KEY TEXT: MATTHEW 7:21
    Sunday: Psalm 40
    Monday: Psalm 143
    Tuesday: Matthew 12:46-50
    Wednesday: Matthew 26:36-46
    Thursday: 2 Corinthians 4:1-18
    Friday: Galatians 2:11-21
    Saturday: James 4:1-16

Questions for Reflection and Discussion

What are some other ways to say "God's will"? When is it easiest to know God's will? When is it hardest?

What are the benefits of knowing you are living in God's will for you? When is it hardest for you to follow God's will for you?

What are some of the ways people can discover God's will for their lives? Are there any practices you have found helpful in discerning God's will for your life? If so, what?

Closing Prayer

Lord, I'd like to be the kind of person who doesn't fret about finding your will, but who confidently obeys what you've already made clear of your intentions for my life and who trusts you for the rest. Help me to do that, I pray in Jesus' name and for his sake. Amen.

WEEK FIFTY:
EVERYTHING WE NEED

Opening Prayer

God, help me to know what I need, and to trust you for it. Thank you that you know what I need before I ask, and that you provide for me so faithfully. Amen.

Heidelberg Questions

QUESTION 125: What does the fourth request mean?

Give us today our daily bread means:

Do take care of all our physical needs[1] so that we may come to know that you are the only source of everything good,[2] and that neither our work and worry nor your gifts can do us any good without your blessing.[3]

And so help us to give up our trust in creatures and to put trust in you alone.[4]

([1]*Psalm 104:27-30; 145:15-16; Matthew 6:25-34;* [2]*Acts 14:17; 17:25; James 1:17;* [3]*Deuteronomy 8:3; Psalm 37:16; 127:1-2; 1 Corinthians 15:58;* [4]*Psalm 55; 22; 62; 146; Jeremiah 17:5-8; Hebrews 13:5-6)*

Exposition

I have seen the Lord supply his people's needs. Evelyne and I lived on an extremely tight budget during our seminary years. We were pouring all the financial resources we had into tuition and books. At times we would be left with twenty dollars for a month's food for us and our two-year-old daughter. And yet, time and time again, God would provide. A family would knock on our door asking if we could use a five-pound block of cheese and a couple loaves of bread. Another would invite us to their home for a pasta dinner. Another day, I would find an anonymous gift of fifty dollars in my mailbox at the school. Soon we learned to laugh at our fears of starvation or of having to drop out of school. How could we have doubted the Lord's kindness?

The fourth request reveals the compassion of the heavenly Father who knows we are needy creatures. He desires to fill our needs and also that we might humbly trust him for them. He tells us to ask for our "daily bread," which sums up all of life's necessities. Just like bread, we need shelter, food, drink, clothing, and transportation — to say nothing of spiritual food, comfort, and shelter. This petition encompasses everything we need to nurture body and soul. Daily bread is everything we need in order to live.

God is the great Giver, concerned not just about our spiritual needs but also our physical. All have a right to their daily bread and are reminded to seek it at the hand of the Father. We are to work diligently in life. But if we must work, we must also pray, because our daily bread comes not simply from our own labor, but from the God who provides for his people. We trust God for our needs even as we work to pay the bills and put food on the table, and we remember to pray that all people might have their daily bread.

The request implies perhaps a limitation. As Dale Bruner points out, we are invited not to pray for cake but for bread.[17] Most of us in the West have been richly blessed materially, yet impoverished spiritually. We are allowed to pray for what we need, but are not given permission to pray for luxury beyond our need. There are times when God gives cake anyway, and then we are free to gratefully receive the gift.

We are to pray for the needs of the day. It is difficult to keep from fretting about the days to come. Many people worry about the future to such an extent that they lose joy and courage needed for today. Jesus knew this when he told his disciples, "You cannot serve both God and Money. Therefore I tell you, do not worry about your life, what you will eat or drink; or about your body, what you will wear. Is not life more important than food, and the body more important than clothes?" (Matthew 6:24-25). Praying for the needs of the future leads to anxiety and covetousness. For the health of our soul we need to come to the Father in prayer every day.

Praying for our daily bread reminds us that God alone is the source of all good. Without his blessing, nothing prospers. Even the material things we need are not products of nature but gifts from God. Rather than strive for more than what we have, we can learn to desire the good that God has for us. In so doing, we will grow in humble confidence in God. Putting confidence in anything else is futile and is what the preacher of Ecclesiastes calls "vanity." Friends disappoint, retirement funds are swindled, business deals collapse, and strength withers. The only sure hope is God, the font of all blessings. Without him, even abundance leaves a sour taste in the mouth.

The children of Israel learned a lesson with bread and meat in the wilderness. Exodus 16 tells how every morning, God covered the ground with flakes of bread called manna; every evening, he drove quail to cover the camp. Each person was to gather as much as was needed for the day, and there was enough for all. The provision was to be for that day; no one was to hoard away for the next day, but simply to trust that God would faithfully provide. The exception to storing away was on the eve of the Sabbath. Then, everyone was to gather for the following twenty-four hours enough food, and it would not spoil. But when someone tried to store food any other day, they would return to find it spoiled.

Manna served to graphically demonstrate to Israel that God would care for his own. God was pleased when they would simply accept his gift, trusting him for what they needed. We are invited to do the same as we come to him day by day.

Other Voices

Now thank we all our God with heart and
    hands and voices,
Who wondrous things hath done, in whom
    his world rejoices;
Who, from our mother's arms, hath
    blessed us on our way
With countless gifts of love, and still is ours
    today.

↶

O may this bounteous God through all our
    life be near us,
With ever joyful hearts and blessed peace
    to cheer us;
And keep us in his grace and guide us
    when perplexed,
And free us from all ills in this world and
    the next.

↶

All praise and thanks to God the Father
    now be given,
The Son, and him who reigns with them in
    highest heaven,
The one eternal God whom earth and
    heaven adore;
For thus it was, is now, and shall be ever
    more.
        — MARTIN RINKART, "Now Thank
        We All Our God"

Now, into the keeping of God I put
    All doings of today.
    All disappointments,
        hindrances,
        forgotten things,
        negligences.

↶

All gladness and beauty,
   love,
   delight,
   achievement.

        ↝

All that people have done for me,
All that I have done for them,
   my work and my prayers.

        ↝

And I commit all the people whom I love
   to his shepherding,
   to his healing and restoring,
   to his calling and making;
      Through Jesus Christ our Lord.
          — MARGARET CROPPER,
  "Prayer," from *The Oxford Book of Prayer*

The first principle we should consider is that the use of gifts of God cannot be wrong, if they are directed to the same purpose for which the Creator himself has created and destined them. *For he has made the earthly blessings for our benefit, and not for our harm.*

No one, therefore, will observe a more proper rule than he who will faithfully observe this purpose. If we study, for instance, why he has created the various kinds of food, we shall find that it was his intention not only to provide for our needs, but likewise for our pleasure, and for our delight.

In clothing he did not only keep in mind our needs, but also propriety and decency.

In herbs, trees, and fruit, besides being useful in various ways, he planned to please us by their gracious lines and pleasant odors. For, if this were true, the Psalmist would not enumerate among the divine blessings "the wine that makes glad the heart of man, and the oil that makes his face to shine." And the Scriptures would not declare everywhere that he has given all these things to mankind that they might praise his goodness.

Even the natural properties of things sufficiently point out to what purpose and to what extent we are allowed to use them. Should the Lord have attracted our eyes to the beauty of the flowers, and our sense of smell to pleasant odors, should it then be sin to drink them in? Has he not even made the colors so that the one is more wonderful than the other? Has he not granted to gold and silver, to ivory and marble a beauty which makes them more precious than other metals or stones?

In one word, has he not made many things worthy of our attention that go far beyond our needs? (Ps. 104:15)
         — JOHN CALVIN, *Golden Booklet*
            of the True Christian Life

Prayer for a Christian is not an attempt to force God's hand, but a humble acknowledgment of helplessness and dependence. When we are on our knees, we know that it is not we who control the world; it is not in our power, therefore, to supply our needs by our own independent efforts; every good thing that we desire for ourselves and for others must be sought from God, and will come, if it comes at all, as a gift from His hands. If this is true even of our daily bread (and the Lord's Prayer teaches us that it is), much more is it true of spiritual benefits. This is all luminously clear to us when we are actually praying, whatever we may be betrayed into saying in argument afterwards. In effect, therefore, what we do every time we pray is to confess our own impotence and God's sovereignty. The very fact that a Christian prays is thus proof positive that he believes in the Lordship of his God.

— J. I. PACKER, *Evangelism & the Sovereignty of God*

Daily Scripture Readings

KEY TEXT: PSALM 23:5
> Sunday: Exodus 16:1-36
> Monday: Job 38:22-41
> Tuesday: Psalm 31:19
> Wednesday: Psalm 121
> Thursday: Joel 2:18-27
> Friday: 2 Corinthians 8:1-24
> Saturday: 2 Corinthians 9:1-15

Questions for Reflection and Discussion

What would you include in the term, "our daily bread"? Why do you think Jesus didn't tell his disciples to ask for cake?

How would you prioritize your basic needs in life?

Describe some ways you have had to trust God's provision. What are some ways you can thank him for it?

Closing Prayer

O God, help me to look to the needs of others before being concerned with meeting my own. Please look with kindness upon all your people, including me, so that we may enjoy the gifts of your salvation. In Jesus' name, amen.

Week Fifty-one:
A Clean Slate

Opening Prayer

*It seems the further I go with you in life,
the more acutely I become aware of my sin.
Unburden me, God, as I come to you.
Amen.*

Heidelberg Questions

QUESTION 126: What does the fifth request mean?

Forgive us our debts, as we also have forgiven our debtors means,

Because of Christ's blood, do not hold against us, poor sinners that we are, any of the sins we do or the evil that constantly clings to us.[1]

Forgive us just as we are fully determined, as evidence of your grace in us, to forgive our neighbors.[2]

(*[1]Psalm 51:1-7; 143:2; Romans 8:1; 1 John 2:1-2; [2]Matthew 6:14-15; 18:21-35*)

Exposition

Renewal always begins when the people of God get on their knees. Repentance is the starting point for a new work of God in us. The time of confession in an order of worship often begins with the call from 1 John, "If we claim to be without sin, we deceive ourselves and the truth is not in us. [But] if we confess our sins, he is faithful and just and will forgive our sins and purify us from all unrighteousness" (1:8-9). We can have courage to come before the living God, confessing our sin, because he has promised his forgiveness in Christ.

God's Law in the Ten Commandments shows us what is our duty to God. If we do not pay what we owe in obedience, then we are in his debt. Every debt must be paid, and if we are unable to pay it, then there must be punishment. This is the punishment Jesus took in our stead. In praying, "forgive us our debts," we recognize that we are unable to pay off our debt. We can do nothing to make things right, but we want to be free from judgment. The fifth petition is a coming-to-terms with the fact that we need refuge in God's grace.

The first thing we have to do is to see sin for what it is. It is not cute or daring and it is not something to be dismissed with "everyone does it." Sin is serious. Our transgressions cling to us. The image of clinging is vivid, calling to mind a pair of boots after slogging through a pigsty. You can try to shake off the mud and grime, but filth stays until you give it a good scrubbing. The sins seen outwardly are symptoms of sin on the inside. It is not only what we do but a rotten root that is the problem. A holy God holds us accountable for what we deserve.

Yet God has not left us to our own devices. We can find encouragement in this prayer that God will be pleased to forgive us and make us clean. Our assurance is strong, because we appeal to the blood of Christ. Because he has paid the price, we do not have to agonize over a payment we can never make.

In praying for forgiveness, as with each of the six petitions of the Lord's Prayer, we use the plural. "Forgive *us* our debts." Our destiny as individuals is tied up in the purpose of a *people* of God. We are to pray that God would cleanse his church and make it ready to reflect his light in the world. We pray that God would forgive all his children because we stand in solidarity with them not only in our redemption and our hope, but also in our sinfulness. We are still a sinful people who keep on sinning daily, and daily we need to pray this prayer.

Jesus taught his disciples that as a *forgiven* people we must also be a *forgiving* people. He said, adding this appendix to the prayer: "For if you forgive men when they sin against you, your heavenly Father will also forgive you. But if you do not forgive men their sins, your Father will not forgive your sins" (Matthew 6:14-15). I have sometimes wished that verse were not included in the Bible. But the Lord saw fit to include it for a purpose. It is not intended as a threat, nor is it an indication that we must earn God's forgiveness. It is a simple statement of fact. Christians are those who enter into a whole new reality. Although outwardly we appear the same as others, we live according to another kingdom than the world. If we have experienced the forgiveness of God, we by *nature* are able to share that forgiveness with others. If we continue in a spirit of revenge, we betray our true self. We bear witness to the fact that we have not come into a saving relationship with Christ.

This is the truth Jesus explains with his parable of the unmerciful servant in Matthew 18. He has just taught about the process of restoring a sinful brother. Peter then asked just how many times he is to forgive. How many times must he forgive a brother who sins against him — seven times? To him, seven times is generous. But Jesus says, no, not just seven times, but seventy-seven times. Jesus is saying, that will be the very character of those who have known his wonderful love. Every time a brother has hurt us, we are to go about the process of restoration that culminates in treating that person like "a pagan or a tax collector" (Matthew 18:17). How did Jesus treat tax collectors and pagans? He loved them, enjoyed fellowship with them, shared the gospel with them, and brought them to repentance. The Father's will, said Jesus, was that he might find the lost sheep, and that not any of "these little ones should be lost" (Matthew 18:14). Jesus hereby reverses the fratricidal vengeance of unredeemed humanity, expressed in Lamech's ancient poem. He exults, "I have killed a man for wounding me, a young man for injuring me. If Cain is avenged seven times, then Lamech seventy-seven times" (Genesis 4:23-24). What a contrast this is with the limitless love of Jesus!

Without the love of God expressed in his forgiveness, life loses its purpose and joy. It appears like nothing more than a brief span between nothingness and nothingness, or a wait for the judgment of a God we cannot appease. But with forgiveness we have assurance that God loves us and is shaping a good future for us. God alone can soften our heart to receive his love and enable us to extend that love to another. Forgiveness offered is proof of forgiveness received.

Other Voices

Out of the depths to Thee I raise
The voice of lamentation;
Lord, turn a gracious ear to me,
And hear my supplication.
If Thou shouldst count our every sin,
Each evil deed or thought within,
O who could stand before Thee?

⏝

To wash away the crimson stain
Grace, grace alone prevaileth.

Our works, alas! are all in vain;
In much the best life faileth.
For none can glory in Thy sight,
All must alike confess Thy might
And live alone by mercy.

⏝

Therefore my trust is in the Lord,
And not in mine own merit.
On God my soul shall rest; God's word
Upholds my fainting spirit.

God's promised mercy is my fort,
My comfort, and my strong support;
I wait for it with patience.

⤝

What though I wait the livelong night,
And till the dawn appeareth,
My heart still trusteth in God's might;
It doubteth not nor feareth:
So let the Israelites in heart,
Born of the Spirit, do their part,
And wait till God appeareth.

— MARTIN LUTHER, "Out of the Depths"

I recall Michael Christopher's play *The Black Angel,* where he tells the story of Herman Engel. Engel, a German general in World War II, was sentenced by the Nuremberg court to thirty years in prison for atrocities committed by his army. He survived his sentence and was released from prison. At the time of the play he is in Alsace, building a cabin in the woods where he and his wife intend to live out the years left to them — incognito, forgotten, at peace.

But a man named Morrieaux, a French journalist, is waiting in the wings.

Morrieaux's whole family had been massacred by Engel's army during the war. When the Nuremberg court had refused to sentence Engel to death thirty years before, Morrieaux privately condemned Engel to die. His condemnation was kept alive and hot by the fire of hate he kept kindling in his heart. Now the time had come.

Morrieaux had stoked up the fanatics in the village close by Engel's cabin. That very night, they were going to come up the hill, burn down the cabin, and shoot Engel and his wife dead.

Morrieaux, however, wanted to get to Engel beforehand. Some gaps in Engel's history plagued the reporter's need for a finished story. So he went up the hill, introduced himself to a shaken Engel, and spent the afternoon grilling the former general about the village massacre that lay like a forgotten shadow in Engel's past.

But Engel's feeble humanity — he seemed less like a monster than just a tired old man — confused Morrieaux. Besides, he was having a hard time putting all the pieces of the terrible story together; and so he was plagued by newborn doubt. His vengeance was blurred; the purity of his hate was contaminated.

Toward the end of the afternoon, as the sun fell deep and the woods became a cavern, Morrieaux blurted out to Engel that the villagers were going to come and kill him that night. He offered to lead Engel out of the woods and save his life.

But the afternoon's inquisition had brought other kinds of doubts into Engel's soul. Engel paused, eyes fixed on a cone just fallen from a black pine: "I'll go with you," he slowly said, "on one condition." What? Is he mad? Does he lay down a condition for having his own life saved? What condition?

"That you forgive me."

Forgive? Morrieaux had exterminated Engel a thousand exquisite ways in the fantasies of hate that he had played in his mind for thirty years. But face to face with the ambiguity of Engel's humanity, Morrieaux's vengeance was unsettled. He would save the man's life. Yes, he would cancel the execution.

But forgive him? Never.

That night, the enraged villagers came with sacks over their heads, burned the cabin, and shot Engel and his wife dead.

Now I ask, why was it that Morrieaux could not forgive Engel? Why was forgiving even harder than saving Engel's life?

It was too much for Morrieaux, I think, because his hatred had become a passion too long lodged in his soul. Morrieaux could not live, could no longer be the person he was without his hatred; he had *become* his hatred. His hate did not belong to him, he belonged to his hate. He would not know who he was if he did not hate Engel.

The tragedy was that only forgiveness, the one thing he could not give to Engel, could have set Morrieaux free.

— LEWIS B. SMEDES, *Forgive and Forget: Healing the Hurts We Don't Deserve*

Alas, O God, save me, I cry.
What will become of me?
No good I see within myself;
All good must come from Thee.

〜

All my salvation lies in Thee;
Without Thee I am lost.
I know the law which for my sin
Would have me pay the cost.

〜

So grant me, Lord, both grace and faith
To shield my troubled soul.
Alone, we're less than naught, unless
It pleases thee to uphold.

〜

Thou art my all, I know it well,
By thee let me be sought;
Extract me from this cluttered life
In which thou seest me caught.

〜

Oh, pay the debt I owe, and then
To Thine own self join me.
Alas, O God, save me, I cry.
What will become of me?

— MARGUERITE OF NAVARRE, "All My Salvation Lies in Thee"

[Elias Chacour, a Palestinian Arab Christian priest, issued an ultimatum to his feuding and bitterly divided congregation: nobody was to leave the church until there was reconciliation with one another.]

Silence hung. Tight lipped, fists clenched, all glared as if carved in stone. Long minutes passed. Outside, the sound of a donkey clattered on the pavement. Chacour knew he was finished as priest.

The Abu Maubib, the toughest of the brothers, the village police officer, rose, faced the congregation. "I am the worst one of all. I've hated my own brothers. Hated them so much I wanted to kill them. More than any of you I need forgiveness."

Then he turned to the pastor, "Can you forgive me, too, Abuna?" (Abuna means "our father," a term of deep affection and respect, the first warm greeting Chacour had ever heard in that circle.)

"Come," said Chacour, and they embraced, giving the double kiss of peace. "Now go and greet your brothers." And as his brothers came to meet him, a chaos of embracing and tears broke out. Cousins who had not spoken to each other in years wept openly. Confessions were offered. Invitations to Arab hospitality were renewed, and people at last left arm in arm. A lifeless body — the church — was returning from the dead.

— DAVID AUGSBURGER, Helping People Forgive

Daily Scripture Readings

KEY TEXT: ISAIAH 40:1-2
Sunday: Psalm 51
Monday: Psalm 73
Tuesday: Psalm 139
Wednesday: Hosea 14:1-9
Thursday: John 8:1-11
Friday: Acts 9:1-19
Saturday: 1 John 1:1-10

Questions for Reflection and Discussion

Can you think of a time when you felt that God wasn't paying attention to you? What was that like? Why did you feel that way?

The Bible teaches that we are accountable to God, because it is he who is ultimately wronged by our sins. How does this truth help keep our actions in perspective?

Does the Christian need to confess his or her sins to another Christian, or just go directly to God? Why or why not?

When has God's forgiveness been most real for you?

Closing Prayer

Loving God, you have given me life and have grown in me. Overcome my sin, so I can be who you want me to be. Because you are the God of fresh starts and new beginnings, I commit to this again. In Jesus' merit, I pray this. Amen.

Week Fifty-two:
Not by Our Own Strength

Often my ears are dull and can't hear your voice. My eyes are dim and can't see signs of your presence. You are able to open my eyes and ears, to renew my heart. Lord, give me the kind of pure heart that is capable of receiving your words. In Jesus' name, amen.

Heidelberg Questions

QUESTION 127: What does the sixth request mean?

And lead us not into temptation, but deliver us from the evil one means,

By ourselves we are too weak to hold our own even for a moment.[1]

And our sworn enemies — the devil,[2] the world,[3] and our own flesh[4] — never stop attacking us.

And so, Lord, uphold us and make us strong with the strength of your Holy Spirit, so that we may not go down to defeat in this spiritual struggle,[5] but may firmly resist our enemies until we finally win the complete victory.[6]

(*[1]Psalm 103:14-16; John 15:1-5; [2]2 Corinthians 11:14; Ephesians 6:10-13; 1 Peter 5:8; [3]John 15:18-21; [4]Romans 7:23; Galatians 5:17; [5]Matthew 10:19-20; 26:41; Mark 13:33; Romans 5:3-5; [6]1 Corinthians 10:13; 1 Thessalonians 3:13; 5:23*)

QUESTION 128: What does your conclusion to this prayer mean?

For yours is the kingdom, and the power, and the glory forever means,

We have made all these requests of you because, as our all-powerful king, you not only want to, but are able to give us all that is good;[1] and because your holy name, and not we ourselves, should receive all the praise, forever.[2]

(*[1]Romans 10:11-13; 2 Peter 2:9; [2]Psalm 115:1; John 14:13*)

QUESTION 129: What does that little word "Amen" express?

Amen means,

This is sure to be!

It is even more sure that God listens to my prayer, than that I really desire what I pray for.[1]

(*[1]Isaiah 65:24; 2 Corinthians 1:20; 2 Timothy 2:13*)

Exposition

The last petition of the Lord's Prayer is echoed in the prayer Jesus offers at his Last Supper with his disciples. John records how he prays there, "I am not asking you to take them out of the world, but I ask you to protect them from the evil one" (John 17:15, NRSV). The great challenge of the Christian life is that we continue to live in the world, a place fraught with danger and temptation. Christians live *in* the world, but are not *of* the world — that is, our identity and motivation come from God and so are counter-cultural.

Temptation comes when the Christian is torn by conflicting motivations. It is when we are incited to evil by that which Scripture describes as the Devil, the world, or our own flesh. While God does test his children to make them stronger, he does not entice them to do evil. While the inner struggle may feel the same, the source and purpose are different. God tests us not to see us fail or because he has pleasure in evil. He does it in order to strengthen us or to make clear to us the condition of our hearts and our dependence on him.

Our prayer is that God wouldn't hand us over to our enemies to be tempted. Having grown in faith and discernment thus far on the adventure of Christian faith, we have also grown in humility. We know how desperately we need God's protection and provision, for we are unable to prevail in the Christian life on our own power. That is why the more progress we make on the journey the more acutely we are aware of our need for grace and forgiveness. Daily we have to go back to the beginning, as it were, and look to Jesus in simple faith for his deliverance.

This should not be cause for despair, but rather for humble confidence. God is not the author of sin, and he gives all Christians the ability to live a Spirit-controlled life. So we pray that God will not allow us to be tempted beyond what we are able to bear. To be faithful in the fight we need to go into battle prepared. We need to put on the armor of God so as not to be struck down. This is the reality and the urgency of the spiritual warfare in which we are engaged.

Our battle is urgent, yet it can also be subtle. The Devil does not always come at us like a roaring lion; the apostle Paul cautions us that the Devil is able to appear as an angel of light (2 Corinthians 11:14). Evil does not often present itself in its raw ugliness, but most often acts subversively. In our culture, where everything presents itself in shades of gray, very few things are clearly labeled as immoral anymore. Coupled with the demands for privacy and the ascendancy of the individual over the community, temptation to all sorts of evil is more profound than ever. Because of the ubiquity of temptation, we are driven to cry out for the help of the Holy Spirit. With his help we are not weakened by the tests that assail us but are strengthened.

The prayer concludes with a threefold praise to God. This is the basis for the whole prayer because it underscores our reasons for praying and God's reasons for answering. First, we pray because God will hear us. As subjects of the King we can go to him for everything we need. Our response is to acknowledge him as King, Creator, and Sustainer of all things. We trust him to protect us and to make us into the persons he wants us to be on the journey from his kingdom of grace to his kingdom of glory.

So then the conclusion of the prayer with its final doxology reinforces the first petitions that the Father's name be glorified and his kingdom be established. Having brought our needs to him, we ask that we might be nourished, healed of sin, and made victorious in our struggle with evil. All this honors his name, and we can pray to this end with confidence. He is able to hear us because he has power over all things. We can trust him to not deny us anything that fits his glory and our good.

When we pray the Lord's Prayer, we are beginning a work of eternal consequence. We will continue until the day we are ushered into his presence to join in a great chorus of praise, wonder, and adoration, and we will worship him forever.

"Amen" is a Hebrew word that means, "Let it be so." It is a word that signifies assent, or assurance. It is how we can put our confidence in God's ability rather than in our own emotions. According to Martin Luther, it reminds us that we are not alone, but that we are joining with the church in all times and places in a "united prayer which God cannot ignore."[18] This resounding affirmation is that God hears our prayers.

Other Voices

As the Israelites poured out their sorrows and called on the Lord to help them in their psalms so the Celtic Christians developed a range of prayers and rituals to invoke God's protective powers against evil and danger. Many were adapted from pagan charms and incantations. One ritual that clearly has pre-Christian origins is the *caim*. In times of danger, the inhabitants of the Outer Hebrides would draw a circle round themselves and their loved ones. Using the index finger of their right hand, they would point and turn round sun-wise while reciting a prayer such as:

The Sacred Three
My fortress be
Encircling me
Come and be round
My hearth and my home

David Adam, the present vicar of Lindisfarne . . . has written of the *caim*:

"This was no magic; it was no attempt to manipulate God. It was a reminder by action that we are always surrounded by

God. He is our encompasser, our encircler. It is our wavering that has put us out of tune. This is a tuning in to the fact that 'in Him we live and move and have our being.'"

— IAN BRADLEY, *The Celtic Way*

The Christian ideal changed and reversed everything so that, as the gospel puts it, "That which was exalted among men has become an abomination in the sight of God." The ideal is no longer the greatness of Pharaoh or of the Roman emperor, nor the beauty of a Greek nor the wealth of Phoenicia, but humility, purity, compassion, love. The hero is no longer Dives, but Lazarus the beggar; not Mary Magdalene in the day of her beauty but the day of her repentance; not those who acquire wealth, but those who have abandoned it; not those who dwell in palaces, but those who dwell in catacombs and huts; not those who rule over others, but those who acknowledge no other authority but God's.

— LEO TOLSTOY, *What Is Art*

I bind unto myself today
the strong name of the Trinity,
by invocation of the same,
the Three in One, the One in Three.

I bind this day to me forever
by power of faith, Christ's incarnation,
his baptism in the Jordan river;
his death on the cross for my salvation.
His bursting from the spiced tomb;
his riding up the heavenly way;
his coming at the day of doom

I bind unto myself today.
I bind unto myself today
the power of God to hold and lead,
His eye to watch, his might to stay,
His ear to harken to my need,
the wisdom of my God to teach,
His hand to guide, his shield to ward,
the Word of God to give me speech,
His heavenly host to be my guard.

Christ be with me, Christ within me,
Christ behind me, Christ before me,
Christ beside me, Christ to win me,
Christ to comfort and restore me,
Christ beneath me, Christ above me,
Christ in quiet, Christ in danger,
Christ in hearts of all that love me,
Christ in mouth of friend and stranger.

I bind unto myself the name,
the strong name of the Trinity,
by invocation of the same,
the Three in One, the One in Three,
of whom all nature has creation,
eternal Father, Spirit, Word.
Praise to the God of my salvation,
salvation is of Christ the Lord.

— PATRICK OF IRELAND

My Lord God, I have no idea where I am going. I do not see the road ahead of me. I cannot know for certain where it will end. Nor do I really know myself, and the fact that I think that I am following your will does not mean that I am actually doing so. But I believe that the desire to please you does in fact please you. And I hope I have that desire in all that I am doing. I hope that I will never do anything apart from that desire. And I know that if I do this you will lead me by the right road though I may know nothing about it. Therefore will I trust you always though I may seem to be lost and in the shadow of death. I will not fear, for you are ever with me, and you will never leave me to face my perils alone.

— THOMAS MERTON, *Thoughts in Solitude*

As Paul makes clear, however, and German theologian Jürgan Moltmann (of *Theology of Hope* fame) reaffirms, before the resurrection was the cross, which "reveals . . . the unredeemed condition of the world and its sinking into nothingness." Thus genuine Christian hope is not an unrealistic refusal to accept the negativities of life but a realization that even those negativities, even a whole world "groaning in travail together" (Rom. 8:22), even something as vicious and damnable as Alzheimer's disease, cannot prevail against the power and love of God. Martin Luther King Jr., with a wealth of experience of the negativities of this world, aptly expressed the Christian hope when he said, "We must accept finite disappointment, but we must never lose infinite hope." Such an attitude is possible for Christians because in Christ's resurrection, as Moltmann affirms,

hope is always kindled anew. In him, the future of righteousness and the passing of evil can be hoped for; in him, the future of life and the passing of death can be hoped for; in him, the coming of freedom and the passing of humiliation can be hoped for; in him, the future of . . . true humanity and the passing of inhumanity can be hoped for.

— DONALD K. McKIM, EDITOR,
*God Never Forgets: Faith, Hope,
and Alzheimer's Disease*

Daily Scripture Readings

KEY TEXT: ISAIAH 65:24
  Sunday: Psalm 103
  Monday: Matthew 10:1-25
  Tuesday: Luke 4:1-13
  Wednesday: 1 Corinthians 10:1-13
  Thursday: 1 Corinthians 10:23–11:1
  Friday: 1 Timothy 6:3-10
  Saturday: 1 Thessalonians 2:17–3:13

Questions for Reflection and Discussion

In the eyes of the world, giving in to temptation sometimes means simply overcoming one's inhibitions and discovering one's self. How would you explain to an unbelieving friend the importance of restraint?

Identify the influences that draw Christians away from a godly lifestyle. Why do you think Christians worry about evil in the world? Is that good or bad? Why?

What are some ways you have found strength to resist when tempted to do what you know is wrong? What are the areas where you need the help of Christian friends to overcome temptation?

Closing Prayer

O God, you are my life. You are wisdom, beauty, purity, light, love, and blessing, the only true good. You are my God and my heart's joy. You have freed me from my darkness, freed me to serve you all my days. Let my love and knowledge of you grow until the day I am complete in your presence. Keep me safe until that day. In the precious name of Jesus, this is sure to be!

To him who is able to keep you from falling and to present you before his glorious presence without fault and with great joy — to the only God our Savior be glory, majesty, power and authority, through Jesus Christ our Lord, before all ages, now and forevermore! Amen. (Jude 24)

Appendix

Application: Devotional Reading

Much of Western Christianity tends toward activism. Devotional reading can help us become better rounded in our Christian experience. In addition to the spiritual benefit from reading contemporary devotional works, the evangelical church has rediscovered classic devotional writing from the contemplative tradition. There is a large body of material available these days to help us in our prayer life. The following guidelines may help.

1. PUT THE MAIN EMPHASIS ON READING SCRIPTURE.

Christian literature can help apply God's truth to the concerns of daily living. But it is not a replacement for Scripture. The Bible is the first essential component in Christian formation, for it was shaped by the Holy Spirit working in the minds and hearts of its writers in their own particular setting. The same Spirit causes the words to come off the page and to come alive in us today. Still, really getting into Scripture takes a measure of commitment — after all, the Bible developed in a different time and place, in a world very unlike the one in which we make our lives. Devotional literature can

seem more accessible, but in the long run, we need the timeless perspectives of Scripture.

2. ATTITUDE MATTERS MORE THAN TECHNIQUE.

It seems that today there is a technique for anything you could possibly want to learn. But when it comes to growing intimacy with the Father, the tendency to want a method to guide us isn't enough. For one thing, the living God who stands above us won't be manipulated. For another, the Father who loves us invites us into a relationship. It's not a matter of mastering a set of truths, but of putting ourselves into a place where God's Spirit can touch us. When reading for information, we read differently than when reading for spiritual formation, that is, in order to be shaped by the content we're absorbing. If not technique, then what? Simply desire — to know God and to see his hand shaping us through all the events of our lives.

3. TAKE DEVOTIONAL READING AT ITS OWN PACE.

We read differently when we pore over a riveting best seller, or distractedly skim the morning newspaper, than when we prayerfully mull over the meaning-packed words of a devotional writer. Something about the words compels a more contemplative reading, a more lingering pace. Since the object is to open ourselves to the changed life that God offers, we ruminate upon the words in order to more fully absorb them. Then they are able to become a part of our subconscious mind, to percolate into the recesses of our being. Take just a small portion of a text, perhaps a paragraph, and dwell over that for several minutes as you examine it in your mind.

4. GET HELP FROM CHRISTIAN FRIENDS IN CHOOSING WHAT YOU READ.

See what has made a difference for others who are deep in Christ; after all, changed lives is what it's all about. Ask those whose faith you admire or who have provided reliable guidance for you what works have proven most helpful. Another way to go about it is to see what authors have influenced the Christian writers you already appreciate (and then, in turn, what authors have been most formative in their thinking). Soon, you will discover writers who consistently inspire and influence the lives of Christians. You'll also begin to discern certain recurring themes and writers who rise above mere fashion and have stood the test of time.

5. CHOOSE FROM A BROAD SPECTRUM OF CHRISTIAN THINKERS.

All of us have the tendency to surround ourselves with people like ourselves. The same is true in the ideas we absorb: it's easy to read what you agree with. While it is important to cultivate discernment, we will gain wider understanding and more healthy practice in the Christian life by encountering a variety of sources within Christian orthodoxy. The kingdom of God is too great a reality for any single expression. Spiritual writers from traditions as divergent as Reformed and Wesleyan, Pentecostal and Catholic can be our mentors. From one we will learn to appreciate the grandeur and holiness of God, from another his sovereignty, from another his beauty, from another his immediacy, from another his compassion, from another his grace and his truth.

6. PROCESS WHAT YOU READ WITH A PRAYER PARTNER OR A COVENANT GROUP.

We are more likely to have it stick and to use discernment if we are in relationship with one another. This is the principle of accountability and balance. Try out a new idea by expressing it to another Christian. The challenge in this is that you will have someone asking you if you're putting into practice what you're learning. Application is the all-important outcome and not simply more "head knowledge."

Application: A Model for Prayer

Most of us could use some help when it comes to prayer. How do we shape our prayer life? How do we know when we are properly focused in our prayer? The acrostic "ACTS" reminds us of the essential components of prayer that comprise the Lord's Prayer itself. You can use this as an outline for your prayer time.

ADORATION

This is the primary form of prayer. It is the basic response of the creature to the Creator. God is absolutely different from everything else that is. He is holy, and adoration may be offered to him alone. Prayer to anything in the created order is not Christian worship but idolatry. We humans need to respond to our incomparable God, and that response takes shape in adoration. Many of the psalms echo this theme — "Worship the Lord in the splendor of his holiness; tremble before him, all the earth" (Psalm 96:9). We adore him by surrendering ourselves to God, recognizing our dependence on him. We offer words of praise for God's majesty, holiness, beauty, truth, goodness, justice, and love.

CONFESSION

An ancient Christian prayer says, "Lord Jesus, have mercy on me, a sinner." That prayer is a very good place for us to start our confession. When we come into God's holy presence, we cannot help feeling tarnished by our sins. When the prophet Isaiah sees the glory of God in a vision of heaven, he cries out, "Woe is me! I am lost, for I am a man of unclean lips, and I live among a people of unclean lips; yet my eyes have seen the King, the LORD of hosts!" (Isaiah 6:5, NRSV). God's purity convicts us of sin.

This is entirely different from the shame and guilt that plague so many. This is not unhealthy self-loathing. Scripture lets us know that repentance is always the beginning of renewal. When we say we're sorry to God, recognizing that we continue to fail,

God will forgive. Sometimes it helps to tell a brother or sister in Christ, as James counsels: "Confess your sins to one another" (James 5:16, NRSV). God intervenes through the body of Christ. In relationship with others it is harder to trick ourselves about our sin, and the forgiveness pronounced is tangible. You can agree to name specific sins with a trusted prayer partner, and remind each other, "in the name of Jesus, you are forgiven." At other times, knowing we need no mediator but Christ, we are glad to be able to go straight to him in prayer.

THANKSGIVING

The most natural reaction to forgiveness and blessing is to give thanks. This is close kin with praise of God. One way to say it is that we praise God for who he is and thank him for what he has done. The categorizations don't hold strictly to form, but it is a good discipline to let our adoration of God really be that — our praise and worship — and to let our thanksgiving reflect on the many ways God has blessed us. The Bible records many examples of outbursts of thanksgiving, from the Psalms to victory songs to letters to the churches. When we begin to list the ways God has cared for us, it is easy to think of things to add. His gifts are many. Notice the sequence — we come to God in a posture of thankful trust before we start asking him to meet our needs.

SUPPLICATION

We properly pray *for* others and ourselves only after having worshiped God and confessed our sin. Even then we do not "make known" our needs, strictly speaking, because God knows them already. Still, he invites us to express them as an act of trust. He will fill our needs according to his good will for us. Our petitions and intercessions are a part of our surrender to what the Father has for us, and that brings us peace.

If we remember to include these four components, our prayer will be fuller and more in line with how God wants us to pray.

Application: Daily Devotions

Find a quiet place where you can be with the Lord. This should be a place with as little risk of interruption as possible. It may help to turn on the answering machine. If you are starting with the practice of daily devotions, you may wish to choose a specific time and write in your calendar, "Time with God." Remember that this time is a gift from God. If you find it difficult to focus, tell God about that.

Begin by closing your eyes for a moment and taking several deep breaths. If you find it helpful, you can imagine that as you inhale, you are breathing in the Holy Spirit. Each time you exhale, you are breathing out your worry, your fretfulness, and your distraction. If thoughts come to mind of things that need to be done, don't condemn yourself over your lack of concentration. Simply write down the concern, set it aside for the time being, and continue to focus on God. Spend a few moments in quietness.

Ask the heavenly Father to be with you in this time. You may begin with a prayer something like this: "Lord, take this time. Thank you that you long to meet me every day. As I read and reflect upon your Word, shape me more into the likeness of Jesus. Amen."

Turn to the Daily Scripture Readings near the end of the week's study. Read the Key Text and the selection for that day. The following questions are a good way to start digesting the meaning of a passage:

1. *What does it say?* Ask the investigative questions of Who, What, When, Why, How. Try to get a handle on the essential action of a story, the main point of a letter, the overriding image used in a psalm.

2. *What does it mean?* Ask what the point was, as best as you can tell, for the audience to whom it was directed. The notes in a study Bible can help you discern who the original audience was and what some of their issues were. This will help you understand the original meaning of the text before too quickly jumping into personal application.

3. *What does it mean for me?* This is the "So what?" of the whole endeavor. As well as we might understand the passage, unless we come to terms with it in our own lives, we will not have gained the full benefit.

THE COMMANDMENT	WHAT IS REQUIRED?	WHAT IS FORBIDDEN?
1. The **focus** of worship: *Have no other gods*	To worship the one true God	To deny God, to worship false gods
2. The **way** of worship: *No image or likeness; Do not bow down to them*	To worship God as he wills	To worship wrongly or to worship idols
3. The **attitude** of worship: *Do not take the Lord's name in vain*	To use God's name honorably	To disrespect God's name
4. The **time** of worship: *Remember the Sabbath*	To worship each week, working six days and resting one day	To make work the center of life
5. The rule of **authority**: *Honor your father and mother*	To obey God-given authority	To disregard God-given authority
6. The rule of **life**: *You shall not murder*	To preserve and build up the lives of others	To take the life of another
7. The rule of **sex**: *You shall not commit adultery*	To maintain fidelity in marriage and chastity in singleness	To engage in sexual immorality
8. The rule of **property**: *You shall not steal*	To respect the physical needs of others	To be destructive of that which belongs to others
9. The rule of **speech**: *You shall not bear false witness*	To promote truth and to uphold the good name of a neighbor	To gossip or speak falsely
10. The rule of **heart**: *You shall not covet*	To be content with what we have and to rejoice with what others have	To envy, to be discontent, or to wish evil on another

Bibliography

Alighieri, Dante. *The Divine Comedy*. New York: W. W. Norton & Company, 1977.

Anderson, Ray. *Soulprints: Personal Reflections on Faith, Hope, and Love*. Pasadena, Calif.: Fuller Seminary Press, 1996.

Appleton, George, ed. *The Oxford Book of Prayer*. Oxford: Oxford University Press, 1989.

Augsburger, David. *Helping People Forgive*. Louisville, Ky.: Westminster John Knox, 1996.

Augustine of Hippo. *The City of God*. Garden City, N.Y.: Image Books, 1958.

Augustine of Hippo. *Confessions*. Oxford: Oxford University Press, 1998.

Authentic Worship in a Changing Culture. Grand Rapids, Mich.: Christian Reformed Church Publications, 1997.

Baillie, John. *A Diary of Private Prayer*. New York: Charles Scribner's Sons, 1977.

Balswick, Judith and Jack. *Families in Pain: Working Through the Hurts*. Grand Rapids, Mich.: Baker, 1997.

Barclay, William. *The Ten Commandments*. Louisville, Ky.: Westminster John Knox, 1998.

Barnes, M. Craig. *Yearning: Living Between How It Is & How It Ought to Be*. Downers Grove, Ill.: InterVarsity, 1992.

Barth, Karl. *Dogmatics in Outline*. New York: Harper & Row, 1959.

Barth, Karl. *The Humanity of God*. Louisville, Ky.: Westminster John Knox, 1960.

Barth, Karl. *The Theology of John Calvin*. Grand Rapids, Mich.: Eerdmans, 1995.

Barth, Karl. *Prayer and Preaching*. London: SCM Press, 1964.

Bernard of Clairvaux. *The Love of God*. Portland, Oreg.: Multnomah, 1983.

Blamires, Harry. *The Christian Mind: How Should a Christian Think?* Ann Arbor, Mich.: Servant, 1978.

Bloesch, Donald G. *Freedom for Obedience: Evangelical Ethics for Contemporary Times*. San Francisco, Calif.: HarperSanFrancisco, 1987.

Bloesch, Donald G. *God the Almighty*. Downers Grove, Ill.: InterVarsity, 1995.

Boesak, Allan. *Black and Reformed: Apartheid, Liberation, and the Calvinist Tradition*. Maryknoll, N.Y.: Orbis, 1986.

Bonhoeffer, Dietrich. *Christ the Center*. San Francisco, Calif.: HarperSanFrancisco, 1978.

Bonhoeffer, Dietrich. *Creation and Fall / Temptation*. New York: Touchstone, 1997.

Bonhoeffer, Dietrich. *The Cost of Discipleship*. New York: Collier Books, 1973.

Bonhoeffer, Dietrich. *Letters and Papers from Prison*. New York: Macmillan, 1972.

Bonhoeffer, Dietrich. *Life Together*. New York: Harper & Row, 1954.

Boyer, Ernest Jr. *Finding God at Home: Family Life as Spiritual Discipline*. San Francisco, Calif.: HarperSanFrancisco, 1988.

Bradley, Ian. *The Celtic Way*. London: Darton, Longman and Todd, 1993.

Brooke, Avery. *Plain Prayers in a Complicated World*. Boston: Cowley Publications, 1994.

Brother Lawrence. *The Practice of the Presence of God*. Orleans, Mass.: Paraclete Press, 1996.

Brown, Robert McAfee. *Speaking of Christianity: Practical Compassion, Social Justice, and Other Wonders*. Louisville, Ky.: Westminster John Knox, 1997.

Bruner, Frederick Dale. *The Christbook: A Historical/Theological Commentary.* Waco, Tex.: Word, 1987.

Brunner, Emil. *Our Faith.* New York: Charles Scribner's Sons, 1962.

Brunner, Emil. *The Christian Doctrine of God.* Philadelphia, Pa.: Westminster, 1950.

Brunner, Emil. *The Christian Doctrine of the Church, Faith, and the Consummation.* Philadelphia, Pa.: Westminster, 1962.

Buechner, Frederick. *Wishful Thinking: A Theological ABC.* New York: HarperCollins, 1993.

Buechner, Frederick. *The Hungering Dark.* San Francisco, Calif.: HarperSanFrancisco, 1993.

Bunyan, John. *The Pilgrim's Progress in Modern English.* L. Edward Hazelbaker, ed. North Brunswick, N. J.: Bridge Logos Publishers, 1998.

Calvin, John. *Calvin's Old Testament Commentaries.* Grand Rapids, Mich.: Eerdmans, 1994.

Calvin, John. *Golden Booklet of the True Christian Life.* Grand Rapids, Mich.: Baker, 1952.

Calvin, John. *Harmony of the Gospels.* Grand Rapids, Mich.: Eerdmans, 1994.

Calvin, John. *Institutes of the Christian Religion.* Philadelphia, Pa.: Westminster, 1960.

Carretto, Carlo. *Letters from the Desert.* Maryknoll, N.Y.: Orbis, 1994.

Catherine of Genoa. *Purgation and Purgatory: the Spiritual Dialogue, Classics of Western Spirituality.* Mahwah, N.J.: Paulist, 1979.

Chambers, Oswald. *My Utmost for His Highest.* Grand Rapids, Mich.: Discovery House, 1992.

Chesterton, G. K. *The Everlasting Man.* Garden City, N.Y.: Image Books, 1974.

Chesterton, G. K. *Orthodoxy.* San Francisco, Calif.: Ignatius, 1995.

Clark, Chap and Dee. *Daughters and Dads: Building a Lasting Relationship.* Colorado Springs, Colo.: NavPress, 1998.

Dallas, Joe. *Desires in Conflict: Answering the Struggle for Sexual Identity.* Eugene, Oreg.: Harvest House, 1991.

Davidman, Joy. *Smoke on the Mountain: An Interpretation of the Ten Commandments.* Louisville, Ky.: Westminster John Knox, 1985.

Dawn, Marva. *Reaching Out Without Dumbing Down: A Theology of Worship for the Turn-of-the-Century Culture.* Grand Rapids, Mich.: Eerdmans, 1995.

Dearborn, Tim. *Taste & See.* Downers Grove, Ill.: InterVarsity, 1996.

Dostoevsky, Fyodor. *The Brothers Karamazov.* New York: Viking Penguin, 1993.

Dunn, James D. G. *Jesus and the Spirit.* Grand Rapids, Mich.: Eerdmans, 1997.

Dykstra, Craig. *Growing in the Life of Faith: Education and Christian Practices.* Louisville, Ky.: Westminster John Knox, 1999.

Ecumenical Creeds and Reformed Confessions. *The Heidelberg Catechism.* Grand Rapids, Mich.: CRC Publications, 1989.

Esquivel, Julia. *Certainty of Spring.* Guatemala: Epica, 1992.

Foster, Richard J. *Celebration of Discipline: The Path to Spiritual Growth.* San Francisco, Calif.: HarperSanFrancisco, 1988.

Foster, Richard J. *Freedom of Simplicity.* New York: HarperCollins, 1997.

Goodpasture, H. McKennie. *Cross and Sword: An Eyewitness History of Christianity in Latin America.* Maryknoll, N.Y.: Orbis, 1989.

Graham, Billy. *Facing Death and the Life After.* Waco, Tex.: Word, 1987.

Graham, W. Fred. *The Constructive Revolutionary: John Calvin & His Socio-Economic Impact.* East Lansing, Mich.: Michigan State University Press, 1987.

Graham, Ruth Bell. *Legacy of a Packrat.* Nashville, Tenn.: Thomas Nelson, 1989.

Granberg-Michaelson, Wesley. *Redeeming the Creation: The Rio Earth Summit: Challenges for the Churches.* New York: World Council of Churches, 1983.

Guder, Darrell L. *Missional Church: A Vision for the Sending of the Church in North America.* Grand Rapids, Mich.: Eerdmans, 1998.

Hallie, Philip. *Lest Innocent Blood Be Shed: The Story of the Village of Le Chambon and How Goodness Happened There.* New York: Harper & Row, 1979.

Hammarskjold, Dag. *Markings.* New York: Knopf, 1981.

Hays, Richard B. *The Moral Vision of the New Testament: A Contemporary Introduction to New Testament Ethics.* New York: HarperCollins, 1996.

Herbert, George. *The Temple: The Poetry of George Herbert.* Cape Cod, Mass.: Paraclete, 2001.

Hoekema, Anthony A. *The Christian Looks at Himself.* Grand Rapids, Mich.: Eerdmans, 1975.

Hornok, Marcia K. "Psalm 23, Antithesis." *Discipleship Journal,* March/April 1990, NavPress.

Houston, James. *In Search of Happiness: A Guide to Personal Contentment.* Oxford: Lion Publishing, 1990.

Hunsinger, George. *Disruptive Grace: Studies in the Theology of Karl Barth.* Grand Rapids, Mich.: Eerdmans, 2000.

Hurnard, Hannah. *Hinds' Feet on High Places.* Carol Stream, Ill.: Tyndale, 1983.

The Hymnbook. Atlanta, Ga.: Presbyterian Church, USA, 1955.

Johnson, Ben Campbell. *Discerning God's Will.* Louisville, Ky.: Westminster John Knox, 1987.

Johnson, Ben Campbell. *Pastoral Spirituality: A Focus for Ministry.* Louisville, Ky.: Westminster John Knox, 1988.

Jones, E. Stanley. *How to Be a Transformed Person.* New York: Abingdon-Cokesbury Press, 1951.

Kempis, Thomas à. *The Imitation of Christ.* Grand Rapids, Mich.: Baker, 1973.

Kierkegaard, Søren. *Training in Christianity.* Princeton, N. J.: Princeton University Press, 1972.

Kise, Jane A. G. *Life Keys: Discovering Who You Are, Why You're Here, and What You Do Best.* Minneapolis, Minn.: Bethany House, 1996.

Koyoma, Kosuke. *Fifty Meditations.* Maryknoll, N.Y.: Orbis, 1994.

Kreeft, Peter. *Making Choices: Practical Wisdom for Everyday Moral Decisions.* Ann Arbor, Mich.: Servant, 1990.

Kreeft, Peter. *Prayer, the Great Conversation: Straight Answers to Tough Questions About Prayer.* San Francisco, Calif.: Ignatius Press, 1991.

Kuyper, Abraham. *Lectures on Calvinism.* Grand Rapids, Mich.: Eerdmans, 1993.

Ladd, George Eldon. *The Blessed Hope.* Grand Rapids, Mich.: Eerdmans, 1994.

Law, William. *A Serious Call to a Devout and Holy Life.* Hopkinton, Mass.: Vintage Books, 1986.

L'Engle, Madeleine. *The Summer of the Great-Grandmother.* San Francisco, Calif.: HarperSanFrancisco, 1987.

L'Engle, Madeleine. *Walking on Water: Reflections on Faith and Art.* Wheaton, Ill.: Harold Shaw, 1984.

Lewis, C. S. *The World's Last Night and Other Essays.* San Diego, Calif.: Harcourt Brace, 1984.

Lewis, C. S. *The Great Divorce: a Dream.* San Francisco, Calif.: HarperSanFrancisco, 2001.

Lewis, C. S. *The Problem of Pain.* San Francisco, Calif.: HarperSanFrancisco, 2001.

Lewis, C. S. *Mere Christianity.* San Francisco, Calif.: HarperSanFrancisco, 2001.

Lewis, C. S. *The Silver Chair.* New York: HarperCollins, 1994.

Lewis, C. S. *The Lion, the Witch and the Wardrobe.* New York: HarperCollins, 1994.

Lewis, C. S. *Letters of C. S. Lewis.* New York: Harvest Books, 1994.

Luther, Martin. *Luther's Prayers.* Minneapolis, Minn.: Fortress, 1994.

Luther, Martin. *Luther's Works, vol. 21: The Sermon on the Mount and the Magnificat.* Minneapolis, Minn.: Fortress, 1960.

Luther, Martin. *The Bondage of the Will.* Grand Rapids, Mich.: Revell, 1990.

MacDonald, Gail. *A Step Farther & Higher: Some Turn Back, Others Never Will.* Sisters, Oreg.: Questar, 1993.

Marty, Martin E. *The Lord's Supper.* Minneapolis, Minn.: Augsburg Fortress, 1997.

McGrath, Alister E. *Studies in Doctrine.* Grand Rapids, Mich.: Zondervan, 1997.

Merton, Thomas. *Thoughts in Solitude.* New York: Farrar, Straus and Giroux, 1998.

Merton, Thomas. *No Man Is an Island.* San Diego, Calif.: Harcourt Brace, 1978.

Meyers, Eleanor Scott, ed. *Envisioning the New City: A Reader on Urban Ministry.* Louisville, Ky.: Westminster John Knox, 1992.

McKim, Donald K., ed. *Encyclopedia of the Reformed Faith.* Louisville, Ky.: Westminster John Knox, 1992.

McKim, Donald K., ed. *God Never Forgets: Faith, Hope, and Alzheimer's Disease.* Louisville, Ky.: Westminster John Knox, 1997.

Middleton, J. Richard and Brian J Walsh. *Truth Is Stranger Than It Used to Be: Biblical Faith in a Postmodern Age.* Downers Grove, Ill.: InterVarsity, 1995.

Milton, John. *Paradise Lost and Paradise Regained.* New York: Penguin, 1976.

Moltmann, Jürgen. *The Crucified God.* Minneapolis, Minn.: Fortress, 1994.

Moltmann, Jürgen. *Jesus Christ for Today's World.* Minneapolis, Minn.: Fortress, 1994.

Morris, Leon. *The Atonement: Its Meaning and Significance.* Downer's Grove, Ill.: InterVarsity, 1984.

Muggeridge, Malcolm. *Jesus The Man Who Lives.* San Francisco, Calif.: HarperSanFrancisco, 1988.

Muggeridge, Malcolm. *Something Beautiful for God: Mother Teresa of Calcutta.* San Francisco, Calif.: HarperSanFrancisco, 1986.

Munger, Robert Boyd. *My Heart – Christ's Home.* Downers Grove, Ill.: InterVarsity, 1992.

Murray, Andrew. *With Christ in the School of Prayer.* North Brunswick, N. J.: Bridge Logos Publishers, 1999.

Newbigin, Lesslie. *The Open Secret: An Introduction to the Theology of Mission.* Grand Rapids, Mich.: Eerdmans, 1994.

Niebuhr, H. Richard. *Christ and Culture.* New York: HarperCollins, 1986.

Nouwen, Henri J. M. *Making All Things New: An Invitation to the Spiritual Life.* San Francisco, Calif.: HarperSanFrancisco, 1981.

Nouwen, Henri J. M. *Beyond the Mirror: Reflections on Death and Life.* New York: Crossroad Publishing, 1991.

Nouwen, Henri J. M. *Life of the Beloved.* New York: Crossroad Publishing, 1992.

Nouwen, Henri J. M. *The Return of the Prodigal Son: A Story of Homecoming.* Garden City, N.Y.: Image Books, 1994.

Old, Hughes Oliphant. *Worship: Guides to the Reformed Tradition.* Atlanta, Ga.: John Knox, 1984.

Oden, Thomas C. *The Event Named Resurrection.* Grand Rapids, Mich.: Zondervan.

Olson, Roger E. *The Story of Christian Theology: Twenty Centuries of Tradition and Reform.* Downers Grove, Ill.: InterVarsity, 1999.

Packer, J. I. *Evangelism & the Sovereignty of God.* Downers Grove, Ill.: InterVarsity, 1995.

Packer, J. I. *God: I Want to Be a Christian.* Downers Grove, Ill.: InterVarsity, 1999.

Packer, J. I. *Knowing God.* Downers Grove, Ill., InterVarsity, 1993.

Pannenberg, Wolfhart. *Systematic Theology.* Grand Rapids, Mich.: Eerdmans, 1997.

Pascal, Blaise. *Pensées.* New York: Penguin Books, 1995.

Pentecost, J. Dwight. *Designed to Be Like Him.* Grand Rapids, Mich.: Discovery House, 1994.

Peterson, Eugene H. *Answering God: The Psalms as Tools for Prayer.* New York: HarperCollins, 1989.

Peterson, Eugene H. *The Message: The New Testament in Contemporary English.* Colorado Springs, Colo.: NavPress, 1993.

Peterson, Eugene H. *A Long Obedience in the Same Direction.* Downers Grove, Ill.: InterVarsity, 2000.

Purves, Andrew. *The Search for Compassion: Spirituality and Ministry.* Louisville, Ky.: Westminster John Knox, 1989.

Recinos, Harold J. *Who Comes in the Name of the Lord?* Nashville, Tenn.: Abingdon, 1997.

Rohls, Jan. *Reformed Confessions: Theology from Zurich to Barmen.* Louisville, Ky.: Westminster John Knox, 1998.

Sayers, Dorothy L. *Catholic Tales and Christian Songs.* Oxford: B. H. Blackwell, 1918.

The Scots Confession. Louisville, Ky.: Presbyterian Church, USA, 2001.

The Second Helvetic Confession. Louisville, Ky.: Presbyterian Church, USA, 2001.

Shenk, Wilbert. *Write the Vision: The Church Renewed.* Valley Forge, Pa.: Trinity Press, 1995.

Smedes, Lewis B. *Union with Christ.* Grand Rapids, Mich.: Eerdmans, 1983.

Smedes, Lewis B. *Shame and Grace: Healing the Shame We Don't Deserve.* New York: HarperCollins, 1993.

Smedes, Lewis B. *Forgive and Forget: Healing the Hurts We Don't Deserve.* New York: Simon and Schuster, 1984.

Springsted, Eric O., ed. *Simone Weil: Writings.* Maryknoll, N.Y.: Orbis, 1998.

Stott, John R. W. *Romans: God's Good News for the World.* Downers Grove, Ill.: InterVarsity, 1995.

Stott, John R. W. *The Cross of Christ.* Downers Grove, Ill.: InterVarsity, 1995.

Stott, John R. W. *The Contemporary Christian.* Downers Grove, Ill.: InterVarsity, 1995.

Stott, John R. W. *Christian Counter-Culture.* Downers Grove, Ill.: InterVarsity, 1978.

Stott, John R. W. *Issues Facing Christians Today.* Downers Grove, Ill.: InterVarsity, 1984.

Teresa of Ávila. *Interior Castle.* New York: Image Books, 1972.

Thielicke, Helmut. *I Believe: The Christian's Creed.* Minneapolis, Minn.: Fortress, 1968.

Thielicke, Helmut. *Encounter with Spurgeon.* Philadelphia, Pa.: Fortress, 1963.

Thompson, Marjorie J. *Soul Feast: An Invitation to the Christian Spiritual Life.* Louisville, Ky.: Westminster John Knox, 1995.

Thurman, Howard. *For the Inward Journey.* Richmond, Ind.: Friends United Press, 1984.

Tolstoy, Leo. *What Is Art.* New York: Penguin Books, 1995.

Troeger, Thomas H. *New Hymns for the Life of the Church: To Make Our Prayer and Music One.* Oxford: Oxford University Press, 1993.

Underhill, Evelyn, ed. *Introduction to The Cloud of Unknowing.* Kila, Mont.: Kessinger Publishing, 1998.

Vajda, Jaroslav. *Christmas Carols for Friends and Families.* New York: Darcy Press, 1997.

Van Gogh, Vincent. *The Letters of Vincent Van Gogh.* New York: Penguin Books, 1998.

Volf, Miroslav. *Exclusion and Embrace: A Theological Exploration of Identity, Otherness, and Reconciliation.* Nashville, Tenn.: Abingdon, 1996.

Wainwright, Geoffrey. *Doxology: The Praise of God in Worship, Doctrine, and Life.* New York: Oxford University Press, 1984.

White, John. *Eros Redeemed.* Downers Grove, Ill.: InterVarsity, 1993.

Wiederkehr, Macrina. *A Tree Full of Angels.* San Francisco, Calif.: HarperSanFrancisco, 1990.

Wilkinson, Loren. "'Art as Creation' or 'Art as Work'?" from *With Heart, Mind & Strength: The Best of Crux, 1979-1989.* Vancouver, Canada: Regent College, 1990.

Willard, Dallas. *The Spirit of the Disciplines.* San Francisco, Calif: HarperSanFrancisco, 1991.

Willimon, William H. *Acts.* Atlanta, Ga.: John Knox, 1988.

Willimon, William H. *On a Wild and Windy Mountain.* Nashville, Tenn.: Abingdon, 1984.

Wilson, Marvin R. *Our Father Abraham: Jewish Roots of the Christian Faith.* Grand Rapids, Mich.: Eerdmans, 1991.

Winn, Albert Curry. *A Christian Primer: The Prayer, the Creed, and the Commandments.* Louisville, Ky.: Westminster John Knox, 1990.

Wolterstorff, Nicholas. *Lament for a Son.* Grand Rapids, Mich.: Eerdmans, 1987.

Wright, N. T. *Following Jesus: Biblical Reflections on Discipleship.* Grand Rapids, Mich.: Eerdmans, 1995.

Wright, N. T. *The Original Jesus: The Life and Vision of a Revolutionary.* Grand Rapids, Mich.: Eerdmans, 1997.

Zwingli, Ulrich. *Commentary on True and False Religion.* Grand Rapids, Mich.: Baker, 1981.

Notes

[1] C. S. Lewis, *God in the Dock: Essays on Theology and Ethics* (Grand Rapids, Mich.: Eerdmans, 1970), p. 90.

[2] Throughout "Other Voices", there are references to "man" or "men" meaning "all human beings." To preserve the writers' voices in the age in which they lived, I have left these unchanged. I ask the reader to mentally amplify them to "women and men," "all humanity."

[3] From a lecture given during a Bible conference at the Community Church in Longview, Washington.

[4] Victor Hugo, *Les Misérables* (London: Penguin Books, 1980), p. 376.

[5] John Calvin, *Institutes of the Christian Religion* (Philadelphia, Pa.: Westminster, 1960), Book II, ch. XV, p. 495.

[6] H. V. Morton, *In the Steps of the Master* (New York: Dodd, Mead, and Company, 1962), p. 48.

[7] Heinrich Bullinger, *The Second Helvetic Confession,* 1566.

[8] Author's translation.

[9] Karen Armstrong, *A History of God* (New York: Random House, 1994).

[10] Lewis Smedes, *Mere Morality* (Grand Rapids, Mich.: Eerdmans, 1983), p. 183.

[11] Smedes, p. 183.

[12] United Nations Development Program, 1998.

[13] Richard Foster, *Celebration of Discipline* (San Francisco, Calif.: HarperSanFrancisco, 1988), p. 80.

[14] David Seamands, *God's Blueprint for Living: New Perspectives on the Ten Commandments* (Wilmore, Ky.: Bristol Books, 1988), p. 133.

[15] Richard Foster, *Celebration of Discipline: The Path to Spiritual Growth* (New York: & Row, 1978), p. 30.

[16] Otto Thelemann, *An Aid to the Heidelberg Catechism,* trans. M. Peters (Grand Rapids, Mich.: Douma Publications, 1959), p. 405.

[17] Dale Bruner, *The Christbook: A Historical/Theological Commentary* (Waco, Tex.: Word, 1987), p. 250.

[18] Herbert F. Brokering, *Luther's Prayers* (Minneapolis, Minn.: Augsburg, 1994), p. 48.

Author

The son of Presbyterian pastors, Randal Working is a graduate of Whitworth College and of the University of Washington, where he completed a Masters in Fine Arts degree in drawing and painting. Randal later earned his Master of Divinity at Fuller Theological Seminary. In addition to occasionally showing his paintings, he uses illustration to enhance his teaching ministry.

For several years he worked as a campus minister with Youth for Christ, Switzerland, and as associate pastor for Christian Education at Celtic Cross Presbyterian Church, a church in Northern California. For the past five years he has served as Associate Pastor for Adult Ministries at the First Presbyterian Church of Bellevue, Washington. He regularly leads study tours to Europe and to the Holy Land, and is an adjunct faculty for Trinity Lutheran college in Seattle.

Randal teaches on issues relating to Christian faith and culture, and has contributed to *101 Devotionals for Christian Leaders* and to *Leadership Resources,* published by *Christianity Today.* Randal is married to Evelyne, a native of Geneva, Switzerland. He and Evelyne have three daughters.